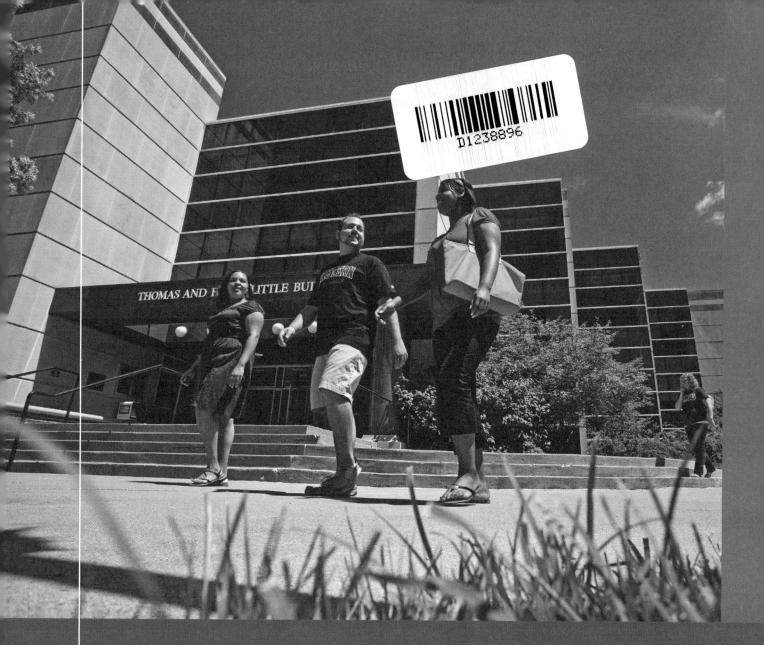

Explore, Evaluate, Expand, Express

ACADEMIC SUCCESS AND THE EKU EXPERIENCE

First Year Courses

Eastern Kentucky University

Hayden-McNeil Sustainability

Hayden-McNeil's standard paper stock uses a minimum of 30% post-consumer waste. We offer higher % options by request, including a 100% recycled stock. Additionally, Hayden-McNeil Custom Digital provides authors with the opportunity to convert print products to a digital format. Hayden-McNeil is part of a larger sustainability initiative through Macmillan Higher Ed. Visit http://sustainability.macmillan.com to learn more.

Printed in the United States of America

10 9 8 7 6 5 4 3 2 1

ISBN 978-0-7380-6587-8

Hayden-McNeil Publishing
14903 Pilot Drive
Plymouth, MI 48170
www.hmpublishing.com

Hearn 6587-8 F14

Table of Contents

3 Chapter Three

Succeed

4 Chapter Four

Practice

5 Chapter Five

Think

6 Chapter Six

Express

7 Chapter Seven

Plan

8 Chapter Eight

Capitalize

9 Chapter Nine

Thrive

Appendix

EKU Resource Guide

Index

Contributors List

Last Name First

Alexander, Ms. Shawne

Arias, Mr. Scott

Ballard, Dr. Michael

Banasiak, Ms. Diane E.

Barnes, Ms. April

Barnett, Ms. Erin

Bauer, Ms. Adrienne

Belluscio, Ms. Teresa

Blythe, Dr. Hal

Bose, Dr. Pradeep

Botts, Dr. Theresa

Bryden, Dr. Phyllis

Capretti, Mr. Paolo

Carlisle, Ms. Kristi

Chandra, Dr. Vigs

Choi, Ms. Laurie

Clement, Dr. Catherine

Clouse, Ms. Ashton

Clouse, Ms. Pamela Jane H.

Collier, Dr. Michael

Conneely, Dr. Rebecca

Creech, Ms. Kim

Dailey, Dr. David W.

Day, Dr. Lisa

Dirks, Ms. Connie

Dunlap, Dr. Scotty

Fairchild, Dr. Jennifer

Frost, Dr. Linda

Gegler, Mr. Jeff

George, Ms. Julie

Gibson, Ms. Karen

Graham, Ms. Gwendolyn

Greenwell, Ms. Lindsay

Haggerty, Mr. Stephen J.

Hale, Ms. Nickole

Harris, Dr. William E., Jr.

Hearn, Mr. John

Howard, Mr. Clay

Hunter, Ms. Karen M.

Isaacs, Ms. Mona

Johnson, Ms. Gladys

Kasitz, Cpt. Michael

Mack, Dr. Felicia

Makinen, Mr. Bryan

Martin, Mr. Billy

May, Dr. David

Miller, Dr. Lori Beth

Moore, Ms. Lisa

Morgan, Dr. Charles H., Jr.

Nguyen, Dr. Minh

Nnoromele, Dr. Patrick

Osbaldiston, Dr. Richard

Raider, Ms. Mary

Radcliffe, Mr. Chris

Richardson, Dr. Ray

Rutherford, Dr. Jack

Sandford, Dr. Katherine

Schumacher, Mr. Matthew

Sehmann, Dr. Karin

Shirey, Mr. Benton D.

Smith, Ms. Shannon

Stevens, Ms. Sandra

Sweet, Dr. Charlie

Taylor, Dr. Missy

Tudor, Ms. Amanda

Valley, Ms. Leslie

Walker, Dr. Jen Colvin

Watson, Ms. Susan

Webb, Ms. Brittany

Wilkins, Mr. Steve

Wilks, Ms. Beverly

Wilson, Dr. Mary

Wilson, Dr. Steffen

Yoder, Mr. Ronald

MICHAEL T. BENSON
PRESIDENT

Dear First Year Student:

Welcome to Eastern Kentucky University. I hope everything is going well with you and that you're adjusting comfortably to your new surroundings and making new friends.

I trust you have already sensed at EKU a strong commitment to your personal growth and academic success. This commitment is reflected in a variety of programs and services designed to help you achieve your educational dreams and grow as individuals.

You have every reason to be proud you're now a Colonel. Our students distinguish themselves in national competitions of all types and compete successfully for some of the most prestigious scholarships. Our graduates have gone on to make headlines all around the world. With hard work and determination you can write your own success story.

One hallmark of the Eastern Experience is that you will graduate as an informed, critical and creative thinker who can communicate effectively. Just as those skills translate to any profession, that goal is embedded in all our academic programs. Simply put, we strive to graduate leaders.

So I encourage you to be an active learner. Talk to our faculty, ask lots of questions, frequent our library, utilize our Noel Studio for Academic Creativity, and take advantage of all the other helpful resources available to you.

Your first year at EKU represents only the first step of a positive, lifelong and life-altering journey. Wherever life takes you, our pledge is to support you all along the way.

Have a great first year, and Go Colonels!

Michael Benson
President

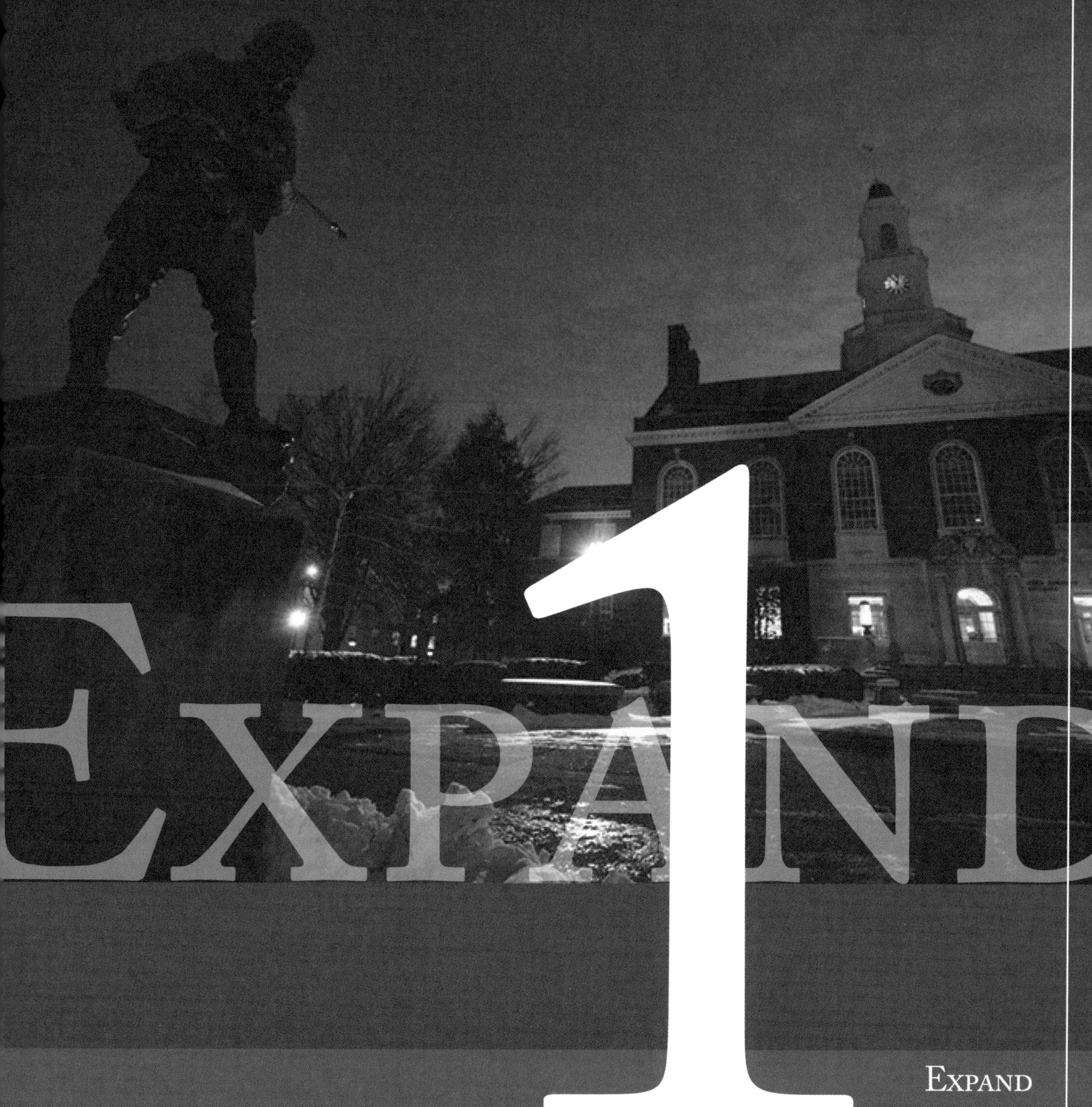

1

EXPAND

Chapter One

Chapter One

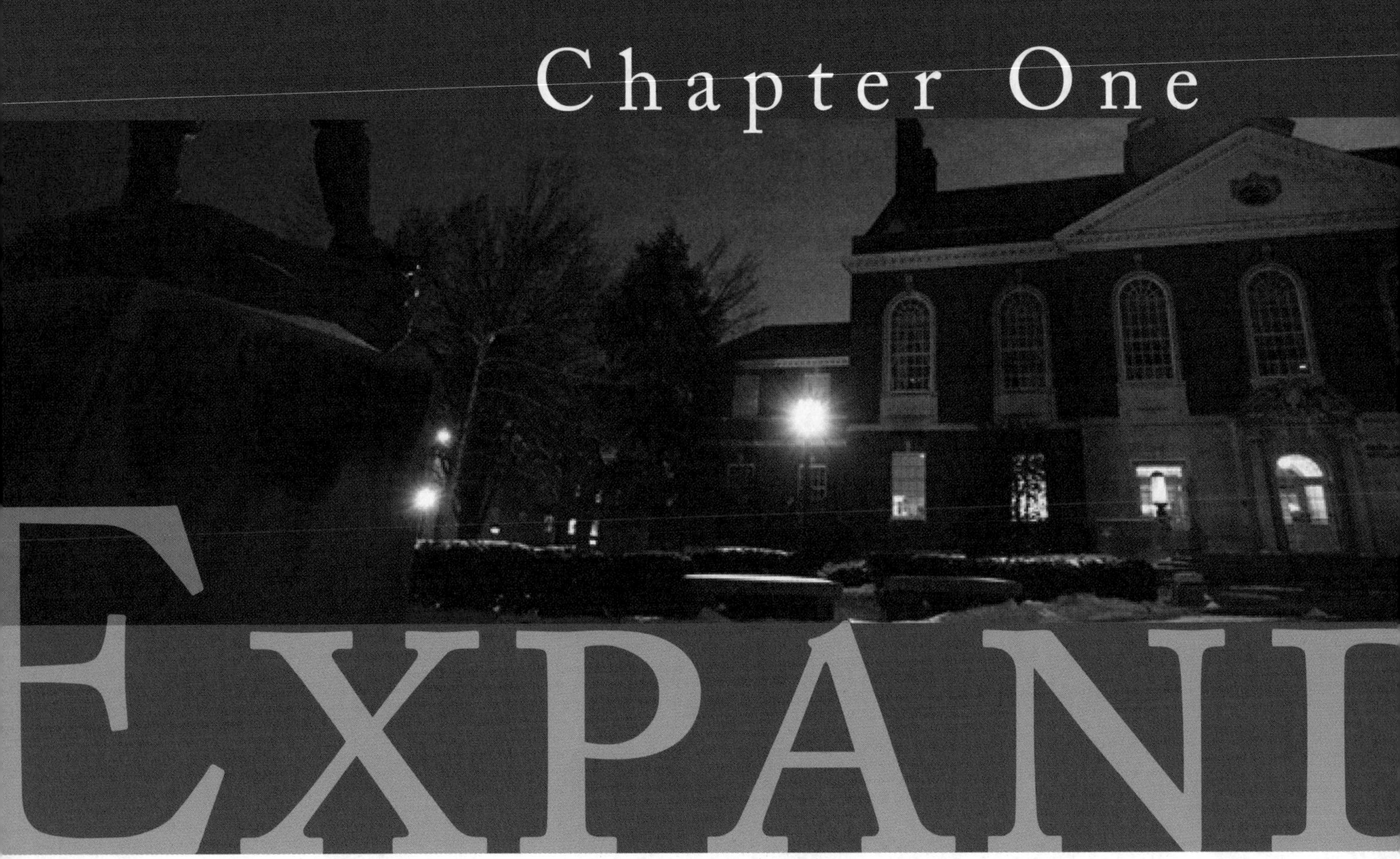

After mastering the content in this chapter you will be able to:

- Articulate the purpose of a liberal education
- Identify essential principles when evaluating ideas and issues
- Identify fundamental questions as a way to process information

Fundamental Question

- How will an EKU liberal education benefit me?

Essential Principles

- Transferable Skills
- Critical Thinking
- Creative Thinking

"If you would hit the mark, you must aim a little above it."
Henry Wadsworth Longfellow
American poet and educator

A Solid Foundation: Critical Thinking and a Liberal Education

■ LIFELONG LEARNING

Why are you in college? Perhaps you are here to learn skills to help you succeed in a specific career field. Or perhaps you are here because it was the next step after high school. Or maybe you're here to experience the college life you've seen portrayed in movies or heard about from friends. There are many reasons a student decides to enroll in higher education. Regardless of why you chose to attend college, while here, our goal is that you will become a lifelong learner and gain skills that will benefit you in all subjects and areas of life. EKU's **liberal arts** education and **curriculum** focuses on developing critical thinking skills and helps students become **self-directed learners**.

■ BLOOM'S TAXONOMY

Educators use the term **cognitive domain** to refer to how people think, and they understand that thinking occurs at various levels. Many educators view higher level thinking through the lens of **Bloom's Taxonomy**. The word "taxonomy" basically means classification. In the 1950s, Benjamin Bloom developed a model to help us classify thinking through a hierarchy of skills and behaviors. The model, which is often portrayed as a pyramid, is depicted below.

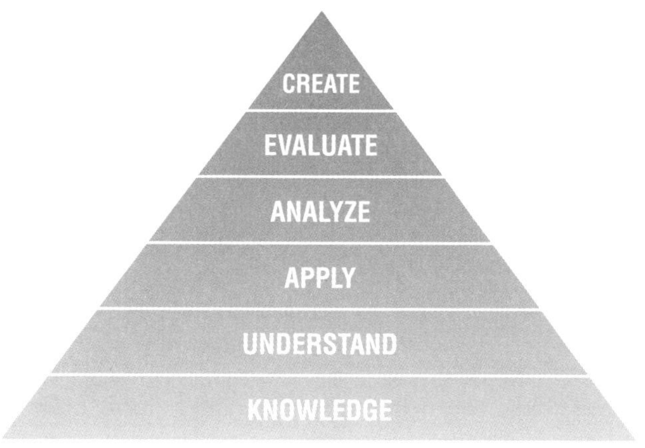

In high school, you were probably asked to memorize information and recall it for a test. That task falls into the "Knowledge" category of Bloom's Taxonomy, or the bottom of the pyramid. You may have also been asked to paraphrase information or explain an idea. Those types of skills fall into the category of "Understand." Most high school curricula focuses on the bottom two categories of Bloom's Taxonomy.

In college, your professors will challenge you to move up the hierarchy by:

- Beginning to use information in new ways ("Apply")
- Breaking information into small parts ("Analyze")
- Justifying a decision or taking a stand ("Evaluate")
- Creating a new product or point of view ("Create")

(Anderson, 2001)

Table 1-1. An illustration of Bloom's classification of thinking.

LEVEL	EXAMPLE
Create	Writing a short story Using context you learned in a history class to help you understand a piece of literature
Evaluate	Selecting the most effective solution Critiquing a classmate's essay based on class criteria
Analyze	Explaining the causes of World War II Analyzing a painting by how well it employs specific techniques
Apply	Computing the area of a circle Identifying a simile in a poem
Understand	Paraphrasing a school policy Explaining what a poem means
Knowledge	Reciting the Gettysburg Address Knowing the steps of the writing process

■ CRITICAL AND CREATIVE THINKING: MOVING ON UP

College classes will require more of you than recalling information, reciting definitions, and explaining your answers. You'll be expected, among other tasks, to analyze information, establish conclusions, and build on prior knowledge. But we don't expect this to happen by itself or to occur overnight. It all begins with the development of critical and creative thinking skills.

Critical Thinking

Many instructors on campus are utilizing the Paul and Elder Framework of Critical Thinking. This framework is explained in Chapter 5 using *The Aspiring Thinker's Guide to Critical Thinking* (2004). Throughout this text, you will see the language and concepts outlined in Chapter 5. It doesn't end there, however. You will continue to encounter these terms and ideas in other classes at EKU. This course lays a foundation for your success by introducing you to the Paul and Elder Framework and preparing you for a life of higher level thinking.

➲Chapter 5 (Think) will help you develop your critical and creative thinking skills.

"My orientation class taught me how to be organized, study well, and plan out my future. I learned what it takes to be a successful student at EKU and even discovered my major through a career exploration project."

Kelsey Gadd
Health Service Administration

Creative Thinking

Have you ever heard someone talk about creativity as "thinking outside the box"? It's the attempt to get thinking out of its normal ruts that led author Arthur Koestler (1964) to pronounce that creativity is "the defeat of habit by originality" (p. 38). When we employ creative thinking, we approach problems and phenomena from a different perspective, often combining several perspectives, and that new point of view allows us to solve things and see things we haven't noticed before.

For most theorists, creative thinking, then, has two distinct traits—it is *novel* and it is *useful*. And when we are able to generate creative thoughts, we find ourselves growing. No wonder the root form of creativity is the Latin *creatus*, meaning "to have grown." Metaphorically, creative thinking is the seed of that growth process.

The Importance of Creative Thinking

In 2010, IBM's Institute for Business Values surveyed 1,500 of our nation's business leaders about the most important skill necessary to succeed. The number one

"If you want to get the particulars correct, don't start with the details. Start with the key ideas and, in hierarchical fashion, form the details around these larger notions."

Dr. John Medina in *Brain Rules*
American developmental molecular biologist

response? Creative thinking (Kern, 2010). In *A Whole New Mind*, Daniel Pink (2005) emphasizes that we are entering the Conceptual Age, where the future will belong to those who can think creatively. Likewise, Australian Erica McWilliam (2008) in *The Creative Workforce* believes creative thinking is the most important subject taught in primary, secondary, and higher education. English educator Ken Robinson says simply that educators should "encourage kids to experiment, to innovate, not giving them all the answers but giving them the tools they need to find out what the answers might be" (p. 26).

Why should you develop creative thinking skills? Perhaps the best answer is that you can't afford not to.

Fundamental Question

One way to categorize information is by determining a question to guide you through exploration. When your thoughts and actions have purpose, there is likely a question in the driver's seat. For example, what question do you expect your orientation class to answer?

We hope that by the end of your time in this course you'll be able to answer: What do I need to know and do to be successful in college and in life? With this question driving the content of the course, you can expect that, come the end of the semester, you'll be able to list different techniques, strategies, and behaviors to help you become a successful person (Nosich, 2008)!

Essential Principles

Now that we have determined a question to guide our thinking, we can identify the key elements necessary to answering this fundamental question. How would you go about answering it?

Your instructor might say that you need to determine a path for academic success, develop as a person, and discover effective strategies. So our key elements are: Academic Success, Personal Development, and Effective Strategies. As you go through this book, each chapter will center on these key elements (Nosich, 2008).

■ THE BENEFITS OF A LIBERAL EDUCATION

A **liberal education** is one of the things all EKU students have in common. The term "liberal" is often related to politics and whether one is a "liberal" or a "conservative" in terms of values. In education, liberal takes on a new meaning. A liberal education equips an individual with a variety of skills and abilities. With a solid liberal arts education, you are not limited in your career exploration, but freed and qualified for a wide range of opportunities for the rest of your life.

Regardless of major selection, all EKU students are required to complete **general education** requirements as part of their liberal education. General education courses are intended to assist you with developing basic, **transferable skills**, which are crucial to success in college, in a profession, and in your personal life. A liberal education prepares you to assume positions of leadership and to be a productive member of your community.

A liberal arts education complements career goals by providing the skills and knowledge that will prepare you for many careers. In today's economy, employers desire transferable skills—skills you take with you to any job, such as written and verbal communication skills, problem-solving techniques, critical thinking skills, research methods, and the ability to work well with others—all skills you can acquire pursuing a liberal arts education.

By identifying your transferable skills, you gain the ability to make connections between your past experiences and future aspirations. On page 7 is a list of skills you may possess. They are not limited to one discipline or knowledge area, but rather they are transferable to many opportunities.

➲**Why do we call them "disciplines"?**
Because the intent is to THINK in a disciplined (specific and structured) way about a particular topic.

The list on the following page contains some of the transferable skills you will likely acquire at EKU through coursework, participation in extracurricular events, working, and volunteerism.

■ GENERAL EDUCATION INFORMATION

The chart below applies the concepts of fundamental questions and essential principles to common areas of a liberal arts education. It shows how these concepts can be applied to the areas of liberal education in the broadest sense. However, individual disciplines, such as economics, geology, or philosophy, could also have fundamental questions and essential principles. If you were to continue to break down the disciplines into specific fields of study, individual classes, or even units of study within the class, fundamental questions and essential principles could still be applied. In this way, fundamental questions and essential principles can help you clarify your thinking on different levels.

Each layer can be assigned fundamental questions and essential principles as in the following example.

Area of Liberal Arts Education: Humanities

Subject Area/Discipline: Literature

Field of Study: British Literature

Class: ENG 474 Shakespeare

Instructional Unit: The Merchant of Venice

Your general education classes provide a breadth of knowledge and skills. Your major, on the other hand, adds depth to your education and prepares you to be a specialist, which is to know a certain content area very well.

Table 1-2. Application of Fundamental Questions and Essential Principles to the liberal arts.

	FUNDAMENTAL QUESTION	ESSENTIAL PRINCIPLES	PRIMARY SUBJECT AREAS
Arts	How can we think differently about our surroundings?	Artistic Expression, Culture, Perspective	Music, Theatre, Visual Arts, Dance
Communication	How can we better articulate our thoughts and opinions?	Clarity, Style	English Composition, Human Communication, Public Speaking, Rhetoric
Humanities	In what ways have humans addressed our existence and meaning of the world?	Diversity, Creativity, Human Condition	Foreign Languages, Literature, Philosophy, Religion
Mathematics	What are the properties of different relations?	Axiom, Formula	Algebra, Calculus, Statistics, Trigonometry
Natural Sciences	What are the truths and laws that pertain to the natural world?	Hypothesis, Natural Phenomena	Astronomy, Biology, Chemistry, Geology, Physics
Social and Behavioral Sciences	How do humans relate to one another and to society?	Diversity, Economics, Human Behavior, Motivation, Social, Political	Anthropology, Economics, History, Political Science, Psychology, Sociology
Wellness	What can we do to stay well and thrive?	Health, Physical, Disease, Choices	Health, Nutrition, Physical Education

"I do think that a general liberal arts education is very important, particularly in an uncertain changing world."

Steve Case

American businessman; co-founder and former CEO of AOL

TRANSFERABLE SKILLS GAINED FROM A LIBERAL ARTS EDUCATION

- ✓ Accommodating multiple demands for commitment of time, energy, and resources
- ✓ Analytical skills
- ✓ Analyzing and learning from life experiences—both one's own and others
- ✓ Analyzing the interrelationships of events and ideas from several perspectives
- ✓ Anticipating problems and responding with solutions
- ✓ Approaching problems from a variety of perspectives
- ✓ Assessing one's values in relation to important life decisions
- ✓ Attending to detail
- ✓ Avoiding bias and preconceptions
- ✓ Behaving ethically
- ✓ Brainstorming
- ✓ Calculating and performing mathematical computations
- ✓ Solving general problems and focusing on details
- ✓ Working on several problems at once
- ✓ Carrying out tasks with thoroughness and precision
- ✓ Collaborating with others
- ✓ Communicating well with diverse groups and at all skill levels
- ✓ Compiling numerical and statistical data
- ✓ Coordinating people, activities, and details
- ✓ Creativity and flexibility in thinking
- ✓ Defining problems and identifying possible/apparent causes
- ✓ Editing and proofreading
- ✓ Effective decision making
- ✓ Effective writing and speaking skills
- ✓ Effective participation in group discussions
- ✓ Evaluating the effects/effectiveness of a decision
- ✓ Explaining difficult ideas and complex topics
- ✓ Expressing ideas
- ✓ Extracting important information
- ✓ Formulating questions relevant to clarifying a particular problem, topic, or issue
- ✓ Formulating and defending positions
- ✓ Gathering information
- ✓ Goal setting
- ✓ Good listening, clarifying, questioning, and responding skills
- ✓ Hypothesizing and testing for results
- ✓ Identifying alternative courses of action
- ✓ Identifying appropriate information sources and resources
- ✓ Identifying possible alternative solutions and selecting the most appropriate one
- ✓ Identifying central issues and key questions
- ✓ Identifying project steps from beginning to end
- ✓ Imagining alternatives
- ✓ Interacting with and appreciating people from diverse cultural, social, and religious backgrounds
- ✓ Interpreting both qualitative and quantitative data
- ✓ Leadership
- ✓ Listening carefully, attentively, empathetically, and with objectivity
- ✓ Making and keeping a schedule
- ✓ Managing time and stress effectively
- ✓ Meeting goals
- ✓ Multitasking
- ✓ Oral and written communication
- ✓ Persuading others to a certain point of view
- ✓ Preparing and writing concise and logically written materials
- ✓ Presenting ideas effectively in speeches or lecture
- ✓ Problem-solving skills
- ✓ Reading accurately, analytically, and critically
- ✓ Research and planning skills
- ✓ Sensitivity to cultural and ethnic diversity
- ✓ Setting and meeting deadlines
- ✓ Structuring and evaluating arguments
- ✓ Summarizing complicated materials
- ✓ Synthesizing facts, concepts, and principles
- ✓ Teaching a skill, concept, or principle to others
- ✓ Technology skills
- ✓ Thinking critically
- ✓ Using a variety of media for presentation

(*Identifying your transferable skills*, 2005)

Here's an **illustration** to help you understand how a liberal education prepares you to be a generalist:

Can Opener vs. Swiss Army Knife

Swiss Army knife, a "generalist"—Completes many tasks, but in a limited way.

Can opener, a "specialist"—Completes one task extremely well.

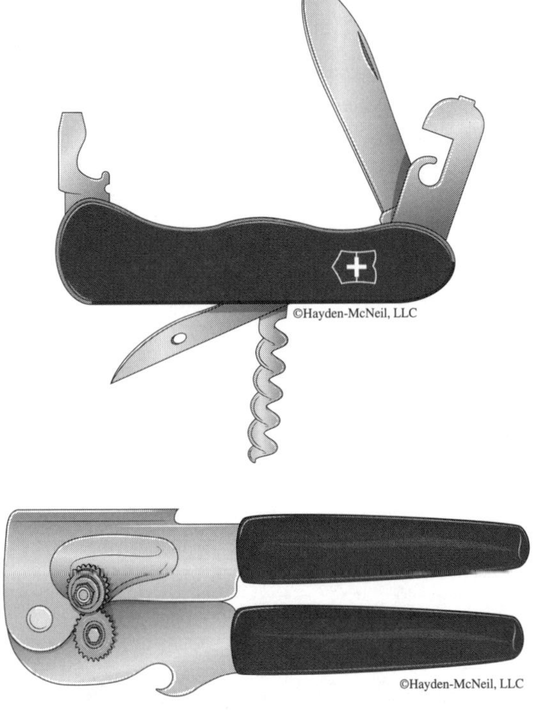

A person in a kitchen with lots of cans to open would use the can opener because it works better and would be more efficient. If the same person became lost in the woods, however, the can opener would only enable that person to eat until the canned food ran out. The Swiss Army knife would accomplish a number of other tasks in addition to opening cans and would be a better survival tool. There will be many times in your life when a can opener isn't the only tool you will need.

By completing the general education requirements, you are filling your toolbox with transferable skills. You will learn to communicate in person and through writing. You will be able to solve complex problems. You will learn how to research. These skills, learned through the completion of various general education requirements, will assist you in becoming a more productive and successful student in your major courses.

➲EKU's General Education program helps students to become informed, independent thinkers by developing competencies in communication, quantitative analysis, and critical thinking and by helping them understand and appreciate the diversity of culture, individuals, the natural environment, and the global society.

How a Liberal Education Impacts You

Becoming a liberally educated individual is important for many reasons:

You will become a citizen of the nation. This means that you will have the knowledge and communication skills to interact with individuals from different backgrounds. You will become a productive member of our democracy, capable of making sound decisions in the voting booth and capable of debating issues and acknowledging various points of view.

➲Attending college is not just about earning a better living; it is also about learning to live a better life.

You will become a citizen of the world. In other words, you will be exposed to non-Western cultures' viewpoints on religion, history, politics, social structures, philosophy, and government. This will, in turn, push you to think about the way you live your life and understand and appreciate differences between cultures.

You will be exposed to issues of ethics and morality. Through your studies at Eastern Kentucky University, you will evaluate issues and ideas that question your beliefs and require in-depth discussion and analysis. You might be exposed to debates on social justice, the environment, or ethics in a profession (such as medicine, business, or law) (Shoenberg, 2005).

"We always hear about the rights of democracy, but the major responsibility of it is participation."

Wynton Marsalis

American musician and composer, and a leading advocate of American culture

HOW CAN BEING "LIBERALLY EDUCATED" ASSIST YOU...

- In being clearer to others when presenting your thoughts, feelings, and ideas?
- In feeling confident you are giving accurate information to others?
- To know you are being specific and precise with your information?
- To add more relevant information to the conversation?
- In being on a deeper level of knowledge and understanding?
- In knowing a broad range of topics to sound worldly?
- In making logical arguments, decisions, and choices?
- In seeing the central idea in a thought, statement, or argument?
- In recognizing whether or not you are being fair in your thinking, or if you are only thinking of yourself and your own goals/values/circumstances?

How a Liberal Education Impacts Your Career

With so much emphasis placed on choosing the right major, it's important to know that the skills employers value the most in recent graduates can be acquired by completing your general education requirements.

So what is it employers are looking for?

- Team player
- An understanding of science and technology
- Top notch communication skills (speaking and writing)
- Clarity of thought about complex problems
- Capability of analyzing a problem and developing a workable solution
- Understanding of a global context
- Creativity in problem solving
- Application of knowledge and skills in new settings
- Ability to understand numbers and statistics
- Strong sense of ethics and integrity

(Peter D. Hart Research Associates, Inc., 2008)

"It is more important than ever to have a college education because getting a degree betters your chances of receiving a job in this increasingly competitive job market!"

Kenton Murphy
Occupational Science

Chapter Summary

Critical thinking will benefit you in many ways. By being a sound critical thinker, you will become a good citizen of your community, be able to justify your decisions, and become an active learner. For example, as a sound critical thinker and a liberally educated individual, you will be better equipped to choose the best candidate in an election, explain to your parents why you want to join a sorority or fraternity, and second guess influential advertisements. Creative thinking skills will enhance your critical thinking abilities by helping you to problem solve and evaluate situations from a different point of view. Not to mention, being a creative and critical thinker will make you a more viable candidate when you enter the job market.

"Making good decisions is a crucial skill at every level."

Peter Drucker

Austrian-born American management consultant, educator, and author

KEY TERMS

Bloom's Taxonomy: A hierarchical classification of learning based on 6 levels of cognition

Cognitive domain: The ability to apply intelligence

Curriculum: Courses and their content

Discipline: An area of knowledge that can be formally taught and researched

General education: Refers to the core curriculum courses which seek to develop basic skills in EKU students

Illustration: An example or demonstration to provide explanation or further clarification

Liberal arts: A curriculum that imparts general knowledge and develops rational thought and intellectual capabilities

Liberal education: "A philosophy of education that empowers individuals with broad knowledge and transferable skills, and a strong sense of value, ethics, and civic engagement" (Association of American Colleges and Universities, n.d.)

Self-directed learner: A person who educates oneself or seeks knowledge independently

Transferable skills: Skills gained which are applicable to many different disciplines and career fields

NOTES

"You are educated. Your certification is in your degree. You may think of it as the ticket to the good life. Let me ask you to think of an alternative. Think of it as your ticket to change the world."

Tom Brokaw

Amercan television journalist and author

■ CAMPUS RESOURCES

First Year Courses
http://www.firstyearcourses.eku.edu
Miller Hall 206, 859-622-7322

General Education Program
http://www.gened.eku.edu

■ REFERENCES

Anderson, L. W., & Krathwohl, D. R. (Eds.). (2001). *A taxonomy for learning, teaching and assessing: A revision of Bloom's Taxonomy of educational objectives* (Complete ed.). Boston, MA: Addison Wesley Longman.

Association of American Colleges and Universities. (n.d.). Liberal education. *Association of American Colleges and Universities*. Retrieved April 9, 2011 from http://www.aacu.org/resources/liberaleducation/index.cfm

Identifying your transferable skills. (2005). Retrieved April 9, 2011, from the Fordham University, Graduate School of Education, Career Services Website: http://www.fordham.edu/images/student_services/career/grad_ed_handouts/transferable%20skills%20cpp.pdf

Kern, F. (2010, May 28). What chief executives really want. *Bloomberg Businessweek*. Retrieved June 3, 2011, from http://www.businessweek.com/innovate/content/may2010/id20100517_190221.htm

Koestler, A. (1964). *The act of creation*. New York, NY: Penguin Arkana.

Longfellow, H.W. (n.d.). *BrainyQuote.com*. Retrieved June 9, 2011, from http://www.brainyquote.com/quotes/quotes/h/henrywadsw105345.html

McWilliam, E. (2008). *The creative work force: How to launch young people into high-flying futures*. Sydney, Australia: University of New South Wales Press.

Medina, J. (2008). *Brain rules: 12 principles for surviving and thriving at work, home, and school*. Seattle, WA: Pear Press.

Nosich, G.M. (2008). *Learning to think things through: A guide to critical thinking across the curriculum* (3rd ed.). Upper Saddle River, NJ: Prentice-Hall, Inc.

Peter D. Hart Research Associates, Inc. (2006, December 28). *How should colleges prepare students to succeed in today's global economy?* Retrieved April 9, 2011, from http://www.aacu.org/leap/documents/Re8097abcombined.pdf

Pink, D.H. (2005). *A whole new mind: Moving from the Information Age to the Conceptual Age*. New York, NY: Riverhead Books.

Shoenberg, R. (2005). *Why do I have to take this course? A student guide to making smart educational choices*. Washington, D.C.: AAC&U Publications.

NOTES

"How we think shows through in how we act. Attitudes are mirrors of the mind. They reflect thinking."

David Joseph Schwartz

American motivational writer and coach

2

Engage

Chapter Two

Chapter Two

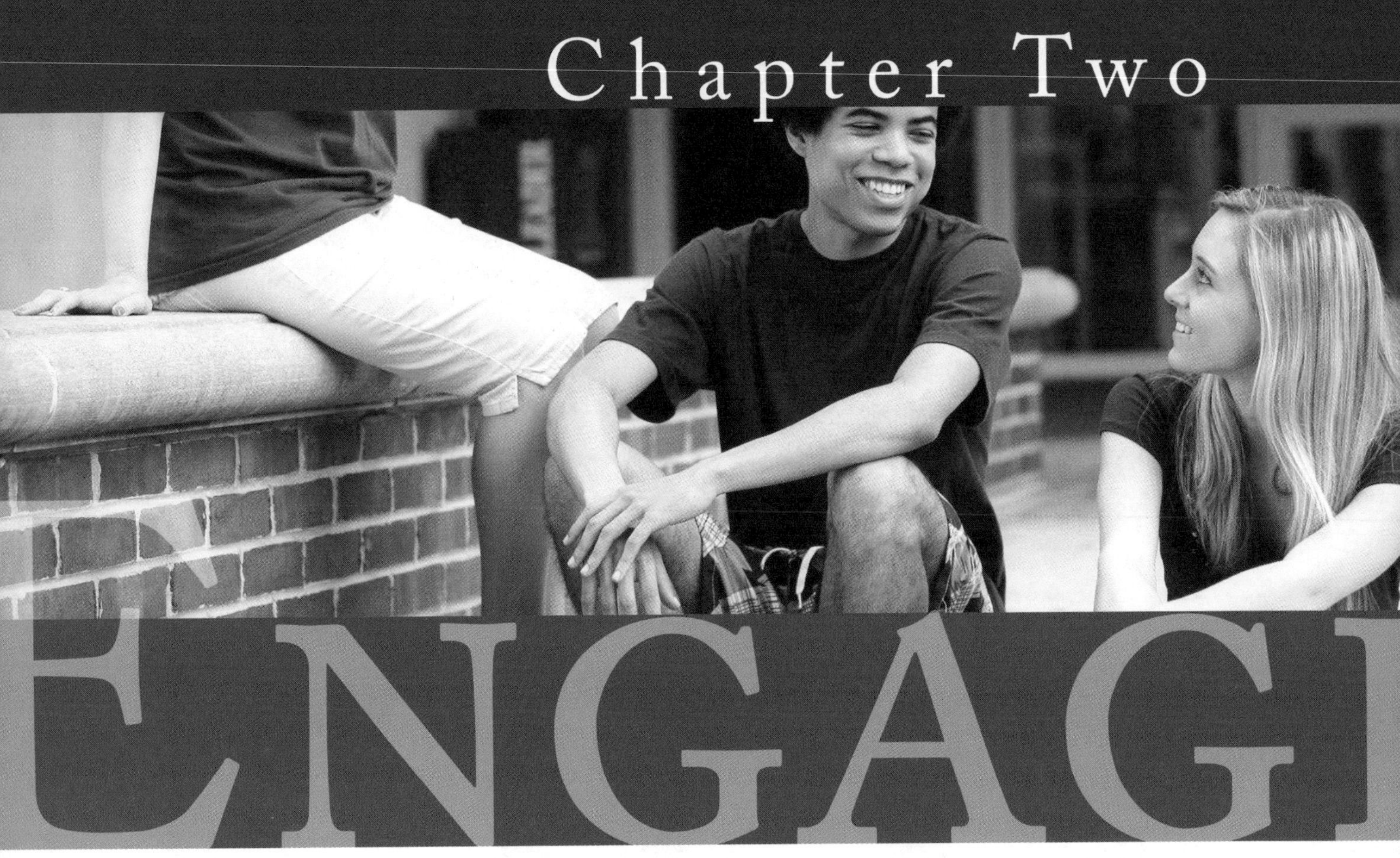

After mastering the content in this chapter you will:

- Be able to identify academic resources and support services important for academic success
- Engage in activities that promote connection to the University
- Be able to locate services on campus
- Increase your awareness of EKU history
- Comprehend campus policies and terminology
- Be able to utilize the Colonel's Compass

Fundamental Question

- How do I become connected to Eastern Kentucky University?

Essential Principles

- Engagement
- Involvement

"You're gonna wish these days/ Hadn't gone by so fast/These are some good times/ So take a good look around/You may not know it now/ But you're gonna miss this."

"You're Gonna Miss This," lyrics by Lee Thomas Miller

Grammy-winning songwriter, EKU alumnus

Welcome to EKU!

Welcome to Eastern Kentucky University, the home of the Colonels! Eastern has a long tradition of educating students from central and eastern Kentucky. Since its inception, the Eastern curriculum has added programs and degrees, including the first doctoral degree in Education awarded in 2010.

As a new student, you are now a part of a student body of over 16,000 students on the main campus in Richmond, or one of the satellite campuses in Corbin, Manchester, Somerset, or Danville. You may choose to pursue one of 11 associate degrees or over 87 baccalaureate degrees, and then go on to further education by choosing from over 30 degrees at the master's level. You may also begin your studies at Eastern in one of the pre-professional programs and then transfer to another institution to complete your degree.

In this chapter, and throughout the book, you will learn more about the university you have chosen to attend—Eastern Kentucky University. You will be able to locate resources to help make your life at EKU more enjoyable and worthwhile. You will find that the University is over 100 years old with many historic buildings, and yet, at the same time, EKU continues to modernize its curriculum and its buildings for the future. As you read about the student resources available, seek out those people who are able to assist you during your college career, get involved in student organizations, and governance and have a great experience at EKU.

➲ In the 1960s and 1970s, freshmen had to wear what were called "beanie caps." Beanie caps were worn to "instill within the new students a real loyalty and school spirit." If freshmen neglected to orient themselves, they were called into "rat court" to be penalized. One such penalty could have been an impromptu song and dance performance in front of a crowd (Couture, Whalen, & Hill, 2007).

1909–1910 Ruric passes away and Dean of Women, Mary C. Roark, assumes leadership as president.

►1922 EASTERN KENTUCKY STATE NORMAL SCHOOL AND TEACHERS COLLEGE IS ESTABLISHED AS A FOUR-YEAR INSTITUTION.

►1925 NORMAL SCHOOL AWARDS FIRST DEGREES.

1916–1928 Thomas Jackson Coates assumes presidency and boosts campus construction.

1910–1916 John Grant Crabbe is appointed president and focuses on EKU libraries.

1906–1909 Normal School Bill is approved. Ruric Nevel Roark serves as Eastern's first president.

The Centennial Man

The Centennial Year Statue, located in front of Powell, was commissioned by the Alumni Association in 1974. Celebrating Eastern's centennial of education and learning, the statue represents America's efforts in science and space research.

(Hay III & Whitlock, 1992)
(EKU Photos—EKU Image Archives Database)

►1874 Central University is founded in Richmond, KY.

1928–1941 Dr. Herman Lee Donovan becomes president and the college is accredited by SACS.

►1935 Eastern establishes Graduate Study and the right to grant a Master's degree.

1941–1960 Dr. Francis O'Donnell takes over as president. Enrollment triples at the end of WWII, and O'Donnell successfully implements integration on campus.

►1965 Eastern creates 5 separate colleges and a graduate school.

►1966 Eastern is officially named Eastern Kentucky University.

1960–1976 Dr. Robert Martin serves his alma mater as president. He constructs 12 new dormitories and expands classroom facilities, student centers, and recreational areas.

1976–1984 Dr. Julius Cherry Powell "the Polisher" becomes president and the Hummel Planetarium is constructed.

1984–1998 Dr. Hanly Funderburk takes over presidency and expands the Danville, Corbin, and Manchester campuses.

1998–2001 Dr. Robert Walter Kustra becomes president. He institutes academic and administrative reforms, seeking to improve student life on campus.

2001–2007 Joanne K. Glasser assumes presidency and creates the first comprehensive capital campaign.

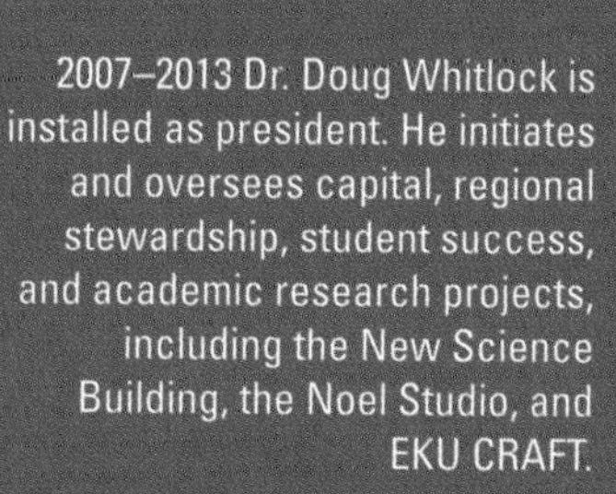

2007–2013 Dr. Doug Whitlock is installed as president. He initiates and oversees capital, regional stewardship, student success, and academic research projects, including the New Science Building, the Noel Studio, and EKU CRAFT.

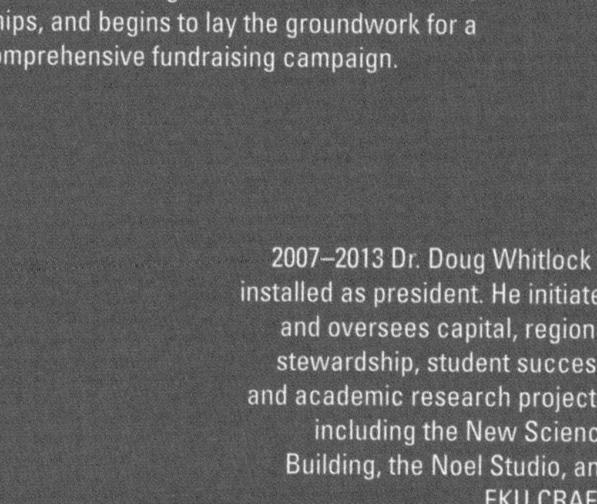

2013–Present Dr. Michael Benson assumes presidency and energetically launches numerous initiatives designed to more effectively brand the University and enhance its visual appeal. He also reveals plans for a new College of Education/ Model Laboratory School complex, announces a move to make the campus tobacco-free, works closely with local and regional officials on numerous partnerships, and begins to lay the groundwork for a comprehensive fundraising campaign.

MISSION AND VISION

At the heart of every organization is its mission statement, which in a very few words describes the major purpose of that organization or institution. The EKU mission statement reads:

> As a comprehensive public institution, Eastern Kentucky University prepares students to lead productive, responsible, and enriched lives. To accomplish this mission, the University emphasizes:
>
> - Student Success,
> - Regional Stewardship, and
> - Critical and Creative Thinking and Effective Communication.
>
> (EKU Office of Institutional Effectiveness, 2011)

Every institution is also guided by a vision statement, which provides guidance and direction for all aspects of the educational institution. The EKU vision statement reads, "Eastern Kentucky University will be an accessible, nurturing, and academically rigorous center of learning that transforms lives and communities, enabling them to adapt and succeed in a dynamic, global society" (EKU Office of Institutional Effectiveness, 2011).

DISTINGUISHED ALUMNI

Since the early days of Eastern, when the University awarded its first degrees in 1925, many graduates have gone on to distinguished service in the local, regional, state, and national arena. They have distinguished themselves in all fields of business, industry, entertainment, government, and education.

SOME NOTABLE EKU ALUMNI INCLUDE:

- Lt. Gen. Keen, Commanding Three-Star General in charge of Haiti Relief/Deputy Director of Southern Command: Class of 1975, Mathematics
- Debbie Dyer, Co-Founder of Central Kentucky Research Associates: Class of 1985, Nursing
- Chad Bratzke, Professional Football Player: Class of 1994, Broadcasting
- Lee Thomas Miller, Grammy-Winning Songwriter: Class of 1991, Music Theory and Composition
- Brian Corcoran, NASCAR Managing Director of Corporate Marketing: Class of 1991, Physical Education; 1995, Master's in Physical Education
- Toni Hacker, N.Y. Fashion Designer: Class of 1997, Art
- Jeff Newton, Emmy Award-Winning Producer—*60 Minutes*: Class of 1997, Journalism
- Amy Kearns, Head of Security for Horse of the Year—Rachel Alexandra: Class of 1998, Journalism

(EKU Alumni, 2007)

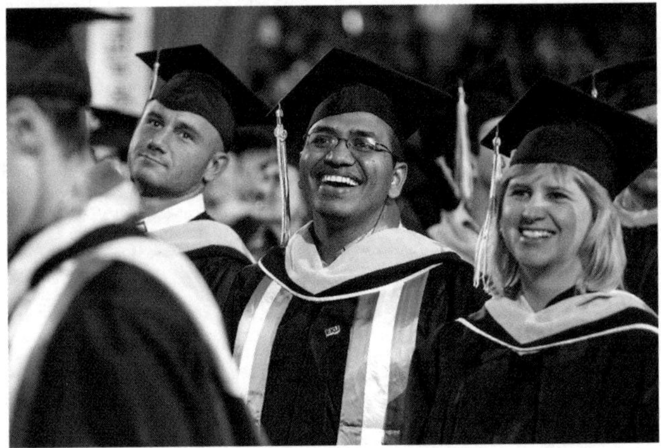

"Curiosity is natural to the soul of man and interesting objects have a powerful influence on our affections."

Daniel Boone

American explorer

Alma Mater

EKU's **Alma Mater** was written by Nancy Evans and arranged by Jane Campbell, the former head music orchestra professor at Eastern. While it is not known when the song was written, the Alma Mater was sung for the first time on record in 1933 at a commencement ceremony. Since then, the Alma Mater is sung at the closing of each fall and spring graduation ceremony.

Hail to thee our Alma Mater,
Faithful guide of youth,
Holding high amid the darkness
Duty, light, and truth;
Still above, the skies attend thee,
Still thy stately columns stand,
Still thy sons and daughters love thee
Sing thy praises o'er the land.
All the earth's resplendent beauty
Nature gathered here,
Rolling lawns and trees and grasses
On thy hillsides fair;
Happy days within thy shadow,
Friends and comrades we have won.
Fill our hearts with exaltation
For thy task so nobly done.
When beloved Alma Mater
Memory recalls
Other days of youth and laughter
In thy gracious halls;
When thy sons and daughters scattered
Turn again to thee,
Still thy lamp is brightly lighting
Us afar, that we may see.

(Evans & Campbell, n.d.)

For a calendar of sporting events and for more information about EKU athletics, visit: http://ekusports.com/

■ COLONEL ATHLETICS

When you think of fall, what comes to mind? Football, tailgating, and cookouts? When spring comes around, can you only think about watching March Madness? You will be happy to find out that ALL athletic events held at home are FREE for EKU students with the verification of your ColonelOne Card. With Eastern's variety of sports, including football, basketball, tennis, soccer, baseball and softball, golf, track and cross country, and volleyball, you will never have a dull moment during the weekend. So come on out and support the EKU Colonels!

■ EKU FIGHT SONG

Eastern Kentucky University is credited with having two fight songs to boost athletic morale. "Yea, Eastern" was written in 1932 by English student Mary Kathryn Burns; the music was arranged by Helen Hull Lutes, a music faculty member. Eight years later another talented student named Frank Wilcox and faculty member Henri Schnabi wrote and arranged "Hail, Hail Eastern Maroons" to revive the Colonel spirit. Memorize the lyrics to these inspiring fight songs, for when the band starts and the fans begin to cheer you'll want to contribute to that Colonel Pride (EKU First Year Programs, n.d.).

Yea, Eastern
(a.k.a. Rally Maroon and White)

Yea, Eastern let's win this fight,
Rally Maroon and White;
We've got the spirit; you've got
the speed,
These two with grit are all that
we need;
So carry and pass that ball;
Show them our boys beat all;
Show them we're right with main and might;
The way to win is fight, fight, fight.

(Burns & Lutes, 1932)

Hail, Hail Eastern Maroons

Hail, Hail Eastern Maroons,
You're the pride of dear old Alma Mater.
Hail, Hail, Eastern Maroons,
For thee we'll give three rousing cheers.
Rah, rah, rah! Hail, Hail, Eastern Maroons,
Loyal to thee we stand,
Ever fight for the right,
We'll make our school the best in the land.

(Wilcox & Schnabi, 1940)

➲Mozart the dog, the unofficial mascot on Eastern's campus during the 1950s and 1960s, is buried in the Ravine behind the Van Peursem Pavilion. This lovable pooch was donated to the housemother of Burnam Hall by a student, Douglas Gaither, when he graduated in 1952. Mozart, named after his frequent appearances at musical events, roamed freely on EKU's campus and could be seen attending classes and sporting events up until his death in 1964 (Couture, Whalen, & Hill, 2007).

■ THE EKU COLONEL

Did you know EKU's mascot wasn't always the Colonel? During the 1920s the name "Maroons" became associated with Eastern due to the school's colors—maroon and white. Students then voted to accept the leopard as the official mascot for the school, but the idea was not enacted. Instead, the Maroons remained the official mascot of EKU until 1963. After the Maroons mascot faded away, beloved campus dogs like Mozart, who is buried in the Ravine, were deemed unofficial mascots. The Colonel figure that is now the official mascot was first introduced in 1963 by President Robert Martin. He had noted that the school needed a "real" mascot, with the result being the Kentucky Colonel (EKU First Year Programs, n.d.; Ellis, 2005).

In 2006, along with the commemoration of the 100th anniversary of the university, the Colonel was redesigned along with the EKU logo (EKU Student Affairs, 2005).

"Every block of stone has a statue inside it and it is the task of the sculptor to discover it."
Michelangelo
Italian artist/sculptor

EKU History

Eastern Kentucky University was founded in 1874 as Central University. Financial problems and enrollment issues eventually led Central University to consolidate with Centre College in 1901, and the institution moved to the Danville campus. After much debate, two normal schools were then created in Kentucky in 1906—one in Richmond (EKU) and one in Bowling Green (WKU).

Eastern became a four-year institution named Eastern Kentucky State Normal School and Teachers College in 1922, offering **baccalaureate degrees**. The normal school title was dropped in 1930, and in 1935, Eastern began to award graduate degrees. In 1948, "Teachers" was dropped from Eastern's name, and the college began to offer non-teaching degrees. During the presidency of Robert R. Martin, Eastern was finally granted the title of a university and became known as Eastern Kentucky University in 1966. Over its existence, EKU persevered through several American tragedies and still developed into one of the most proficient institutions in the education and learning of students. With over 100 majors and several nationally recognized colleges and professional programs, Eastern has established itself as a leading university with a rich historical background that has shaped its beautiful and brilliant future (Couture, Whalen, & Hill, 2006; Hay III & Whitlock, 1992).

➲ The Richmond campus of EKU is also known as "the Campus Beautiful."

■ EKU STATUES

Daniel Boone Statue

If you've ever walked past the Keen Johnson Building you may have noticed the 9-foot-tall, 3,500-pound bronze statue of Daniel Boone. The statue is completely green except for the toe. It is said that rubbing the toe of the left boot will bring you good luck.

The statue is actually a replica casting of an 1893 Daniel Boone sculpture of plaster by Enid Yandell from Louisville, Kentucky. The plaster was then cast in bronze, thanks to the donation by a local businessman, C.C. Bickel, and presented to the city of Louisville in 1906. The original statue is on display at Cherokee Park's main entrance in Louisville. The replication of the statue was commissioned by EKU President Robert R. Martin in 1966. The statue was dedicated on May 1, 1967 (Couture, Whalen, & Hill, 2007).

The Centennial Year Statue

Just outside of the Powell Building stands the statue of a muscular man launching the Saturn rocket from the palm of his hand. The earth and moon orbit above him. Beneath his feet are dolphins, representing the landing of the space shuttle in the ocean. The person who conceptualized the statue was Felix de Weldon, known for his statue of the Iwo Jima flag raising. Weldon wanted the statue to emphasize the research of scientists, the space program, and the American people who supported those efforts. The statue was commissioned in 1974 for the celebration of EKU's centennial. The statue was made in Rome, Italy, and cost approximately $75,000, which was raised by EKU alumni. The names of those who donated amounts of $500 or more can be found on the base of the statue (Couture et al., 2007).

Equestrian Statue

Standing proud in front of the Stratton Building is a statue depicting a Kentucky State Trooper atop a mighty steed. The equestrian statue was commissioned in 1974 along with the new Law Enforcement Complex. The statue was funded by the Alumni Association and EKU Foundation and cost approximately $150,000. The statue symbolizes the elite law enforcement program at EKU, one of the most prominent in the nation (Couture et al., 2006).

➲The Office of Student Life supports a variety of activities for students to enjoy and experience EVERYDAY! Below is just a sample of the activities available to students:

- BINGO!
- EKU Sporting Events
- Community Service Events
- Concerts
- Cultural Events
- Alternative Break Trips
- Intramural Games
- Comedians
- Adventure Programs & Events

Student Involvement: A Key to Success

Being actively involved in the classroom is not the only factor fundamental to your success at EKU; becoming involved in the campus community outside of the classroom is also essential. Research suggests that "the stronger the individual's level of social and academic integration, the greater his or her commitment to the institution and to the goal of college graduation" (Tinto, 1975, as cited in Pascarella, Terenzini, & Wolfe, 1986, pp. 155–156). In fact, in one study, which incorporated more than 1,600 college student interviews, four out of five students cited an incident outside the classroom as having the most significant or profound influence on their college career (Light, 2001).

This engagement outside the classroom reflects the combination of both academic application and social integration. Through this combination of experiences inside and outside of the classroom, you identify your own community and niche within the larger EKU community. Students who are involved in the University community are more likely to succeed than those who are not involved (Pascarella & Terenzini, 2005; Tinto, 2000; Yokomoto, Rizkalla, O'Loughlin, El-Sharkawy, & Lamm, 2001).

"Action is the foundational key to all success."

Pablo Picasso

Spanish artist

Getting involved on campus is one of the best ways for you to take charge of your college experience at EKU. With over 200 Registered Student Organizations (RSOs) and Honors Societies, the opportunities are unlimited. So what are you waiting for? Get involved!

■ SOME WAYS TO GET INVOLVED

- Apply for an on-campus job
- Join a student organization
- Join a fraternity or sorority
- Attend campus events
- Participate in community service
- Play intramural sports

Student Life

Student Life is the home for involvement and leadership for EKU students. We encourage students to get involved and are dedicated to providing a wide range of opportunities, activities, and events designed to enhance the Eastern experience! Student Life consists of Registered Student Organizations (RSOs), Greek Life, Student Activities, Community Service, and Leadership. Each of the entities offers programming and involvement opportunities for Eastern students. You can see all of our upcoming events at http://studentlife.eku.edu/

Connecting with an RSO or starting an RSO is easy; for more information visit http://eku.orgsync.com

Registered Student Organizations

With over 200 Registered Student Organizations (RSOs), there are unlimited opportunities to get involved. Our RSOs are divided into 8 categories, so it is easy to find an RSO that interests you. RSO categories include:

Activity/Interest—founded purely out of the interest of the organization's members.

Club Sport—competitive club teams (non-NCAA sanctioned).

Departmental—associated with academic departments and majors.

Governance—carry out and establish various policies/procedure.

Greek Fraternity/Sorority—nationally affiliated social organizations (see Greek Life description).

Honorary—often linked to majors/colleges and recognize academic achievement.

Religious—based on spiritual beliefs and needs.

Service—focused on community service and helping those in need.

If you can't find an RSO that interests you, it's very easy to get one started. Making the decision to join a student organization will not only enhance your collegiate experience, but will also create lasting friendships and contribute to your professional and personal growth.

OrgSync

OrgSync is an online student organization management program. Through OrgSync you can manage your RSO membership and track your involvement during college. OrgSync will automatically keep track of your extracurricular activities so at the end of your college experience you will have a Co-Curricular Transcript to show potential employers all that you were involved in. You can also log in to discover various events and activities that are happening on campus. Every EKU student with an email address has an OrgSync account—it's that easy to get involved on campus! Make sure to bookmark https://orgsync.com/login/eastern-kentucky-university to sign in with your campus ID.

Departmental Opportunities

Most departments offer opportunities for you to get involved in clubs and societies that are associated with your career and major. Building contacts and references for resumes, learning about scholarships and internships, and meeting other undergraduates in your field of study are just some of the many benefits a departmental organization offers.

➲ Looking for something to do on campus? Check your email! *EKU Students Today* arrives in your inbox each weekday with a list of announcements and events!

EKU Honors Program

The EKU Honors Program is designed for students who want an in-depth college classroom experience with a strong grounding in the liberal arts. As an EKU honors student, you'll thrive in interdisciplinary, team-taught classes with a maximum of 20 students. These challenging and inspiring courses will replace most, if not all, of your general education and University requirements. Our curriculum is flexible, so it benefits students of all majors and won't delay your progress to graduation. As an EKU honors student, you'll also be eligible to live in special honors housing.

EKU honors students get to know their professors at monthly pizza suppers and take trips with fellow honors students to local theater and dance performances, as well as to the Kentucky Opera in Louisville. EKU honors students also have the experience of attending a number of state, regional, and national honors conferences including the National Collegiate Honors Council Conference where more students from EKU present than from any other honors program in the nation.

Applications for the EKU Honors Program are due by January 7; you must have already been admitted by EKU to apply. All applications are submitted online at http://www.honors.eku.edu.

The Honors Student Advisory Council (HSAC)

This 8-member RSO is the student governing body of the EKU Honors Program. EKU Honors Program members interested in gaining leadership experience, organizing social and community service events, fundraising, and bringing greater visibility across and beyond campus to EKU Honors are encouraged to explore this opportunity. Elections for HSAC are held each spring; for more information, see the EKU Honors website at http://www.honors.eku.edu/web10.

"One of my favorite and most beneficial extra-curricular activities has been student government. Not only was it a great way to meet people and get to know the university, it has also given me skills to use in other opportunities beyond the classroom."

Tina Thomas
Accounting

"Exploration is really the essence of the human spirit."

Frank Borman

American astronaut

Governance Organizations

These organizations carry out and establish University changes and/or laws that typically concern the welfare of the student body. The Student Government Association (SGA) is the largest governance organization, but there are many others including Greek government (Interfraternity Council [IFC], National Pan-Hellenic Council [NPHC], and Panhellenic Council), the Residence Life Council, and the Student Senate. Joining a governance organization is one of the most accessible ways to make a difference during your years at EKU.

Greek Life

Social Greek fraternities and sororities offer great involvement opportunities here at EKU. Being Greek is more than wearing letters on your chest. It is about experiences you will have in college that will mold you, shape you, and enhance your out-of-the-classroom experience. Fraternities and sororities offer friendships and connections that last longer than your time at EKU and reach across the country. Greek Life is more than what is portrayed in the media, so make plans to participate in a recruitment event to see what Greek Life is all about.

2.1 Reflection

How do you think you can you "put yourself out there" so you can meet new people and experience new things?

Community Service

Community Service, located within Student Life, directs the University's community service programs. There are a variety of service opportunities throughout the year that EKU students, faculty, and staff can participate in both on and off campus. From working to protect sea turtles over spring break, to building a home for a family over the summer in Honduras, to planting trees on reclaimed mine sites in eastern Kentucky, to volunteering at the local food bank, there are a multitude of opportunities to give back locally, nationally, and internationally. Please contact us (or look on OrgSync) to find out more about the different ways you can get actively involved in your world through service.

Community Service also puts together Alternative Breaks. The mission of the Alternative Break Program is to provide opportunities for students to develop into engaged and mindful citizens who think about and engage in service to meet unmet needs in their host communities. The EKU Alternative Break Program places teams of students in communities across the United States and the world to engage in volunteer service and experiential learning. An EKU Alternative Break trip is an immersion experience in the community—students will experience different cultural, environmental, and socioeconomic backgrounds. While meeting identified communities' needs through service, students will learn about the social and cultural issues facing the host communities.

Why get involved on campus?
- Meet people
- Add to your resume
- Try new things

Honorary Organizations

These organizations are often linked to majors and recognize outstanding academic achievement. Honorary organizations usually have GPA and course requirements and are often by invitation only. A few of EKU's include: Alpha Kappa Psi, Golden Key International Honor Society, and Mortar Board.

Student Interest Organizations

Student Interest Organizations are very diverse and each club, committee, or group was founded purely out of the interest of the organization's members. Some prominent organizations include: Black Student Union, Caduceus Club, EKU Marching Colonels, Feminists for Change, Mock Trial, Older Wiser Learners, and PRIDE.

"Get involved. You'll be spending the next four years of your life here so enjoy it. Get out and meet new people!"

Casey Emerson
Nursing

Peer Education Organizations

Peer Education programs aid in the teaching and assistance of making better informed decisions for the general student population. Some Peer Education Organizations, such as the Health Education Action Team (H.E.A.T.), have student Peer Educators who help the organization facilitate various informative programs. If your major is affiliated with any Peer Education Organization, it is beneficial to get involved.

Recreation Clubs and Intramural Sports

EKU offers many opportunities for students to stay active on campus. Several club sports offered include: club swim team, ice hockey club, soccer, basketball, and wrestling. Students can also form their own less formal intramural teams for a variety of sports throughout the year.

Learn more about campus recreation, recreation clubs, and intramural sports by visiting http://campusrec.eku.edu/

Religious Organizations

Religious organizations on campus fill your spiritual needs. Many of these religious organizations have church services, social events, and formals, as well as volunteer opportunities. Campus Crusade for Christ (CRU), Campus Outreach, Colonels for Christ, Muslim Student Organization, and Latter-Day Saint Student Organization are just a few of the religious organizations offered at EKU.

Chapel of Meditation

Dedicated May 13, 1972, the Chapel of Meditation is a nondenominational facility used primarily for meditation, weddings, and memorial services. A special memorial service is held there each year to commemorate faculty, staff, and students that have passed away the previous year. Many campus organizations reserve the chapel for special ceremonies, such as inductions or initiations. Various campus ministry services meet there as well to meditate and pray.

The fountain outside of the chapel symbolizes the water of knowledge the University provides.

Residence Hall Leadership and Service

Meeting new people and making a connection with both EKU and the student community are vital aspects of enjoying the start of your collegiate experience. Putting yourself out in the community can not only impact your Colonel experience, but also impact the lives of future students. Residence hall organizations are a simple way to get involved.

Residence Hall Council

Every year Hall Council members are elected to fulfill leadership positions and represent fellow students within each residence hall. Hall councils are responsible for co-curricular programming, creating a diverse social and educational atmosphere, and serving as liaisons between residents and the University Housing office. You are qualified to participate in one of these organizations based on the residence hall where you reside.

"We can no more do without spirituality than we can do without food, shelter, or clothing."

Ernest Holmes

American spiritual writer, teacher, and leader

Resident Assistant (RA)

The RA is one of the most important resources a resident has in the campus community. They are selected upper-class students assigned to individual floors. Chosen to provide leadership and assistance to the residents of the hall, they offer opportunities for academic enrichment and personal growth through hall programming. To apply for this position a student must have lived on a college campus for two semesters, have above a 2.5 GPA, and their judicial record will be reviewed. Many of the student leaders on EKU's campus have been a Resident Assistant at one point during their college career.

SOME EXAMPLES OF STUDENT LEADER POSITIONS AT EKU:

- RSO Officer
- Alternative Break Leader
- Intramural Sports Official
- Peer Educator
- Resident Assistant
- Event Planner

CO-CURRICULAR PROGRAMMING OPPORTUNITIES

New Student Days

Start your college experience off right by attending one of the most important events of your first year at EKU. New Student Days (NSD) is when new students come together to participate in a variety of both academic and social events. The mission of New Student Days is to help students transition to EKU, learn about campus services and activities, and meet other new students. You will have dinner with the president, meet faculty and administrators, participate in campus traditions, and much more!

New Student Days kicks off the Sunday before classes begin and programs continue throughout the first weeks of classes. New Student Days is encouraged for all new students.

For more information on New Student Days, visit: http://www.firstyear.eku.edu/nsd

"The various Chautauqua lectures presented on campus are always interesting. It's great to have the opportunity to hear such accomplished people speaking on what they are passionate about."

Courtney Leggett
Nursing

Chautauqua Lecture Series

Students have an opportunity to directly encounter some of the leading thinkers and activists of our time tackling provocative but vital issues thanks to the Chautauqua Lecture Series. The Chautauqua Lecture Series aims to address both local concerns and global imperatives and to extend your liberal arts education beyond the classroom. By striking a balance between the local and the global, we help to serve the students' regional needs.

For more information on the Chautauqua Lecture Series, visit: http://www.chautauqua.eku.edu

Get Engaged in the Arts

Dance Theatre

Enjoy the art and performance of dance? Then consider auditioning for Dance Theatre at EKU! Dance Theatre is a program for students and faculty alike to perform art and social forms of dance. They hold a community-wide concert at the end of every semester that showcases original pieces of choreography and the work of professors and upperclassmen throughout the themed and exciting performance. Dance Theatre is a great way to express art and stay in shape.

EKU Theatre Arts

EKU's Theatre Arts is a distinguished and busy program. The Department of English and Theatre offers teaching and non-teaching degrees and is in charge of the co-curricular production program. Each year, EKU Theatre puts on four major productions ranging in style from modern-day art, to musicals, to classical scripts. From productions such as *Romeo & Juliet* and *Sweeney Todd*, EKU Theatre welcomes all forms of talent to fill the many roles of a theater production which includes directors, stage managers, actors, singers, costume and set designers, and more. With a state-of-the-art stage and theatre facility, EKU Theatre welcomes all to come and enjoy an escape into drama, art, and action!

Giles Art Gallery

The Fred Parker Giles Gallery, named for a distinguished past Professor of Art, is located off the main lobby of the Campbell Building and is the most important venue for the display of art in Richmond. Spacious, well-lit, and flexible, the gallery extends through two levels and can accommodate large, or even multiple, exhibits. The gallery changes exhibits approximately once a month.

The Arts at EKU

Dance Theatre:
http://www.dance.eku.edu/dance-theatre

EKU Theatre Arts:
http://www.theatre.eku.edu/

Art Focused Student Organization:
http://www.art.eku.edu/student-organizations

Giles Gallery:
http://www.art.eku.edu/fred-parker-giles-gallery

EKU Music:
http://www.music.eku.edu

EKU Music

EKU's Department of Music is home to future band directors, music teachers, composers, soloists, and music professionals in music industry fields of recording, arts management, and music marketing. With over 100 performances each year, there's always an ensemble, student, faculty, or guest artist recital being presented in one of the many performance venues on campus. The majority of these events are free and open to the public, so take a break from studying and join us for some live music! Listening not enough for you? The Department of Music has many non-auditioned groups open to all student musicians, regardless of your academic major. Visit our website (music.eku.edu) or come by the Foster Building for more information on how to get involved.

EKU's Center for the Arts hosts live entertainment, theater performances, and music concerts throughout the year, often at a discount for EKU students. To see the EKU Center for the Arts schedule, visit http://ekucenter.com/

Academic Resources

■ OFFICE OF THE REGISTRAR

The Office of the Registrar is the official location for your academic transcript and all academic records. This is the office you will visit when you have questions about dropping

"There's something about the theater which makes my fingertips tingle."

Wole Soyinka

Nigerian dramatist

and adding courses, **academic bankruptcy**, enrollment or degree verifications, **academic holds** on your registration, changing your name or address, and withdrawing from the University.

To find more information about your academic record and other topics, visit http://www.registrar.eku.edu/procedures-services-policies.

■ ACADEMIC ADVISING

Academic advising is an important aspect of the college experience. Advising can help students determine life and career goals, create solid academic plans, and ensure that you reach your academic potential. We recommend you meet with your academic advisor at least once a semester, or more often if you are having academic or personal issues that could keep you from being a successful student. Advisors provide academic assistance, major and career exploration, work with you to solve problems or refer you to other areas or departments that can help you, explain your DegreeWorks audit (your graduation road map), and select the courses needed to become a college graduate.

Check out Academic Advising online for more information: http://www.advising.eku.edu/

You will find that the advising process takes various forms depending on the college and department in which you declare your major. Some students are advised by faculty who teach major courses in a degree program, while others are advised by professional advisors. If you have not declared a major, or you have more than one college readiness need (090 or 095 level course), the University Advising Office (Whitlock Building, Room 347) is where you will find your advisor.

■ STUDENT OUTREACH AND TRANSITION OFFICE

The Student Outreach and Transition Office (SOTO) serves as a one-stop shop for a variety of adult, transfer, veteran, and re-entry students' needs. Current students can receive individualized consulting services in the areas of degree audits, major selection, academic bankruptcy, the transfer credit process, degree completion via distance learning, and course registration. The office also strives to have answers to basic questions regarding filing for financial aid, financial aid appeals and professional judgment, securing veteran's benefits, and receiving credit for prior learning.

For more information about SOTO, visit http://soto.eku.edu/

Transfer Center

Have you taken courses at another institution before coming to Eastern Kentucky University? If so, you will want to visit the Transfer Center. They can answer questions about how your previous coursework is reflected in your degree audit and work to help maximize the number of transfer hours that can be applied to your selected degree. If you elect to take summer courses elsewhere, they can help you identify courses that will apply to your outstanding degree requirements.

Military and Veterans Affairs

EKU has been recognized as one of the top veteran-friendly campuses by *G.I. Magazine*. Approximately 450 veterans and their families currently receive veteran's benefits.

EKU's Office of Military and Veterans Affairs is located in the Burnham House. Military and Veterans Affairs offers a variety of services and opportunities for students who have served in the United States Military, including targeted tuition rates, priority registration, adventure programming, and a textbook lending program.

The Office of Military and Veterans Affairs houses a VA certifying official who assists with the completion of important paperwork each semester. This office also facilitates a number of opportunities for vets to connect with fellow vets through peer-to-peer mentoring and tutoring, adventure programming, and special workshops designed to meet the needs of our vets. The staff also serves as advocates for our valued service members and their families.

Learn more about Veterans Affairs at:
http://soto.eku.edu/veterans

➲Did you know?
EKU offers a Minor in Military Studies.

Education Pays

The Education Pays Center offers qualified students a world of benefits, from tutoring and computer labs to financial aid, cultural enrichment, work experience, and career counseling. To qualify, you must be a recipient of Kentucky Transitional Assistant Program (K-TAP) and a full-time student at EKU. Visit the SOTO website for more information.

■ COLONEL'S COMPASS

The Colonel's Compass is your online one-stop shop to answer many questions about EKU. You will find the Compass link on the EKU homepage. The Compass is essential to navigating the often rough waters of being a student, so be sure to check it often.

Here's a list of some of the questions the Colonel's Compass can answer:

- What are course abbreviations? What do they stand for?
- How do I contact the dean or chair of a department?
- What does it mean when I receive an error while registering for classes?
- Where can I find deadlines for Add/Drop, Withdrawal, and Refund dates?
- I need a calendar of all important EKU dates; where do I go?
- Where can I look up my final exams schedule?
- When can I see my advisor for career advising and to receive my RAC number?
- I don't know anything about registering for classes. What do I do?

Check out the Colonel's Compass:
http://www.eku.edu/compass

"Twenty-five million veterans are living among us today. These men and women selflessly set aside their civilian lives to put on the uniform and serve us."

Steve Buyer

Former U.S. Representative

UNDERGRADUATE CATALOG

The EKU Undergraduate Catalog is one of the more important resources you should become familiar with as an EKU student. The catalog provides information about the University, required general education courses, grading, and lists all of the majors and minors at the University. All degree requirements are listed by college and department, and descriptions of all courses are located at the end of the catalog.

Check out the current Undergraduate Catalog online:
http://www.undergradstudies.eku.edu/catalog/

ACADEMIC SUPPORT AND TUTORING

Adjusting to college courses and the expectations of professors can be overwhelming. That is why tutoring is available to EKU students free of charge in a variety of disciplines. EKU offers tutoring in math, accounting, physics, chemistry, economics, foreign languages, and communications. Below you will find information on a few of the tutoring centers available on campus.

Find more information about tutoring online:
http://tutoring.eku.edu

Math Tutoring Lab

Located in the Wallace Building, the Math Tutoring Lab has consultants who are available to work one-on-one with students on their math assignments and test preparation. The Math Tutoring Lab may be reached by calling 859-622-6508.

Noel Studio for Academic Creativity

The Noel Studio opened in 2010 to provide a space for EKU students to bring a variety of communication projects, including traditional print-based essays, oral presentations, digital productions, notes, and outlines. Students can even visit the Noel Studio without anything substantial on paper. They can discuss ideas and questions about their work with consultants or just use the invention or practice spaces to develop ideas.

University Housing

University Housing offers individual and group tutoring in math, sciences, English, and the humanities. They also offer a variety of workshops throughout the year on topics such as time management, test prep, study skills, and more. Call 859-622-6480 for more information.

Common Knowledge—Home of the EKU GURU

Common Knowledge is a new program run by EKU student GURUS dedicated entirely to your success! A GURU will answer any question you may have and help you with your homework. A GURU can also assist you with financial aid, locating classes/buildings, registration, Blackboard, finding a job, and a whole lot more.

- Friend the GURUs on Facebook: C.K. Gurus and ask them anything about EKU live via Facebook chat.
- GURUs offer homework help in over 25 different subject areas.
- Can't make it to campus for homework help? SKYPE with the GURUs @ Common_Knowledge and they'll help you with your homework.Follow them on Twitter @ CKGurusEKU.
- Can't find where you need to be on campus? Drop by the Tech Commons and a GURU will walk you there.
- Need to check out a laptop, projector, or camera for a class project? Just ask the GURUs.

Common Knowledge is located in the Tech Commons behind the Food Court on the lower level of the Powell Building, in the Whitlock Building Computer Lab,and in Crabbe Library near Java City.

Don't struggle with your most challenging subjects alone when help is available. For hours and contact information for these and other tutoring centers on campus visit: http://tutoring.eku.edu/directory-and-hours

EKU LIBRARIES

Eastern Kentucky University Libraries are the academic heart of campus. EKU Libraries inspire creativity,the exploration of new ideas,the generation of new knowledge, and the development of new skills.

Stop by one of three locations:

1. John Grant Crabbe Main Library, University Drive
2. Elizabeth K. Baker Music Library, Foster Building
3. Business Library and Academic Commons, Business and Technology Complex

There are many ways to get answers to your reference questions:

- Instant message: http://www.library.eku.edu/ask-us
- Email: reference.library@eku.edu
- Phone: 859-474-0EKU
- Or visit the John Grant Crabbe Main Library Help Desk

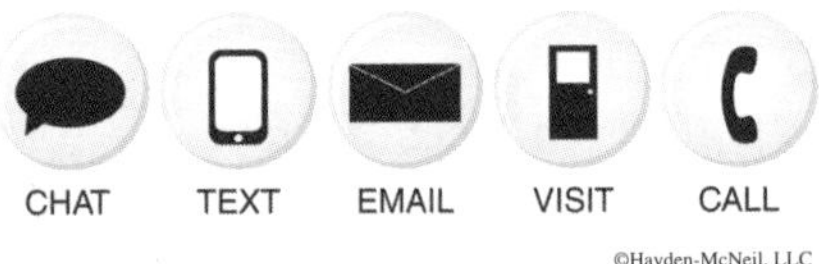

Do you need something fun to read? Check out the Library's popular and staff picks collections in the Main Library's Grand Reading Room. Here you'll find an assortment of fiction and non-fiction best sellers you're sure to enjoy.

Looking for peace and quiet? Visit the Main Library's fourth floor, an entire space devoted to quiet study. The fourth floor is perfect for relaxing between classes, reading, and of course studying!

Visit EKU libraries online:
http://www.library.eku.edu
http://www.facebook.com/ekulibraries
https://twitter.com/ekulibraries

INFORMATION TECHNOLOGY (IT.EKU.EDU)

Student Computing Services (studentcomputing.eku.edu)

Student Computing Services is a collection of integrated IT support services focused on empowering student success. We collaborate with EKU's diverse student population in one single, convenient location in room 230 of the Combs Classroom Building.

We offer technical support (e.g., email, ResNet, wireless), charging stations for mobile devices, equipment checkout services (Windows and Mac PCs, iPads, cameras), and tech tutoring.

Computer Labs

EKU has four Information Technology (IT) computer labs providing Windows and Mac computers, printers, scanners, and a large selection of software. These labs are on the lower floor of the Powell Building, the main floor

> "I have always imagined that Paradise will be a kind of library."
>
> Jorge Luis Borges
>
> Argentine writer

of the Whitlock Building, Combs 230, and the Crabbe Library. Hours vary widely, so check the IT website.

For computer lab hours and locations visit: http://www.it.eku.edu/computerlabs

EKUDirect is the official site for student account tasks involving accounting, financial aid, registration, housing, and more: http://it.eku.edu/ekudirect

Visit EKU myMail to access your student email: http://mymail.eku.edu/ (EKU email is the official communication service for the University).

Printing

Campus computer labs employ the Pharos Uniprint system, which encourages you to print responsibly and control costs and waste. Each student begins each new semester with a full $25 allocation, which cannot be rolled over to the next semester or be refunded. You will be billed for exceeding your allocation. The Pharos Uniprint system makes it easy for you to print from any computer lab on campus without carrying cash or a debit card!

Blackboard

Just as soon as classes begin, some of your instructors may direct you to the course **Blackboard** site. The majority of professors on campus use Blackboard, although there are some that use other software for special purposes.

The login to this learning site is the same as your normal login that you use for all of your computing activities on campus. When you open Blackboard, you will see a list of courses in which you are enrolled and the professor has made available.

Clicking on the class link will open the Blackboard site for that particular class. Blackboard is used for a variety of purposes. Some instructors use Blackboard to post announcements, distribute lecture notes, store assignments, and give quizzes. Your professor may also request that you submit papers you have written through the Blackboard site. One way a paper is submitted is through **Safe Assignment**, which compares your paper with papers all over the web.

Blackboard also has links which allow you to communicate with other members of the class individually or as a part of a group, check your grades, or contact your professor.

To visit the EKU Blackboard site, go to: http://learn.eku.edu

■ DISABILITIES SERVICES OFFICE

To address the accessibility and academic needs of individuals with disabilities, the Office of Services for Individuals with Disabilities (OSID) will review, evaluate, and determine eligibility for any requested services and accommodations from students, faculty, or staff. To qualify for services an individual will need to complete the application for services and provide the University with current **disability** documentation that meets our disability documentation guidelines. Qualified disabilities may include learning disabilities; ADHD; Asperger's; physical, visual, and hearing impairments; mental health; and chronic health impairments. While accommodations are determined at the OSID, the University also has an ADA Coordinator and the ADA Compliance Committee to ensure that disability rights are protected and addressed appropriately.

For more information, visit the Disabilities Office website:
http://www.disabilities.eku.edu/

■ COUNSELING CENTER

College life is a new experience for most students who arrive on the Eastern Kentucky University campus each fall. Life as you know it may be turned upside down as you experience residence hall life for the first time and are far from home and the familiar experiences you have had for so many years. You may be completely on your own for the first time in your life, having to learn to set your own schedule, arrive to class on time, eat a proper diet, and get a good night's sleep. There is no one to make sure you get your homework done and papers written. College life can be downright overwhelming at times, leading to a stressful first semester.

The Counseling Center can help you work through your concerns and learn tools for dealing with your stress, improving your friendships and relationships, developing skills for improving academic performance, choosing a major and/or career, and identifying strategies for improving your overall happiness. This office is staffed by trained counselors who are here to help you in any way they can. Anything you share with a counselor is held in the strictest confidence, and there is never a charge for the time you spend.

Visit the EKU Counseling Center's website for a variety of helpful resources:
http://www.counseling.eku.edu/

How can I meet with an EKU counselor?
To talk with a counselor, please call 859-622-1303, or stop by the Counseling Center in the Whitlock Building, room 571.

Fall and spring semester hours are Monday–Thursday, 8 am–5 pm, and Friday, 8 am–4:30 pm.

Career Counseling Seminar

GCS 199, Career Counseling Seminar is offered by the Counseling Center to help you choose a major and career direction based on your interests, skills, personality characteristics, and values. You will learn how to select possible majors and careers where you would be most successful. This course, meeting for eight weeks, is offered every semester for one credit hour on a pass/fail basis.

Chapter Summary

As you can see in this chapter, EKU is a university that has numerous opportunities available to provide you with a complete college education. The University has a long and varied history of preparing students to enter the work world in successful careers. Reaching that goal requires work, using available resources and opportunities, and involvement in campus life.

"If a window of opportunity appears, don't pull down the shade."
Tom Peters
American business writer

■ KEY TERMS

Academic bankruptcy: A policy in which a student's previous college-level course work is not considered in the calculation of GPA and credit is not applied to the current university attended (though the work remains on the student's record)

Academic hold: An account restriction which prevents a student from registering until all outstanding materials are submitted

Alma Mater: A school's official song; also refers to the school or university from which one graduated

Alumni: Graduates or former students of a particular school, college, or university (singular: alumnus)

Baccalaureate degree: An academic degree awarded for studies in an undergraduate major generally lasting four years; a bachelor's degree

Blackboard: A comprehensive education technology website that connects students and instructors to facilitate and enhance classroom/online learning

Disability: A physical or psychological condition that may limit one's ability to access physical spaces or activities, or may present a psychological or emotional barrier to success in education

Safe Assignment: An automated system on the Blackboard site that detects plagiarism

NOTES

"Go as far as you can see; when you get there, you'll be able to see farther."

J.P. Morgan

American financier, banker, philanthropist, and art collector

■ CAMPUS RESOURCES

Academic Advising
http://www.advising.eku.edu
Whitlock Building, room 347, 859-622-2276

Alumni Association
http://www.alumni.eku.edu
Richards Alumni House, 859-622-1260

Athletics
http://www.ekusports.com
Alumni Coliseum 115, 859-622-2120

Common Knowledge
http://www.facebook.com/CKGurus
Tech Commons, Powell Building, 859-622-2496

Counseling Center
http://www.counseling.eku.edu
Whitlock Building, room 571, 859-622-1303

***Eastern Progress* Newspaper**
http://www.easternprogress.com
Combs Building, room 230, 859-622-1881

EKU Libraries
http://www.library.eku.edu
103 Libraries Complex, 859-622-1790

EKU Theatre
http://www.theatre.eku.edu
Campbell Building, room 306, 859-622-1315

First Year Programs
http://www.firstyear.eku.edu
Whitlock Building, room 372, 859-622-1682

Giles Gallery
http://www.art.eku.edu
309 Campbell Building, 859-622-6139

Greek Life
http://www.greeklife.eku.edu
Powell Student Center, room 136, 859-622-2050

Honors Program
http://www.honors.eku.edu
Case Annex, room 168, 859-622-2924

Information Technology
http://www.it.eku.edu
859-622-1682

Milestone Yearbook
http://encompass.eku.edu/yearbooks/
Combs Building, room 328, 859-622-2569

Noel Studio for Academic Creativity
http://www.studio.eku.edu
Crabbe Library, 859-622-7730

Registered Student Organizations
http://www.studentlife.eku.edu
Powell Student Center, room 128, 859-622-3855

Registrar
http://www.registrar.eku.edu
Whitlock Building, room 239, 859-622-3876

ResNet
http://studentcomputing.eku.edu
Combs Building, room 230, 859-622-3050

Student Life
http://www.studentlife.eku.edu
Combs Building, room 328, 859-622-2569

Student Outreach and Transition Office (SOTO)
http://www.soto.eku.edu/
Whitlock Building, room 442, 859-622-7686

Tutoring
http://www.advising.eku.edu/tutoring/
Whitlock Building, room 347, 859-622-6778

University Housing
http://www.housing.eku.edu
Whitlock Building, room 552, 859-622-1515

■ REFERENCES

BrainyQuote. (n.d.). *BrainyQuote.com*. Retrieved June 9, 2011, from http://www.brainyquote.com/

Burns, M.K. (Songwriter), & Lutes, H.H. (Composer). (1932). Yea, Eastern. In *EKU First Year Programs* (n.d.), Family resources, *EKU First Year Programs*. Retrieved March 17, 2011, from http://www.firstyear.eku.edu/family-resources

Couture, J., Whalen, D., & Hill, C. (2006). *Eastern Kentucky University 1906–1956*. Chicago, IL: Arcadia Publishing.

Couture, J., Whalen, D., & Hill, C. (2007). *Eastern Kentucky University 1957–2006*. Chicago, IL: Arcadia Publishing.

EKU Alumni (2007). Alumni awards. In *EKU Alumni Awards*. Retrieved March 18, 2011, from http://alumni.eku.edu/awards/a-z.htm

EKU First Year Programs. (n.d.). Family resources. In *EKU First Year Programs*. Retrieved March 17, 2011, from http://www.firstyear.eku.edu/family-resources

EKU Office of Institutional Effectiveness. (2011). *2011–2015 Mission Values Vision Draft*. Retrieved from Eastern Kentucky University, EKU Office of Institutional Effectiveness Website: http://www.oie.eku.edu/spc/StrategicPlan/2011–2015%20Plan/2011-2015%20Strategic%20Plan%20Mission%20Values%20Vision%20Final%20Draft%20010711.pdf

EKU Student Affairs. (2005). *Family calendar and handbook*. Retrieved March 18, 2011, from Eastern Kentucky University, EKU Student Affairs Website: http://www.studentaffairs.eku.edu/resources/family_calendar_05.pdf

EKU Undergraduate Studies. (2010). Section one: The university. In *Eastern Kentucky University Undergraduate catalog 2010–2011*. Richmond, KY: Eastern Kentucky University. Retrieved March 18, 2011, from Eastern Kentucky University, EKU Libraries, Encompass archive Website: http://www.undergradstudies.eku.edu/catalog/2010-2011/easternkentuckyuniversity.pdf

Ellis, W.E. (2005). *A history of Eastern Kentucky University: The school of opportunity*. Lexington, KY: The University Press of Kentucky.

Evans, N. (Songwriter), & Campbell, J. (Composer). (n.d.). Eastern Kentucky University alma mater. In EKU First Year Programs (n.d.), Family resources, *EKU First Year Programs*. Retrieved March 17, 2011, from http://www.firstyear.eku.edu/family-resources

Gorley, A., & Miller, L.T. (2007). You're gonna miss this [Recorded by Trace Adkins]. On *American man: Greatest hits, vol. II* [CD]. Los Angeles, CA: Capitol Nashville.

Hay III, C. C., & Whitlock, C. D. (1992). Eastern Kentucky University: A long look back (R.E. Harrell, Ed.). In C. Usher, *Eastern Kentucky University: Then and now* (R. E. Harrell, W. Butler, & W. Strode, Eds.) (pp. 65–112). Louisville, KY: Harmony House Publishers.

Light, R. (2001). *Making the most of college: Students speak their minds*. Cambridge, MA: Harvard University Press.

Pascarella, E. T., Terenzini, P. T., & Wolfe, L. M. (1986). Orientation to college and freshman year persistence/withdrawal decisions. *Journal of Higher Education*, *57*(2), 155–175.

Pascarella, E. T., & Terenzini, P. T. (2005). *How college affects students: A third decade of research*. San Francisco, CA: Jossey-Bass.

Tinto, V. (1975). Dropout from higher education: A theoretical synthesis of recent research. *Review of Educational Research, 45*(1), 89–125.

Tinto, V. (2000). Taking retention seriously: Rethinking the first year of college. *NACADA Journal*, *19*(2), 5–10.

Yokomoto, C., Rizkalla, M., O'Loughlin, C., El-Sharkawy, M., & Lamm, N. (2001). Developing a motivational freshman course in using the principle of attached learning. *Journal of Engineering Education*, *88*(1), 99–106.

Wilcox, F. (Songwriter), & Schnabi, H. (Composer). (1940). Hail, hail Eastern Maroons. In EKU First Year Programs (n.d.), Family resources, *EKU First Year Programs*. Retrieved March 17, 2011, from http://www.firstyear.eku.edu/family-resources

3

SUCCEED

Chapter Three

Chapter Three

SUCCEED

After mastering the content in this chapter you will:

- Recognize your academic responsibilities
- Understand the impact of and be able to calculate your Grade Point Average
- Be able to demonstrate active learning habits
- Be able to demonstrate a successful application of study skills
- Be able to construct and use time-management tools
- Demonstrate academic integrity

Fundamental Question

- How can I become a successful college student?

Essential Principles

- Time Management
- Responsibility
- Self-Awareness

"High expectations are the key to everything."

Sam Walton

American entrepreneur and founder of Walmart

For most new students, the transition from high school to college is both exciting and challenging. This chapter will center on the changes and responsibilities a new college student will encounter. It will feature the differences between high school and college, your instructors' responsibilities, and your responsibilities as a college student.

Stepping Up

As soon as possible, you should become aware of the importance of stepping up and taking responsibility in college in ways you were not expected to in high school. In high school, your parents and teachers bore much of the responsibility of helping you get your diploma. Your parents made sure you got up in the morning and went to school, they fed you balanced meals, they did your laundry, etc. Your teachers reminded you of assignments, gave you work when you were absent, offered extra credit, etc.

In college, there is a substantial shift in responsibility. You are responsible for enrolling in, and successfully passing, the courses required to earn your college degree. You bear the weight of responsibility for your own success here and in the future.

Table 3-1. High School vs. College: What's the Difference?

IN HIGH SCHOOL	IN COLLEGE
Your time is structured by others.	You manage your own time.
You are not responsible for knowing what it takes to graduate.	Graduation requirements are complex and differ from year to year. You are responsible for knowing those that apply to you.
You are in classes 30+ hours/week.	You are in classes 12–18 hours/week.
Instruction is by lecture, learning activities, games, group work, etc.	Instruction is mainly by lecture.
Class size is around 30–35 students per class.	Class size can range from 10 to 500+ students per class.
Teachers approach you if you need assistance.	Professors expect you to initiate contact if you need help.
You have little control over your own class schedule.	You arrange your own class schedule.
Grades are based on multiple homework assignments, quizzes, tests, projects, etc.	Grades are usually based on one or two tests and possibly an essay paper or group project.
Teachers check all your homework and remind you of incomplete work.	You are expected to read the syllabus for assignment due dates—no hand holding. Professors may not always check homework or remind you of incomplete work.
Teachers are often available to talk before, during, or after class.	Professors expect and want you to attend their scheduled office hours.
If you are absent, teachers provide you with information you missed.	Professors expect you to get any missed notes from your classmates.
Class attendance is closely monitored.	Monitoring of attendance varies by class. There is a "1st Day Attendance—Faculty Drop" policy.

(Shoenberg, 2008)

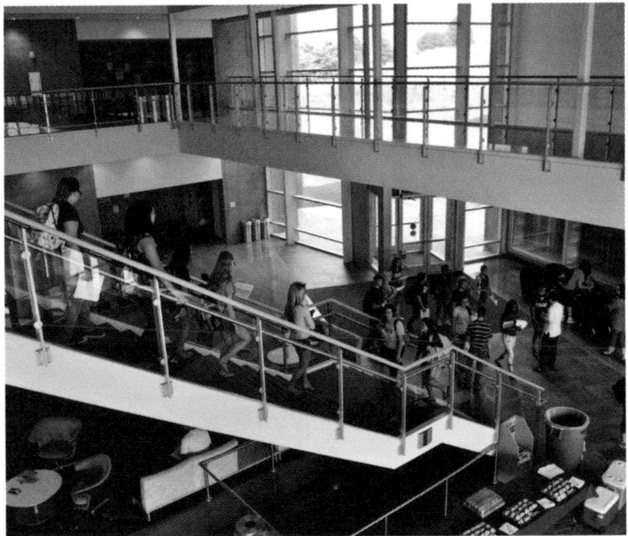

"For me, the biggest difference between high school and college is the amount of independence. However, it is up to the student to use this freedom in a positive way that helps their college experience, not damages it."

Ashley Stearns
Political Science

ACADEMIC WORKLOAD

The easiest way to envision your next few years in college is to recognize that college is like having a new full-time job! Between attending classes and studying, being a full-time student usually takes around 36 to 40 hours a week.

In general, you should study two hours for each hour you are in class. Studying can include reading, note taking, projects, Blackboard assignments, and other homework. Studying does not include things such as busy work or finding the "best spot" to study. So, for example, if you take a class that meets three hours per week, you should study six hours outside class for that course each week. Adding the three hours of class time and the six hours of study time gives you an academic workload of nine hours for that class every week.

As you can see, being successful in college will require a greater commitment of your time and energy than what was required in high school. Likewise, your performance in college will have a much greater effect on your future than your performance in high school. The next section discusses an important tool you can use to measure your academic success and make sure you stay on track along the way.

UNDERSTANDING THE IMPACT OF YOUR GPA

At Eastern Kentucky University, you are expected to maintain a minimum of a 2.0 cumulative **grade point average** (GPA). However, you should strive to achieve much higher. Keeping a high GPA is vital to your academic success. If you slack off or don't take your classes seriously, you could find yourself on academic probation, or even suspended or dismissed by the University. Your GPA is also important in regards to maintaining scholarships, being admitted into certain academic programs, and advancing to graduate school. Table 3-2 shows some of the consequences of falling below EKU's minimum 2.0 GPA requirement.

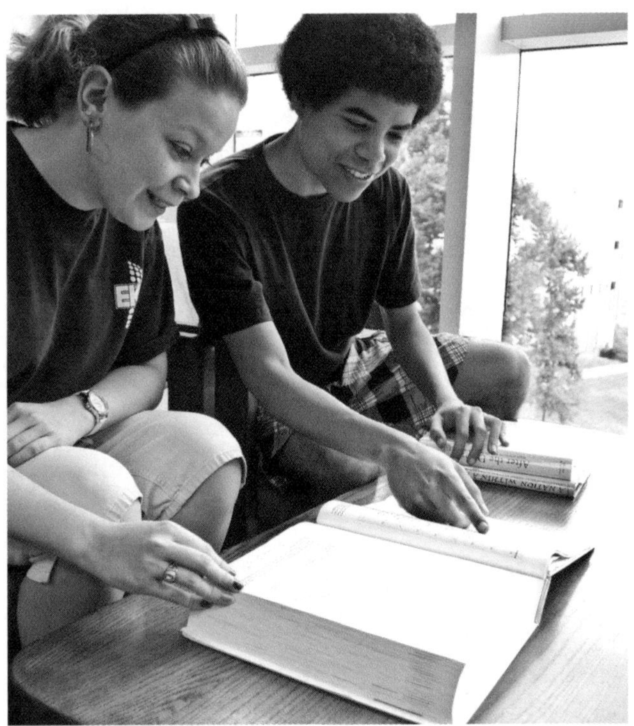

"Accept responsibility for your life. Know that it is you who will get you where you want to go."
Les Brown
American businessman

Table 3-2. Impact of Your GPA.

IF YOU. . .	ACADEMIC STANDING	LOOKING AHEAD
Earn a GPA of 2.0 or above	Good	No registration limitations
Are a first-year student and earn below a 2.0	Academic Warning	May not enroll in more than 16 hours in fall/spring or more than 6 hours in summer
Are a second-semester student and your cumulative GPA is below 2.0	Academic Probation	May not enroll in more than 13 hours in fall/spring or more than 6 hours in summer
At the end of a semester on Academic Probation, if you do not earn a 2.0 term GPA *and* your cumulative GPA remains below 2.0, you will be placed on Academic Suspension.		
SUSPENSION TYPE	**IF YOU. . .**	**SUSPENSION PERIOD**
1st Suspension	Earn a GPA below 2.0 in fall semester	Spring Semester
1st Suspension	Earn a GPA below 2.0 in spring semester	Summer and Fall Semesters
2nd Suspension	Earn a semester GPA below 2.0	1 Calendar Year
3rd Suspension	Earn a semester GPA below 2.0	2 Calendar Years
At the end of a 3rd Academic Suspension, you must earn and maintain a term GPA of 2.0 or better each semester. If you have a term GPA below a 2.0 at the end of *any* term, you will be dismissed from the University and will not be able to reapply for admission to the University for 5 calendar years.		

(EKU Undergraduate Studies, 2010)

"Let's face it, you can't be good at every subject! If you need help don't hesitate to go to EKU Tutoring Services. That is what they are there for!"

Callie Northern
Bachelor of Fine Arts

Want to quickly calculate your semester GPA? Use the online GPA Calculator by visiting: http://www.advising.eku.edu/gpacalculator/

How Do I Calculate My GPA?

Your GPA is calculated by dividing the total number of **quality points** by the number of attempted hours. Your hours attempted are the sum of your credit hours (not including courses below the 100 level or classes taken as Pass/Fail or Satisfactory/Unsatisfactory). In order to find your quality points, you must take the grade point value for each course and multiply it by the credit hours for the course.

Grade Point Values:

A = 4.0 C = 2.0 F = 0.0

B = 3.0 D = 1.0

Table 3-3 shows an example of how to find your quality points.

Table 3-3. Quality Points for One Semester.

QUALITY POINT EXAMPLE FOR ONE SEMESTER						
Course	Grade	Grade Value	Multiply	Credit Hours	Total	Quality Points
GSD 101	A	4.0	×	3	=	12
ENG 101	B	3.0		3		9
MAT 095	B	3.0		N/A		N/A
PHE 180	A	4.0		3		12
SOC 131	B	3.0		3		9
PHE 190	A	4.0		1		4
			Totals	13		46

In this example, the semester GPA would be calculated as follows:

GPA = 46 (Total Quality Points) / **13** (Hours Attempted) = **3.538**

To calculate your cumulative GPA for the year, add your total attempted hours and total quality points for all semesters. Divide the total quality points by total attempted hours.

Program Acceptance, Scholarships, and Awards

Several programs at EKU require a certain minimum GPA to be considered for acceptance. Two programs that require a minimum GPA are Education and Nursing. However, they are not the only programs with these requirements. Consult with your advisor and the Undergraduate Catalog about program requirements. In addition, many academic scholarships require you to maintain a minimum GPA.

Scholarships

To find information about GPA requirements for scholarships, programs, and awards, check out the Undergraduate Catalog: http://www.undergradstudies.eku.edu/catalog

A **scholarship** is money you have been awarded to pay for school-based academics, activities, or other qualifying factors. By now, you may have already been awarded a scholarship or two and you can continue to apply for scholarships while you're in college. Scholarships can be divided into three basic categories: merit based, need based, and criteria based.

Merit scholarships are based on academic performance. They are awarded for grades, standardized test scores, and academic achievement. **Need-based scholarships** are available to students with financial need. This means that the family demonstrates some type of financial hardship. Some need-based scholarships have other requirements like academic success or a specific criteria. **Criteria-based scholarships** are based on an activity, a physical attribute or heritage, or a specific course of study.

There are literally thousands of scholarships available if you meet the required criteria. Of course there are the obvious ones like football, music, and alumni scholarships, but are you left-handed? Do you breed rabbits? Are you an expert at duck calls? A vegetarian? Is your last name Van Valkenburg? If you can answer yes to questions like these, there is a scholarship out there waiting for you to find it. After you've checked with EKU for scholarships, look online, go to the library reference section, or look for scholarship guidebooks.

Once you've gotten the scholarship, you need to know what you have to do to keep it. Some scholarships have a one-time payout but many will continue to pay on a semester or annual basis as long as you meet certain requirements. It is important to know which of your scholarships are recurring and the requirements for keeping them. Most will require you to maintain a certain GPA or be enrolled for a certain number of hours each semester. Some may be tied to an activity or an organization you participate in. Losing scholarships can be financially costly! You worked hard to earn them so work hard to keep them!

SCHOLARSHIP TIP

One of the most common recurring scholarships is the Kentucky Educational Excellence Scholarship, or KEES.

Kentucky high school graduates earn KEES money while in high school. This scholarship is good for 8 semesters, as long as you stay on track to graduate and meet the GPA requirements.

Students who have earned fewer than 60 credit hours must maintain a 2.5 GPA to continue receiving KEES money.

Once you have earned more than 60 credit hours, you must maintain a 3.0 GPA to keep the full scholarship amount. You can still receive half of the scholarship amount if you maintain a GPA between 2.5 and 3.0.

Awards

Dean's List

EKU recognizes students who achieve academic excellence. One of those recognitions is the Dean's List. The eligibility requirements for the Dean's List are:

"March on. Do not tarry. To go forward is to move toward perfection. March on, and fear not the thorns, or the sharp stones on life's path."

Khalil Gibran

Lebanese-American poet

Table 3-4. Eligibility for Dean's List.

HOURS ATTEMPTED (100 LEVEL OR HIGHER COURSES)	MINIMUM GPA REQUIRED
12	3.75
13	3.65
14 or more	3.50

Students who are taking fewer than 12 semester hours are not eligible to be placed on the Dean's List. Courses below the 100 level will not be counted in determining eligibility.

EKU recognizes students who are on the Dean's List three times with the Dean's Award. Students receive a recognition pin by the dean of their college for this award.

President's Award

"As a further recognition of academic achievement, the University presents the President's Award to students who completed a full time course load, with normal grading, and who attain a 4.0 GPA for the semester. Students receiving the President's Award receive a letter of recognition from the President. In addition, the Division of Public Relations sends the names of the recipients to appropriate news media, including their hometown newspaper" (EKU Undergraduate Studies, 2010).

The Instructors' Role

While you are in college, you will take classes from a variety of instructors who you should view as future colleagues. Some of your instructors teach for the University full-time while others teach part-time. You may even have the opportunity to work with a graduate student, though this is most common in lab classes. Think carefully about how you represent yourself toward instructors, as you may need to call on them to serve as references or to write letters of recommendation.

The position of your instructor will determine his or her academic responsibilities at the University. Your high school teacher spent seven hours a day in the classroom teaching. Your college instructor may only spend two or three hours teaching, but the rest of his or her time may be spent researching, publishing, or performing committee work.

■ THE SYLLABUS

One of the responsibilities of all instructors at EKU is the course syllabus. A **syllabus** is a document that is essentially a contract between you and your instructor. Your instructor is responsible for giving you a syllabus early in the semester. It describes the course content and explains how you can successfully complete the course. Keep your course syllabus in a safe place until your semester grades are posted, as it is your responsibility to be aware of and adhere to all policies listed. The following sections give you a brief introduction to the components included in a typical syllabus.

Misplaced your syllabus? Many professors will have your syllabus available all semester on Blackboard at http://learn.eku.edu

Office Hours

Your instructor will note office hours on the syllabus. These are the days and times when your instructor is committed to being available for consultation outside of class. If these hours are not compatible with your schedule, email your professor to set up a time that better fits into your schedule.

> **Remember**—if you have an appointment with your instructor, it is important to keep it and be on time. If you can't keep the appointment, it is best to give at least a twenty-four hour notice, when possible. Missing appointments portrays you as unprofessional.

Instructor Contact Information

Besides office hours, each syllabus will include information on how you can reach your instructor outside of class, including their academic department, office location, phone number, and email address.

Textbook Requirements

You will find that most of your classes require textbooks, as outlined in the syllabus. In addition to textbooks, you may find that some classes require additional supplies. For example, your math class might require a specific calculator and your art class might require charcoal pencils.

Visit EKU's Barnes & Noble Bookstore online and even pre-order your textbooks: http://eku.bncollege.com

Student Learning Outcomes

Student Learning Outcomes outline what knowledge or skills a successful student in your class will be able to demonstrate upon completion of the course. Instructors design their courses with the end in mind, identifying the purpose, significance, and value of their classes. You will notice that each chapter in this textbook also has Student Learning Outcomes.

Evaluation Methods

A syllabus should outline how your learning will be assessed, whether through exams, essays, projects, or other means. This is a road map for the semester and will help you gauge your progress in the course.

Attendance Policy

Attendance policies vary between departments and instructors. Each instructor will outline his or her specific policy on the course syllabus. Pay attention to each syllabus to know what's expected from you if you miss class and how to stay ahead.

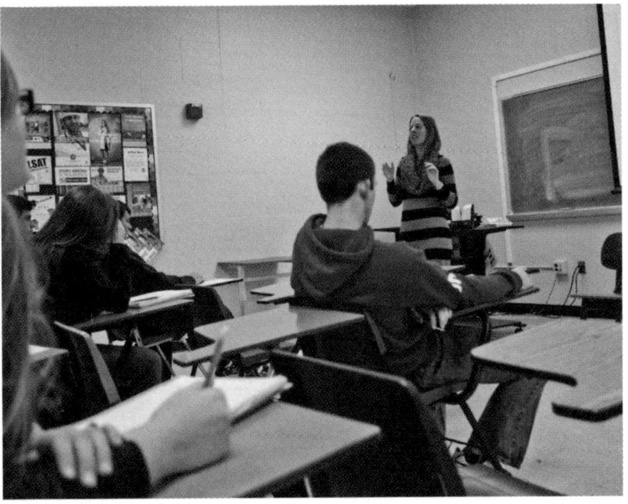

OTHER INSTRUCTOR RESPONSIBILITIES

The Classroom Environment

Instructors are responsible for fostering a safe, open learning environment for their students. You should feel comfortable voicing your opinion and feel respected by your instructor and peers.

"I believe the professors at EKU are a lot more personal with their students than they are at bigger universities. They take time out of their busy lives to make sure we succeed. Without my professors, I would not have made it as far as I have today. My professors all have past experiences that relate to the material they are teaching, which makes learning a more fun experience."

Jacqueline Dean
Social Work, Minor in Veteran Studies

"One worthwhile task carried to a successful conclusion is worth half-a-hundred half-finished tasks."

Malcolm S. Forbes

American businessman

Timely Feedback

In high school, feedback was probably continuous. There were also likely to be many assignments on which to base your grades. In college, you will find that your final grade may come from only three or four items during the entire semester. Turnaround time for grading will depend on your instructor's course load, total number of students, and other University responsibilities, but you should expect to receive feedback from your instructors consistently throughout the semester. Many instructors use Blackboard to post grades quickly.

The Students' Role

■ ATTITUDE AND OUTLOOK

Your attitude is one of the biggest determining factors in future success. Entering into classes and situations with the right attitude will open your mind to new ideas, relationships, and opportunities. On the other hand, entering into classes and situations with the wrong attitude will form barriers between you and your instructors, as well as between you and other students. Learning to listen, not just hear; having patience and persistence; and keeping an open mind will allow for new experiences to help you grow. Attitude should be your asset, not your liability.

■ LOCUS OF CONTROL

Your **locus of control** is where you place the responsibility for events that occur in your life. Do you take ownership of your successes and failures, or do you project the responsibility elsewhere?

External Locus of Control

When events occur in your life and you feel that you do not have control over them, you display an **external locus of control**. This is someone who believes that outside sources control his/her academic and life success. These individuals tend to blame others for their misfortunes and failures and even put the responsibility for their successes on outside sources instead of looking at themselves. They tend to feel that they have no control over their lives or the situations that affect them.

> **For example:** Tia stayed at a party and did not return to her room until 6:00 am. She knew she only had two hours before her first class but wanted to take a nap, so she set her alarm clock to wake her at 7:15 am. When Tia woke up, it was 9:00 am; she had missed her math class. Tia was very upset at her roommate for not waking her for class.
>
> Instead of Tia placing the blame on herself, she put the blame on her roommate (Lefcourt, 1984).

Internal Locus of Control

When events occur and you feel that you have control over them, you display an **internal locus of control**. This is someone who believes that they can be successful academically and in life through hard work, their abilities, and dedication. Students who have an internal locus of control have a strong personal motivation to succeed.

> **For example:** Jill wanted to stay at the party, but instead of staying, she left to go back to her room so she could study. Jill was being a responsible student, showing that her education has priority over partying (Lefcourt, 1984).

Locus of Control Test
To take an online locus of control test, visit: http://www.psych.uncc.edu/pagoolka/LC.html

CREATIVE THINKING TIP

Take risks.
Learn to live with the possibility that you will make mistakes. Thomas Edison admitted that in trying to make a workable light bulb he came up with some 3,000 theories on how he might accomplish the task, but in only two trials did he succeed. That's not much of a success rate, but it was enough for Edison to persist.

Are You a Creator or a Victim?

Creators are those individuals who take responsibility for their actions and situations. Creators have choices and believe they have full control over the events and situations that may occur in their lives. Creators have an internal locus of control.

Someone is a creator when they look at their situation and try to find ways to change.

> **For example:** Jill goes to purchase her GSD 101 textbook. When she arrives at the bookstore, she discovers all the GSD 101 textbooks are sold out and the bookstore will not be getting more in for a week. Jill goes and speaks to her instructor and explains the situation. The instructor has an extra copy of the book and gives it to Jill to use until the bookstore receives more books.

Jill was a creator by going to talk to her professor about not having a textbook for class. She knew it was her responsibility to find an alternate solution until the books arrived (Hazard, 1997).

Victims are those who do not take responsibility for their actions. Victims place the blame on others and do not look within themselves. Victims have an external locus of control.

> **For example:** Tia's GSD 101 class is meeting in Career Services to work on their Career/Major exploration papers. Tia did not write down the location of Career Services, so she missed class. Tia feels that her professor should have placed a note on the classroom door reminding the class of the location change.

Tia displayed the mindset of a victim by putting the blame on the professor when it was her responsibility to find out and write down the location of Career Services (Hazard, 1997).

Change Your Mind

It is possible to move from being a victim to being a creator. You can start this change in thinking by starting with a change in the language you use. Practice by replacing the "victim" language you use in the first column with the "creator" language in the second.

Table 3-5.

"VICTIM" LANGUAGE	"CREATOR" LANGUAGE
"I should do my history homework."	"It would be better if I. . ."
"This is horrible. . . My favorite TV show comes on in 20 minutes but I have a test in the morning!"	"This is inconvenient. . ."
"This research paper is too big."	"I can take this one step at time. . ."
"I have to go to algebra tutoring."	"I choose to go. . .."

(Hazard, 1997)

CREATIVE THINKING TIP

Be bold.
Take chances that initially seem a little off-center. In a world that believed the earth was the center of the universe, Galileo was willing to suffer the consequences of asserting that the universe was in fact heliocentric.

> "If it's never our fault, we can't take responsibility for it. If we can't take responsibility for it, we'll always be its victim."
> Richard Bach
> American novelist

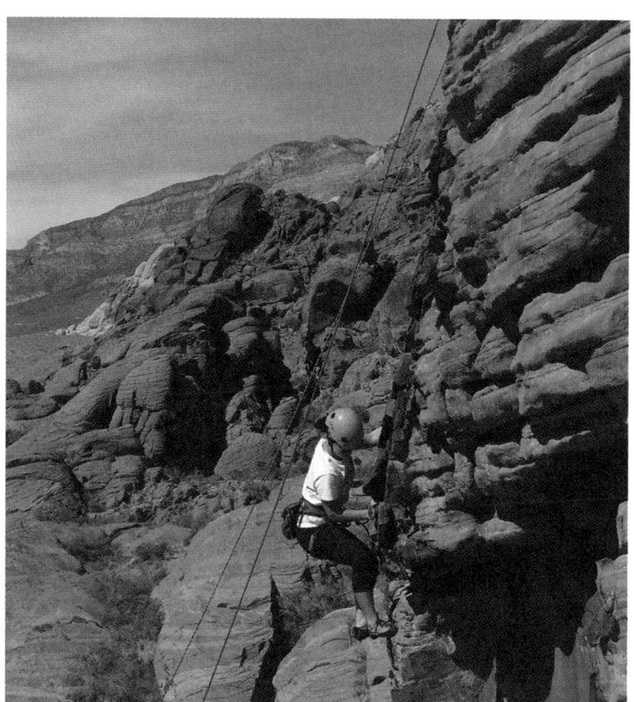

Photo credit: EKU Adventure Programs

Classroom Engagement

Learning is when "change takes place." Therefore, in order to learn effectively, you cannot merely be a passive observer. You must make it a point to be actively engaged in the learning process.

■ BE PREPARED FOR CLASS

This is as simple as doing your reading, taking notes, and completing homework on time. Even if your instructor does not collect your work, it will be relevant pre-work for the topic of an upcoming lecture, quiz, or test.

Also, if you've read the assignment for that class period and done the homework, you will be prepared to ask questions about things that are unclear to you.

Another part of being prepared for class is leaving your cell phone turned off. If you have an emergency situation, you should discuss it with your instructor before class.

■ BE ON TIME (EVEN EARLY) FOR CLASS

It is hard to be an active participant if you come in late or leave early. This is disruptive to others and to the instructor. Arriving early allows you time to gear up for class by taking out your reading notes, reviewing for quizzes, or speaking with your instructor.

■ MOTIVATION

Motivation can come from many sources. It may come from your instructors, your parents or other family members, your friends, or your income. However, true motivation comes from within you. Ultimately, you will be the one to choose to complete assignments on time and with academic integrity, to participate fully or partially, and to work toward your long-term and short-term goals, or not. True motivation lies within you and only you have the power to develop it.

Often, we have to be creative when convincing ourselves that something that we would rather forget about is, in fact, important. The next time you do not feel like completing an assignment or attending a class, make a connection to something important to you. Do you really want to disappoint that family member? Do you really want to settle for a lower grade? Reach deep within and find the motivation that works best for you.

In most college courses, the beginning and ending five minutes are critical times for announcements, quizzes, etc. You should not expect to be given make-ups because you come in late or leave early and miss something. If this happens, ask a classmate for notes.

During the first days of class, it is advisable to swap contact information with at least two other students in each of your classes. This way if you must miss class, you have someone to contact for notes or assignments.

EKU has a "1st Day Attendance—Faculty Drop" policy. According to this policy, students who do not attend the first day of class can be disenrolled from the class at the instructor's request, providing the student has not given the instructor prior notice of his/her absence. Students should log in to EKU Direct and view their "printable class schedule" to verify what courses they have officially registered for. Courses that have officially been dropped will not show up on this schedule.

■ SIT IN THE FRONT OF THE ROOM

Students who sit in the first couple of rows perform better. Why do you think this is so?

It is easier to be an active participant in the front row. It is more difficult to zone out, be distracted by other students, or to engage in side conversations if you're in the front of the room. It is also easier for the instructor to remember you and typically, instructors who remember your face and name already have an impression that you are serious about your coursework. Better proximity to the instructor is better for you academically (Lindquist & McLean, 2011).

■ ACTIVELY LISTEN AND TAKE NOTES

Take notes in each class because taking notes:

- Requires active listening
- Keeps you actively participating in your learning
- Makes it easier to ask questions about things you don't understand

(Active listening and note taking will be discussed in detail in Chapter 4: Practice.)

■ ASK GOOD QUESTIONS

If you are prepared for class and take lecture notes, you will be more aware of when you need to ask your instructor for clarification. If you go to class without reading and do not take notes, you will be less likely to recognize areas where you need more information.

"Growth is the greatest achievement!"

Carla Couch
Social Work

■ STRATEGIZE

No one expects freshmen to arrive at college with academic strategies that will make them a success in every class. However, if you utilize strategies you learn in one class and practice them in other classes, you can become a better college student. If you learn a successful strategy in your freshman orientation class but never use it again, you are doing yourself a disservice.

■ MEET WITH INSTRUCTORS

If you take the time to introduce yourself to your instructors, you will discover that they want you to succeed and will often go out of their way to help you become a successful student.

Manage Habits

Everyone has habits. Some are productive and others are not.

Focus on developing positive habits while you are in college. Manage your life well (e.g., exercise, eat well, manage stress).

"People often say that motivation doesn't last. Well, neither does bathing—that's why we recommend it daily."

Zig Ziglar

American author and motivational speaker

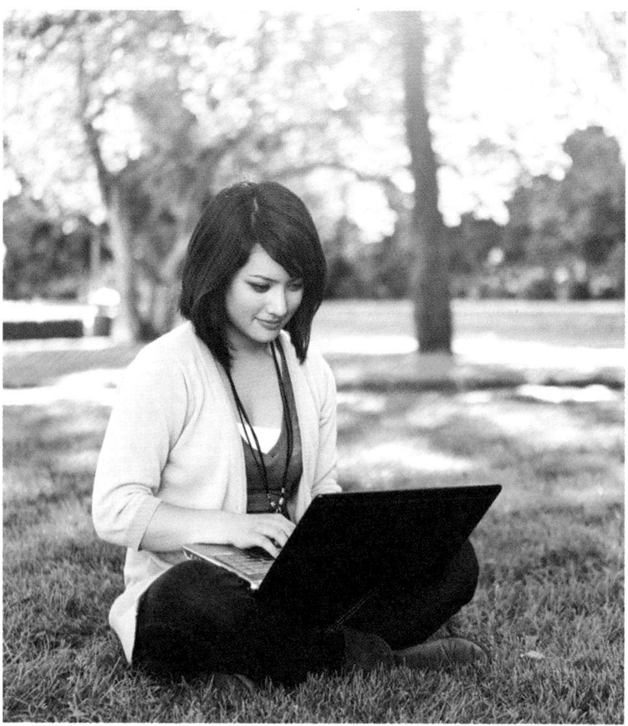

Also, don't let bad habits that you brought with you to college get any worse. Sometimes in high school, for example, you may not have always gotten a good night's sleep. That wasn't a big deal because you still had your parents to wake you up and get you to school. However, in college, this can be detrimental to your academics since you likely won't have your parents to help you get out of bed in the morning. Form positive academic habits early in your college career to ensure a successful academic experience.

BE RESPONSIBLE: MISSING CLASS

On the first day of class your instructor will go over the rules for absences/tardiness in that specific class. These may vary by department, course, and instructor, so be sure you know and understand the specifics.

Best practice: do not miss class. If you approach your college academics like a job, as discussed earlier, you won't miss classes except under extreme circumstances. If you miss a lot of days in a job, you will get fired. If you miss days in a class, your grade can be negatively impacted. Remember that your instructors understand emergencies, so be honest with them and always produce written proof.

Unacceptable excuses for missing classes:

- "I just can't get up at 8 am for this class!"
- "The breakers were flipped in my residence hall last night and reset my alarm clock. I overslept."
- "I was at a Rush party last night so…"

Don't expect your instructors to supply missed information to you. They expect you to be responsible for your own learning and proactive enough to catch up when you need to miss. Be careful about using Blackboard as a crutch when you miss class. Unless you're taking an online course, lecture notes and assignments may not appear on Blackboard. If you do have to miss class, try to contact your instructor beforehand. This shows that you are serious about the class.

TIME MANAGEMENT

Effective time management is very important to learn as you begin your academic career because it reduces stress and is a skill you will use throughout your life.

Organize Your Time

Once you evaluate your time, you'll be better prepared to begin time-management practices. These are skills that will follow you into your professional life, and they're a good thing to learn and perfect now.

EKU's Counseling Center offers Time Management Workshops: http://www.counseling.eku.edu

Planner/Calendar

A planner or calendar is one tool you can use to help you manage your time and stay organized. You can purchase an EKU planner at the campus bookstore. Other options are electronic versions you can set up on your computer (e.g., Google Calendar) or a mobile device. Regardless of what you use, always have it with you! Start each semester by recording each syllabus on your calendar. Find your important dates (e.g., tests, homework due dates, daily readings, projects) and record them on your calendar like this:

	MONDAY, MARCH 1
	HON 205 - Chapter 4
	ART 200 - Chapter 4/5
	Paper 1 due
	ENG 102 - Draft 1
	Paper 2 due
	Chapter 5

©Hayden-McNeil, LLC

"Having a planner in college allows you to map out not only your homework schedule, but aspects of your everyday life, whether that includes volunteer opportunities, social events or basic errand reminders. Without a planner to document the homework assignments in your classes, you can become easily overwhelmed and forgetful. Without my planner by my side throughout the day, I feel lost! It is extremely beneficial to be able to open it up and gauge how to spend my day and how to accomplish my work."

Heather Zimmerman
Nursing

3.1 Reflection

List tasks you are procrastinating on:
Are there certain types of tasks you are more likely to procrastinate on?

How do you know you are procrastinating?

To-Do List

A to-do list will give you a list of everything you need to do for a specific amount of time (e.g., day, week) in one spot. They are handy to post around your desk where you do your homework. Your to-do list should be prioritized. This means you put things on the list in order of importance—most important to least important. Importance can be determined by the amount of time left to complete

"Who questions much, shall learn much, and retain much."

Francis Bacon

British philosopher and statesman

the task before the due date and the complexity of the task. You should also put non-academic items on the list, such as breaks and your personal activities that must be done during that time period (e.g., laundry). You can also break large tasks down into smaller tasks that could span multiple weeks/to-do lists.

To-do list tips:

- Do "unpleasant" work first so you get that out of the way
- Consider the priority level of the tasks
- Assign each task a time limit
- Check off tasks as you complete them
- At the end of the day or week reward yourself for your accomplishments
- At the end of the day or week create the next list

Procrastination

Procrastination is avoiding doing things that need to be accomplished.

Every day holds 24 hours and how you decide to spend those hours is up to you. There are different situations and events that can steal hours from your day. Some of these are occurrences that you create yourself. Others are occurrences which happen to you and are often out of your control. Remember the discussion earlier in the chapter about the locus of control?

Within Your Control:

- Visiting with friends
- Talking on the phone
- Listening to music
- Watching TV
- Computer games, email, Facebook
- Daydreaming
- Worrying
- Alcohol/drugs
- Making avoidable mistakes
- Poor concentration
- Lack of planning
- Poor reading/study skills

Often Out of Your Control:

- Music/noise in area
- Waiting/delays
- Roommate problems
- Unclear assignments
- Too many demands
- Other people's problems
- Mechanical failures
- Illness
- Lack of authority
- Emergencies
- Family
- Meetings

CONTROL PROCRASTINATION TIPS

Procrastination adds a lot more stress to your day, but it is easily controlled. Some ways to control procrastination include:

- Realize you are not perfect—no one is.
- Keep a calendar and to-do list so you can manage your time properly.
- Change your environment, if needed, and control distractions. It is important to have a good work environment, but you don't want to waste too much time looking for perfection either.
- Study in short bursts of 30–60 minutes with 10-minute breaks worked in.
- Form study groups.
- Get tutoring if you need extra help in a subject. There is no shame in asking for help if you need it.
- Break large assignments down into smaller chunks that spread out over time.
- Set realistic goals.
- Don't cram.

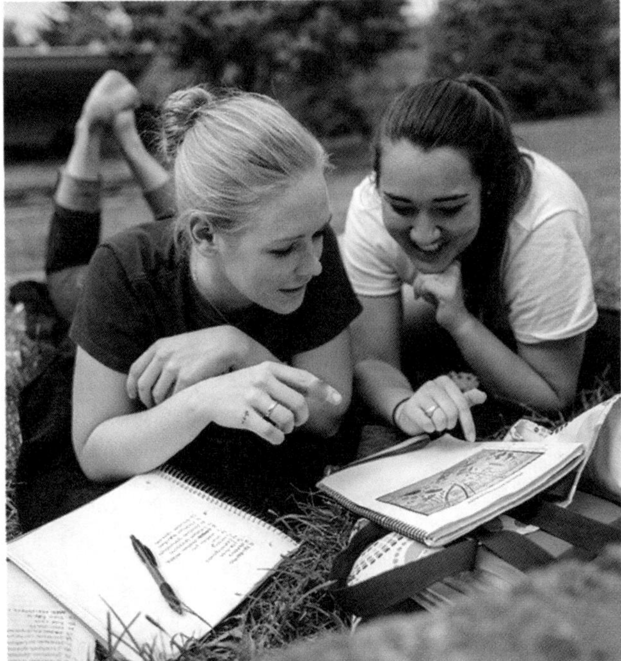

Time Management Matrix

The time management matrix in Table 3-6 (Covey, Merill, & Merill, 1994) is a tool to help you categorize and visualize the different tasks in your life. It shows you how you can use your time more efficiently and helps you identify where you are wasting time.

Table 3-6. Time Management Matrix.

TIME MANAGEMENT MATRIX		
	Urgent	Not Urgent
Important	1 • Crisis • Emergencies • Pressing problems • Deadline-driven projects • Last-minute studying or assignment completion If you include papers or exams here, you're probably not giving yourself enough time to prepare.	2 • Preparation/planning • Exercise • Pressing problems • True recreation/ relaxation • Spending time with family and friends This is where your priorities should fall.
Not Important	3 • Some calls • Mail and text messages • Some meetings • Some "pressing" matters • Pleasant conversations Too much time here will reduce study time and cause you to feel pulled in too many directions.	4 • Busywork • Junk mail • Some phone messages • Some email • Television • Surfing the web Too much time here means you're doing a lot of procrastinating. Balance is the key.

(Chart adapted from: Covey et al., 1994)

Time Management Summary

- Keep a calendar/planner.
- Create a daily or weekly to-do list.
- Be aware of and avoid ways that you procrastinate.
- Eliminate time wasters such as Facebook or video games.

> "In college, you learn how to learn. Four years is not too much time to spend at that."
>
> Mary Oliver
>
> American poet and Pulitzer Prize winner

Academic Integrity

Academic integrity is the ability of scholars to share information and build off each other's work while their intellectual property rights are respected and protected.

Academic integrity is the responsibility of both the instructor and student. The student must follow the rules, but if they don't, the instructor must follow up with the Academic Integrity Committee.

EKU takes the responsibility of protecting intellectual property very seriously. In this vein, EKU has adopted an Academic Integrity Policy (AIP):

Academic Integrity at EKU

"Eastern Kentucky University is a community of shared academic values, foremost of which is a strong commitment to intellectual honesty, honorable conduct, and respect for others. In order to meet these values, students at Eastern Kentucky University are expected to adhere to the highest standards of academic integrity. These standards are embodied in the Eastern Kentucky University Academic Integrity Policy, which all students shall pledge to uphold by signing the Eastern Kentucky University Honor Code. By honoring and enforcing this Academic Integrity Policy, the University community affirms that it will not tolerate academic dishonesty."

(EKU Academic Integrity, n.d.)

To read the full Academic Integrity Policy for EKU, please visit: http://www.academicintegrity.eku.edu/

■ WHAT CONSTITUTES ACADEMIC DISHONESTY?

According to EKU's Academic Integrity Policy, **academic dishonesty** includes, but is not limited to, cheating, plagiarizing, fabricating, or assisting another to commit the same act (collusion).

Cheating

Cheating is an act of deceiving an instructor that the student has sufficiently mastered the content material in a course. This may include giving or receiving assistance on an assignment or task that is not authorized by the instructor, collaborating on an assignment or task without authorization, or using electronic aids during a task (EKU Academic Integrity, n.d.).

Fabricating

Fabricating is an attempt to misrepresent information in an exercise. There are several methods of fabrication. They include citing information from a source that it was not taken from, listing sources that were not used, distorting findings by the use of fictitious data or concealment of relevant data, or submitting work as your own that was partially or entirely completed by another person (EKU Academic Integrity, n.d.).

Plagiarism

Plagiarism is an act of representing someone else's work as one's own. This can include words, ideas, or images and can be done accidentally or purposefully. Improperly citing sources in a manner that obstructs the degree to which a source was used may be considered plagiarism as well. For instance, failing to place quotation marks around a direct quote is an act of plagiarism even if the source of the idea is cited (EKU Academic Integrity, n.d.).

There is a special type of plagiarism called **self-plagiarism.** This is the use of information from an essay or paper previously written for another class without proper citation. Most students do not think of citing themselves, but they should get permission from their instructors to reuse all or parts of a previous assignment and supply appropriate citations.

■ WHAT IF ACADEMIC DISHONESTY IS SUSPECTED?

EKU has a comprehensive procedure for suspected violations of its Academic Integrity Policy. This section is taken from that policy but will provide only a very brief overview of these procedures. The entire process may be found on the EKU Academic Integrity website at http://www.academicintegrity.eku.edu.

Possible Sanctions

The minimum sanction for a violation of the academic policy for a student with no previous violations is an assigned grade of "F" for the work in question. If the student has a previous violation, the minimum sanction is an "FX" on the student's transcript, which denotes failing for academic dishonesty.

Safe Assignment

Safe Assignment is a feature of Blackboard that gives EKU faculty an easy and reliable method for checking students' work for plagiarism. Students submit work and instructors can usually have a results report in 30 minutes that identifies passages that may have been plagiarized. The service compares students' work with millions of websites and previously submitted papers.

Questions about Academic Integrity

If you have any questions regarding what constitutes a violation of EKU's policies about academic integrity, please ask your First Year Course instructor for clarification. You may also contact the Office of Student Rights and Responsibilities.

Chapter Summary

This chapter has outlined the tools you can use to become a successful college student. College is very different than high school and you will be expected to step up to new challenges and responsibilities. By taking charge of your academic career, forging relationships with your instructors, and staying on top of assignments through time-management skills, you are well on your way to a successful career at Eastern Kentucky University!

"Time stays long enough for anyone who will use it."

Leonardo da Vinci

Scientist and artist

■ KEY TERMS

Academic dishonesty: Any type of misconduct that occurs in relation to an academic examination or exercise which includes, but is not limited to, cheating, plagiarism, fabrication, and collusion

Academic integrity: Refers to the ethical code of conduct in which the intellectual property rights of scholars are respected and protected

Cheating: Deceiving an instructor that the student has mastered course material

Creators: Individuals who have an internal locus of control

Criteria-based scholarship: Money awarded based upon specific criteria such as participation in an activity, physical attributes, heritage, field of study, etc.

External locus of control: Believing that your life is controlled by external forces (e.g., fate, luck)

Fabricating: Any attempt to misrepresent or falsify information in an exercise

Grade point average: A measurement of a student's academic performance in a given term or cumulatively over several terms, calculated by dividing total grade points by total number of credits

Internal locus of control: Believing that your life is controlled by internal forces (e.g., individual behavior and choices)

Locus of control: Your belief regarding the control you possess over your own life

Merit scholarship: Money awarded to students based upon academic performance

Motivation: Reason or reasons for acting in a particular way; the incentive for achievements

Need-based scholarship: Money awarded to students based on demonstrated financial need

Plagiarism: Using someone else's work and representing it as one's own original work

Procrastination: The act of avoiding completing tasks that need to be accomplished

Quality points: The grade point value multiplied by credit hours

Scholarship: Money awarded to a student to pay for school costs based upon academic achievements, activities, need, or other factors

Self-plagiarism: Reusing content from one's own previous work without appropriate permission or citation

Syllabus: An instructor's written description of a course, given to students at the start of the course; typically details the course content, assignments, examinations, grading, and class policies

Victims: Individuals who have an external locus of control

NOTES

"You may delay, but time will not."

Benjamin Franklin

American author, scientist, statesman, and Founding Father

CAMPUS RESOURCES

Blackboard
http://www.learn.eku.edu

EKU Student Rights and Responsibilities
http://www.studentrights.eku.edu
Turley House 1, 859-622-1500

Noel Studio for Academic Creativity
http://www.studio.eku.edu
Library 207B, 859-622-6229

Tutoring Centers
http://www.advising.eku.edu/tutoring
859-622-6778

REFERENCES

BrainyQuote. (n.d.). *BrainyQuote.com*. Retrieved June 9, 2011, from http://www.brainyquote.com/

Covey, S.R., Merrill, A.R., & Merrill, R.R. (1994). *First things first: Coping with the ever-increasing demands of the workplace*. London, England: Simon & Schuster UK Ltd.

EKU Academic Integrity. (n.d.). EKU honor code and pledge. In *EKU Academic Integrity Policy*. Retrieved from http://www.academicintegrity.eku.edu/

EKU Undergraduate Studies. (2010). Section one: The university. In *Eastern Kentucky University Undergraduate catalog 2010–2011*. Richmond, KY: Eastern Kentucky University. Retrieved March 18, 2011, from Eastern Kentucky University, EKU Libraries, Encompass archive Website: http://www.undergradstudies.eku.edu/catalog/2010-2011/easternkentuckyuniversity.pdf

Hazard, L.L. (1997). The *effect of locus of control and attitudes toward intelligence on study habits of college students*. (Doctoral dissertation.) Retrieved from ProQuest Dissertations and Theses database/UMI. (UMI Order No. ABA98-04550)

Lefcourt, H.M. (1984). *Research with the locus of control construct*. New York, NY: Academic Press, Inc.

Lindquist, S.I., & McLean, J.P. (2011, April). Daydreaming and its correlates in an educational environment. *Learning and Individual Differences*, *21*(2), 158–167.

Shoenberg, R. (2008). *What will I learn in college? What you need to know now to get ready for college success*. Washington, D.C.: AAC&U Publications.

RESOURCES & REFERENCES

NOTES

"Every time I've done something that doesn't feel right, it's ended up not being right."

Mario Cuomo

Italian-American politician

4

Chapter Four

Practice

Chapter Four

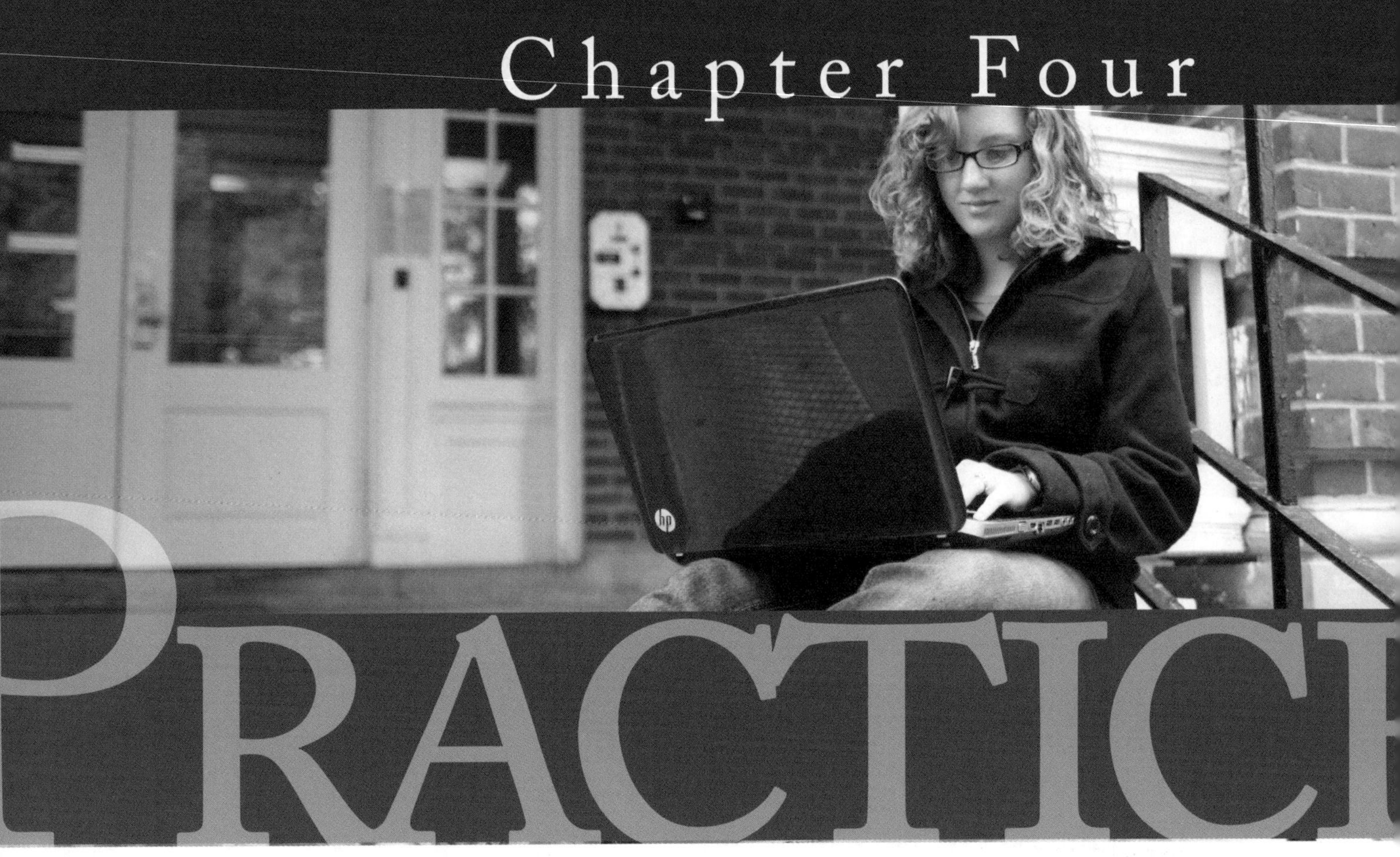

PRACTICE

After mastering the content in this chapter you will be able to:

- Apply effective strategies in preparing for, attending, and following up on classroom lectures
- Take relevant and consistent lecture and chapter notes
- Read for maximum learning and retention of information
- Describe the importance of concentration in your study habits
- Develop note-taking and reading strategies

Fundamental Question

- How do I become a more academically prepared student?

Essential Principles

- Active Listening
- Test Preparation
- Note-Taking Strategies
- Test Anxiety Management
- Reading Strategies
- Concentration

"Education is the process in which we discover that learning adds quality to our lives. Learning must be experienced."
William Glasser
American psychologist

In Chapter 3 you learned that you are ultimately the only person who can ensure that you have a successful college experience. Since you now understand, among other things, the importance of time management and regular class attendance, you are ready to delve into some strategies and resources for **active learning** that will help you achieve your academic goals.

Active Learning

To understand active learning, let's use an illustration. Suppose you move to a new house with a large forest behind it. A friend points out that your new house is close to his if you take a straight path through the forest. Unfortunately, there is no path and the forest is overgrown. The first trip through, you use your hands to fight your way through the trees. Without a set path before you, you are not certain of the direction, and your progress is slow. Yet you are determined. Next time you take an old machete and cut brambles as you go; a path begins to form and your progress is quicker. Yet again you go through the forest, but this time you slice your way through with the best clearing tool—a sharpened ax.

After these three trips, always going the same direction and using different tools to make your way, you now have a cleared and familiar path through the trees that is so smooth you could ride your bicycle on it. You continue to keep the path clear of stray debris, but without large obstacles and with certainty of the direction to take, you now barely have to think about making the trip and can spend your time thinking about what you'll be doing when you arrive.

Your brain is like the forest while your friend represents a new concept, set of information, or skill you need to learn. If the concept is unfamiliar, you have to make the first path, often before you know the end result. However, some strategies will help make the path smoother more quickly. The active learning basics below will get you headed in the right direction.

Active Learning Basics

- Have to have a clear destination. Know what you need to know. Take good notes, ask good questions.
- Make more than one trip. Cramming is only a temporary fix; if you don't go back over the path, it becomes overgrown again rapidly.
- Use more than one tool—attack the problem in more than one way.
- Do maintenance work and review every now and then.

The more times and ways your brain is exposed to new information, the faster and smoother neuron connections (the path) will grow. In most classes, students are exposed to new ideas through reading and hearing about them. If you read material before lecture, listen in class, take good notes, and participate in class discussions, you will already have had four exposures in four different forms and at different levels of involvement. If you then go home and review your notes, jot down questions and annotate, do the homework assignment, talk about what you're learning, and spend some time reflecting on the new ideas—connecting them to what you already know—you will soon have a nicely cleared path of understanding.

Instruction on listening? You're kidding, right? I thought all I needed to do to listen was to be in the room!

■ ACTIVE LISTENING—BE PREPARED TO HEAR

To begin an exploration of active learning strategies, we need to start with some instruction on **active listening**.

While listening may seem synonymous with hearing, we are actually talking here about something a bit more deliberate than simply being in the room. Active, effective listening is not a passive activity. To benefit from and understand what you hear, you need to be actively involved in the process.

Active listening ensures that you are more engaged in learning, processing what you hear, and finding ways to make that information more meaningful. Active listening can help you take better notes and contributes to better retention of information. To be active in your learning, you must also be active in your listening.

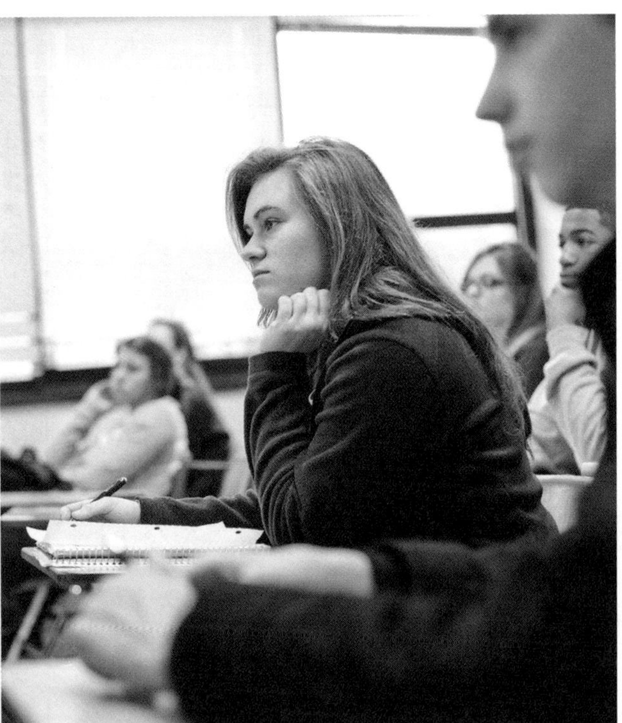

Pre-Class Preparation

The first step in active listening actually occurs before you enter the room. If your intent is to stay focused and learn new information, the first thing to do is to come prepared to hear. How do you do this? By reading or reviewing material that is to be discussed. (Yes, we are talking about reading the assignments and reviewing notes from the previous class!) Instructors don't assign reading just to keep you busy. Exposure to new material prior to discussion provides you with concepts and ideas to listen for and relate to during class.

Eliminate In-Class Distractions

Another factor in being prepared to hear is getting rid of the "background noise" in your brain. Once you arrive in class, spend just a few minutes clearing your mind of unrelated thoughts (like your professor's ugly shirt or interesting hairstyle). Think about the important concepts from your reading, try to identify the **fundamental question** from the chapter, or recall where the professor ended the last lecture. This will help put your mind in a state of readiness for learning.

Where you sit in the room is another important factor in active listening. Sitting near the front means you will be less distracted by other sounds. The professor's words will be clearer and you will be less likely to miss important information. You also get a better view of the speaker's body language and visual elements, which can aid your understanding. Furthermore, being up front and visible is great motivation for staying attentive and on task!

"The minute that you're not learning I believe you're dead."

Jack Nicholson
American actor

The last step in getting ready to hear is to dispense with anything that could interfere with the task at hand. Remove everything from your desk or table top except what you need to follow the lecture and record information. Phones and music devices need to be silenced and put away. Not only are they distracting to you, they are rude to the professor. Unrelated books, homework from other classes, and food should be stowed away.

■ ACTIVE LISTENING—BE PHYSICALLY ATTENTIVE

In addition to your preparations for hearing, other aspects of active listening are **attending behaviors**—things you consciously do that help you pay attention. Open posture and body position, non-verbal responses, and verbal responses are three examples of good attending behaviors that contribute to active listening.

Open Posture and Body Position

An **open posture** is one in which your body is in a position that looks and feels ready to receive information. You are sitting up straight and alert, or even leaning slightly forward. Your feet are on the floor and you are poised to write, with materials for note taking at the ready. Additionally, your appearance is one of someone who is eager to learn.

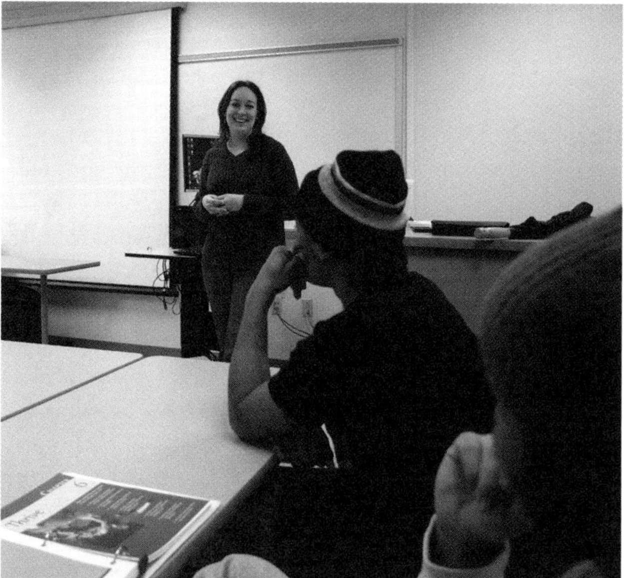

Non-Verbal Responses

A speaker can always tell who is really listening. They are the ones who nod, smile, frown, or have looks of recognition or confusion cross their faces—**non-verbal responses** that they are processing information. The eyes may be "a window to the soul," but they are also a window to our thought processes. Our eyes tend to move up and to the sides when we are visualizing something or recalling information. Be sure to make eye contact with your professor. Turn your head toward the speaker and really look at them. Do not stare at them continually, but making occasional eye contact will let them know you are listening.

If you are paying attention to the lecture, all of these non-verbal responses will happen naturally, but do not be afraid to let your non-verbals show. Your professors use these visual cues to gauge how well their students are following, so your non-verbal responsiveness can actually have a positive impact on the lecture.

Verbal Responses

Active listening also involves the component of **verbal responses**—being able to articulate what you have heard and check your understanding for accuracy. This is where you put your hand in the air and summarize what you have heard or ask for confirmation that you heard correctly. While it may seem awkward at first, making comments such as, "So, Professor, what you are saying is..." will not only help you get better information, it will demonstrate to the instructor that you have been listening. (Chances are your classmates will also appreciate the clarification!)

■ YOUR INSTRUCTOR'S PRESENTATION STYLE

In addition to active listening, one of the most helpful things you can do is to learn your instructor's lecture style. Identifying this early in the semester will be helpful to you as you listen and participate in the classroom. Keep in mind that sometimes their teaching style and your preferred learning style will not mesh well. These differences are why it is very important that you keep up-to-date on your reading and homework and communicate one-on-one with your instructors.

It is important to be aware of your instructor's verbal or mannerism cues during a lecture. You should always make a note of these. They are your instructor's way of letting you know something important is being said.

COMMON VERBAL OR MANNERISM CUES

Phrases such as:

- For example…
- For instance…
- In conclusion…
- This is key…
- Let me emphasize…
- First... second... etc.

Other indicators:

- Repeating words or phrases
- Speaking more slowly or loudly
- Changing their tone of voice
- Asking students a question
- Writing on the board
- Including terms on a PowerPoint

Take the opportunity before, during, and after class to ask questions. Students who ask questions stand out in their instructors' minds. Do not just ask questions to kill class time, but do not hesitate to ask when you need more help.

AFTER CLASS

Learning is not finished at the end of a lecture. If you have a break after your classes, you should sit down and immediately review the day's lecture and classroom activities. This process helps strengthen ideas and concepts from the reading and lecture while they are still fresh in your mind and will assist you in studying later. If you don't have a free period after your class, do the review as soon as you can later in the day.

Note-Taking Strategies

Another key element of active learning and *one of the most valuable things that you can do to ensure academic success* is note taking. Taking notes during class will help you to absorb the material being presented and will be *hugely important* when it comes to studying for exams. Just as every student has a different style of learning, you will also have a different style of note taking. Three note-taking methods that are often effectively used are the Cornell method, mind mapping, and the outline method.

CORNELL METHOD

The **Cornell method** of note taking began at Cornell University in the 1950s and has become a standard at many universities. Before class, divide your page into two columns, with the column on the right (about 6 inches wide) being larger than the column on the left (about 2 inches wide). The column on the right, the larger of the two columns, will be where you take notes during class. The column on the left is for after class. Don't forget to leave room at the bottom of your page for your summaries.

Now, follow the 5 Rs:

Record: Take notes during class, as you normally would, in the larger of the two columns. Use abbreviations and symbols to save time. You should leave yourself extra space at the bottom of your page for a brief summary.

Reduce: Not long after class, summarize your notes by writing important points and main ideas in the summary block. Then reduce your notes even further to just one or two key words; record these in your cue/key word column. By reducing large chunks of information into one or two key words, you are forcing yourself to memorize and learn the information from class. During the reduce process, you will be determining essential principles from the class lectures (similar to the Essential Principles listed at the start of each chapter in this book).

Recite: Fold your paper in half or cover the note-taking column. Go through the key words you recorded and try to recall the main ideas of the lecture by using your own words.

"I like to listen. I have learned a great deal from listening carefully. Most people never listen."

Ernest Hemingway

American author, Nobel Prize winner

Reflect: Building on previous knowledge is one of the best ways to retain information. Go through your notes and think about the significance of the facts or how you can apply them to other facts from your text. Think about how the content from this class relates to what you have learned in other classes to help build baseline knowledge.

Review: Review your notes frequently. This will keep the information fresh and help you prepare for exams.

See the example below to help you visualize this process (Campus Grotto, n.d.).

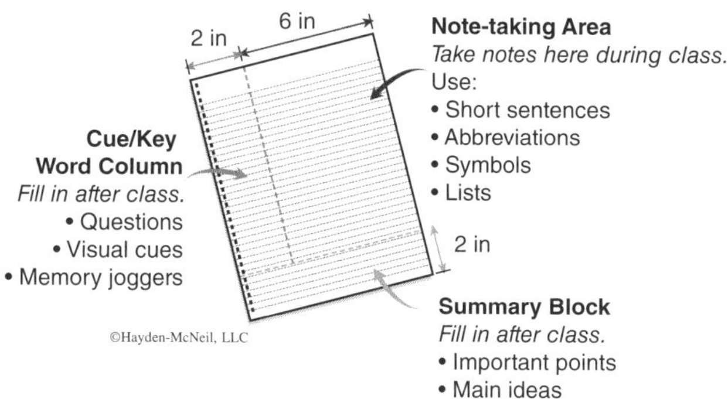

■ MIND MAPPING

A **mind map** is a diagram of ideas or tasks that can be used for organizing notes or for brainstorming. Start with your main idea in the center and branch out from that. You can be as simple or as creative as you want, and it is an excellent visual tool!

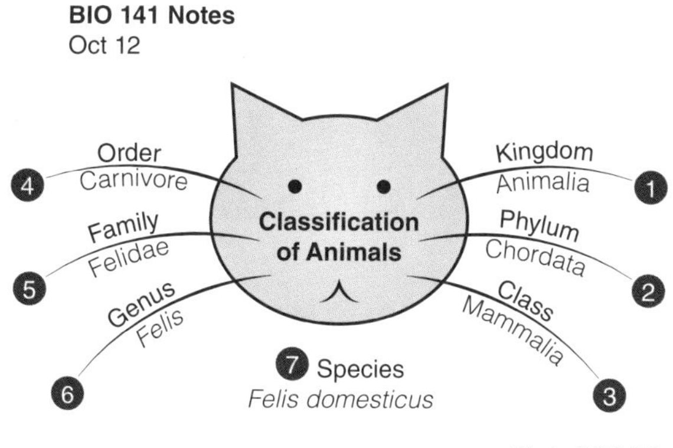

Find more information on mind maps online: http://www.mindtools.com/pages/article/newISS_01.htm

■ OUTLINE METHOD

Outlines are a common tool to help us organize information. They can be used as a tool to organize lecture notes, information in a textbook, or prewrite an essay.

The outline method of note taking starts on the left-hand side of the paper. The main points are placed at the left edge of the paper. Less important points, or supporting information, are indented to the right. Each set of supporting points is indented more to the right. Outlining helps you to visually grasp the levels of significance that ideas carry as well as to sow the relationship of these ideas to other information. The sample outline below shows a basic outline format.

SAMPLE OUTLINE

Fairy Tale Motifs

I. Good versus Evil
  A. Kind and innocent character battles evil
    1. Witch
    2. Enchantress
      a) Rapunzel
    3. Stepmother
      b) Cinderella
      c) Snow White
    4. Demon

➲ Did you realize that Wikipedia uses outlines at the beginning of every entry to organize content?

Beyond the Classroom

So you went to class, engaged in active listening and note taking—your work should be finished for the day, right? While you might want to spend the rest of your day enjoying the sunshine in the Ravine, your active learning is not yet complete. Doing homework and studying are key aspects of active learning and are equally important to attending classes. Just as there were certain preparations and behaviors to enhance your time in class, there are also specific decisions you can make and strategies you can use to make your time studying and completing homework worthwhile.

"There are several great places to study on campus. Noel Studio offers one-on-one or group consultations with their staff, the 4th floor of Crabbe Library is a quiet zone, and Tech Commons offers free popcorn and music to relax students as they study."

Josh Hartlage
Physical Education
(K–12 Teaching)

CONCENTRATION IN THE STUDY ENVIRONMENT

Eliminating Distractions

When it is time to study, you have to limit distractions. This means that wherever you work best, that environment must be free from the things which will keep you from your goal. If your goal is to study for tomorrow's test, then you should leave your cell phone in your room, work away from the computer, and avoid getting caught up in conversations with friends on campus.

4.1 Reflection

Do I study best in the library?

Do I prefer natural or fluorescent lighting?

Am I more productive studying by myself or with a friend?

Do I need a very quiet space or do I like background noise?

At what time of day am I the most productive?

Choosing the Conditions

Not everyone produces their best work under the same conditions. Some students prefer the library. You might prefer to study in your room. You may have a preference for sitting in a comfortable chair rather than at a desk. However, if you study in a comfortable chair and you are apt to fall asleep in that chair, then perhaps you have to make a change. You may not study well with background noise, but what if your roommate likes to have music playing in the background? If this is the case, you will not be able to study together very well. However, if your roommate uses earphones, then you can share the same environment and work well in the same space together.

POSITIVE STRATEGIES FOR CONCENTRATION

Using Your Best Time

It is common to use your best times of the day for the things you enjoy the most. However, if you want to take your academic goals and plans seriously, then you have to

"He listens well who takes notes."
Dante Alighieri
Italian poet

change your thinking. If you are someone who has lots of energy late at night, then this is the time you should devote to reading, studying, and writing papers. If you are someone who has lots of energy in the morning hours, consider getting up early to review material before class begins. Take advantage of the extra energy that you have at that time. Work during those times of day when you are naturally more engaged in your learning and more creative.

Taking Breaks

Taking regular breaks while studying is a good idea. After an hour, take a stretch break, eat a snack, or take a brief walk. Be sure to give yourself a time limit on your break as well—too much time devoted to breaks can get you further from your goal!

A FEW STUDYING TIPS

1. Read the material before going to class.
2. Annotate the text and make outlines.
3. Go to class prepared to find answers. Be involved in discussions.
4. Take good lecture notes; be involved by actively listening.
5. After class, edit and review your notes; look for terms or ideas you don't fully understand.
6. Talk about those areas with others—a fellow classmate would be great, but a good friend will serve quite well.
7. Complete related homework.
8. Start over for the next assignment.

Making an Investment

Everyone has his or her favorite things to do. You probably do, too. When studying you should keep in mind those projects, athletic events, or activities that you enjoy. You easily can get lost in a project, a sport, or even an activity. Why do you do this? Usually this is because you are invested in the outcome. You want to do well, and you enjoy what you are doing.

Think of your academic work as a vehicle for personal growth. How important and valuable is that growth? What are you willing to do to achieve it? If you are willing to make an investment in your academic work, then the payoff will be tremendous.

If you train for a road race, work on a school play, or create a dynamic Facebook page, then you know how success feels. It is great to work hard on something, to achieve, and to feel proud about your efforts. Education is the same way. Make an investment in it.

■ READING STRATEGIES

Now that you have chosen a good study environment and are able to concentrate, it is time to talk about your **reading strategies**. It is not just enough to attend lecture and study your class notes. Lecture and reading go hand in hand, and you need to take the time to carefully read what is assigned from the course text.

During the course of your studies, you will be required to read many different genres of texts (including arts, humanities, science, and mathematics). You will also be required to comprehend, analyze, decode, and summarize the material from these readings, and you must be prepared to document your understanding with some form of verbal or written discourse! Chances are great that you will have writing or speaking assignments based on your readings.

Though there is great variety in the material you have to read and even in the assignments that will be drawn from these texts, there are a few strategies you can use to help make your reading for any subject the most effective it can be.

Pre-reading Your Textbooks

Pre-reading is a reading strategy that has been proven to increase comprehension. So before you start the heavy lifting of reading your text, it is important to note the key elements in your book. Although no textbook is perfect, they are designed to help you learn. Use the features of your textbooks to your benefit!

Some of you may already engage in a bit of pre-reading on a subconscious level as you make mental notes of important items from the text. However, writing down preview information can be helpful for all students as it provides a permanent copy to store in your notes for future reference.

➲Helpful Hint: Place a sticky note where the glossary begins so you can find it easily!

After pre-reading, you will have a better idea of the difficulty of the text and the range of information you are expected to learn. You will have a general idea about the content and will have predictions and questions about the specifics.

Pre-reading will enhance your learning from your reading assignments and help prepare you for additional assignments and for any discussion that might take place in lecture. Do not neglect to pre-read. You wouldn't leave your house without preparing by getting dressed—don't begin to read your text without preparation through pre-reading.

ASK QUESTIONS

Experts estimate that when you were in middle school, you asked around a hundred questions a day. For various reasons, that number diminishes to almost zero when you reach college.

Identifying with Your Author

Take a look at the different books you have for math, science, and English. Would you agree that each of these books has its own vocabulary? Of course there is an overlap of some general language, but math and science textbooks generally use specialized terms, signs, and symbols. Each of these may be absolutely critical to your understanding. But before you can read a math textbook, for example, it is necessary that you begin by thinking like a mathematician. Let's face it—it is very difficult to skim or scan a math textbook. But if you begin to think like a mathematician—analyzing patterns of text, studying concrete details, formulating abstract concepts—and really focus on the meaning of the mathematical terms and symbols, it is easier to transform your reading interpretations into math learning. In other words, you may find it beneficial to look at your math text from a different point of view—from the perspective of the author.

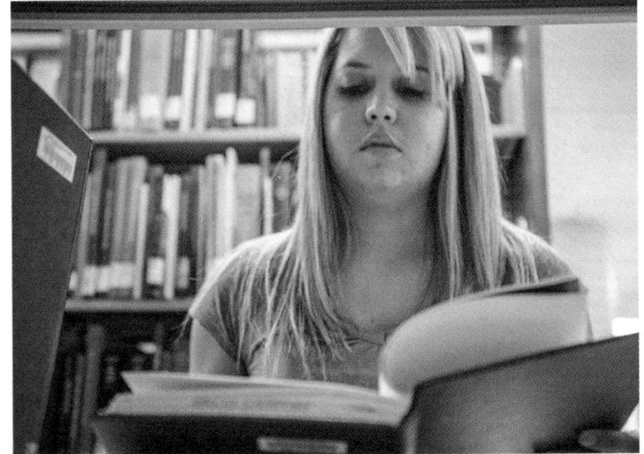

"To do two things at once is to do neither."

Publilius Syrus

Latin writer of maxims

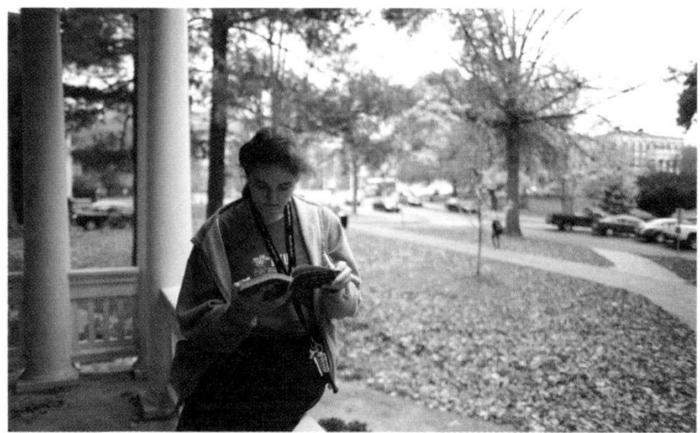

Ask questions as you read:

- What was the time frame in which the text was created?
- What was the culture?
- What was the political climate?
- Does the writer have a bias?
- Is the writer credible?

Be open-minded and prepared to investigate different cultural values and beliefs honestly and without bias.

This strategy of identifying with the author is a helpful tool that can be applied to books for any course or subject. For texts that are more based in fact and logic, such as those math and science books, try to adopt the thinking strategies of mathematicians and scientists. Rely on logic, observation, and step-by-step processes. For more narrative or creative texts, perhaps from an English literature course, try to imagine the historical period in which the author lived. What was the world like in that time and place? What was the author's life like? Approaching the subject matter of any book from the perspective and mindset of the author will provide you with deeper insight and interpretation of the text.

Drawing from Personal Experience

In addition to identifying with the author of a book, it is also important that you bring your own personal interpretations and background knowledge to your reading. Think about what you already know about the subject matter being discussed and see how your knowledge is enhanced by the new text or how differing views by authors you experience come into discussion with one another. Does the text confirm or challenge the views of other authors you have read?

Your own personal experiences will also influence how you interpret a text as you will read from a particular perspective that will enhance and complicate what you read. Do you agree with what is written in the text, or do you have a different take on the subject being discussed? For example, how does one's experience growing up in Appalachia compare to the descriptions of the region found in literature books? Also think about your beliefs and values as you read your books; does the text challenge those beliefs? Does it influence you to adopt new beliefs? For example, if you previously knew little about climate change, do you now believe that this issue is in fact a reality? You will explore many issues in your college classes and will ultimately develop your own beliefs and values in response to the variety of arguments you encounter as you read your course texts.

Whenever you engage with a new text, take the time to think about how it relates to your personal values, background, and knowledge. You will be able to engage more fully with the text as you build upon previous knowledge, personally connect with the writing, and enter into discussion with the topics being presented.

> CREATIVE THINKING TIP
>
> **Recognize, pursue, and develop glimmers of ideas.** Trust your unconscious. Sometimes the best ideas aren't the ones that hit you squarely in the face, but are seen out of the corner of your eye. Take notes on things you suddenly think of so you don't lose them. When you are typing a paper, if something you want to deal with strikes you, just get it down before you forget it. You can always edit your paper later.

Reading Like a Writer

All of your courses, regardless of subject matter, require your engagement as a student learner. You can expect to be reading—and writing. Your professors will often ask you to do some writing based upon the material in your textbooks. This could be anything from a short paragraph response to a full-length essay. So when you work through your texts, you need to think and read like a writer.

As you read for class, think about the text:

- What was the author's purpose?
- Did the author provide details? If so, what details were important?
- Was the author's use of word choice effective or ineffective? Why or why not?
- Was the vocabulary conversational or academic?

When you read, make note of themes, important discussion points, key vocabulary, the intentions of the author, whether the arguments were supported and successful or not, the way language was used, etc. Writing assignments will require you to think critically about the text and might test your knowledge on any number of aspects of the material—from a synopsis of the author's main argument to an analysis of the specific syntax used.

So as you read, don't just run your eyes over the words—pay close attention to what you are reading. Read like a writer!

> CRITICAL THINKING TIP
>
> **Use your critical thinking skills when you read!**
>
> - Think about the author's purpose and point of view.
> - Identify key information and assumptions.

Note Taking while Reading Your Text

While reading, it is important to remember that activity and engagement are the keys to success. The more you interact with the text, the more likely you are to learn and remember the material. This means having a pen, highlighter, and/or pencil at hand, as well as a notebook to record key information.

Spiral-bound notebooks have their place, but to maintain good organization, consider a three-ring binder for each class. It is a good idea to head each page of notes with the date, chapter number, and chapter title. Also, create vocabulary pages for each chapter. While you are reading, make pages in your notebook that list important terms, their meanings, and pictures or diagrams to create word associations. Textbooks are useful for identifying vocabulary; they are usually *italicized*, in **bold**, or colored text. Making index cards with terms and definitions is another excellent method for learning vocabulary. Consider which process works best for you.

> "When I am reading a book, whether wise or silly, it seems to me to be alive and talking to me."
>
> Jonathan Swift
>
> Irish essayist, author of *Gulliver's Travels*

You cannot expect to read a textbook chapter from beginning to end and comprehend its content without actively taking notes. After pre-reading, read the chapter from beginning to end, then reread and actively take notes while rereading—if this suits your style of learning. Remember, extensive rereading is critical to note taking and understanding. Sometimes, you have to read, reread, and reread again.

"What you read for class is what professors will test you on. So when I read, I underline or write on a Post-It parts that I think are important, words I do not know, things I have questions about, and comments that I have."

Paige Aponte
Elementary Education

Do whatever it takes to understand the content of your textbook chapters. It takes a considerable amount of effort to be a successful college student. The amount of time and energy spent reading textbooks will depend on the difficulty of the material. You will comprehend some textbooks during the initial read and will require fewer notes. Other textbooks will take considerably more time and energy. You will learn to gauge this for yourself as time goes by, but it will not happen unless you dive into college reading and note taking full force. Unfortunately, many students learn after midterm, or after their first semester, or after their first year of college, that the expenditures of time, energy, and effort are necessary to reap the rewards of success and self-confidence.

DID YOU KNOW?

In one hour, the average student can read:

- Eight to ten pages of a natural science book
- Ten to twelve pages in a social sciences book
- Twelve to fifteen pages of narrative text such as plays, novels, etc.

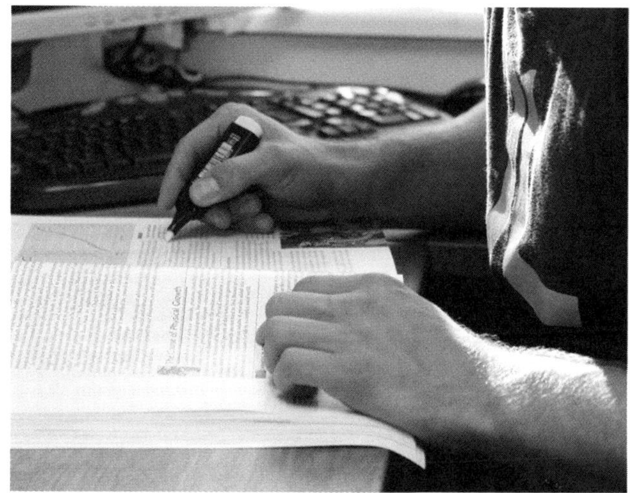

Annotating the Text

What's the difference between taking notes when you read and annotating a text?

Whereas note taking typically has you jotting down notes on a separate piece of paper, **annotating** a text is writing and taking notes directly on the pages of your textbook. Annotating can be done while you are in lecture as well as when you are studying your text outside of class. One advantage to annotating is that all of the information is in one place and less likely to be lost. Having your notes directly on the pages also makes it easier to relate your initial thoughts and classroom notes to the text. This will prove especially valuable when it comes time to review for exams.

SOME TIPS FOR ANNOTATING A TEXT

- Circle words that are unfamiliar
- Underline or highlight definitions or key information
- Number main ideas
- Use margin space to summarize passages
- Write a question mark by any concepts on which you are unclear

The following example of annotated text will give you a better idea of how to use this technique to improve your reading comprehension and retention.

Effective & Efficient Studying
How to Make Your Study Time Pay Off
Catherine Clement -Psychology Department

Your primary goal in studying is to understand the material you are studying. You also need to remember material. It turns out that understanding and remembering are closely connected.

put ideas into own words

(1) **Explain ideas to yourself.** For example, explain why Lincoln made certain decisions just before the Civil War. Explain why a particular equation is appropriate for a particular problem. Many ideas cannot be automatically understood. You have to actively figure them out, and express them in your own words. Once you figure something out, your chances of remembering it increase. Memory often comes along for free with a solid understanding.

link information to prior knowledge

(2) **Make connections.** Memory is based on connections -- one idea cues you to remember another idea. When you study you must actively make links between ideas, and the more meaningful the link, the better. Thus, thinking about why Lincoln made a particular decision will cue you to remember that decision.

Categorize information

(3) **Make outlines and organize concepts.** Making an outline and putting concepts into categories of related ideas helps you understand, gives you interconnections, makes the set of material less overwhelming, and makes remembering much easier.

focus on 1 task at a time

(4) **Do one thing at a time.** Devote your whole mind to your study task. If half your attention is on the studying, and the other half is on Facebook, you are working against yourself. Research shows that distractions impair memory for material you are studying. Research also shows that people do tasks less quickly and less accurately when they are doing more than one task at a time.

Take breaks-pace studying

(5) **Space out your studying of a particular set of material.** For example, if you plan to spend six hours studying the events leading up to the Civil War, space that time out across three occasions, rather than studying all at once for six hours. One reason that spaced studying is helpful is that on each new occasion you think about the material in a new way; you think about the material from a new perspective. These different perspectives create different connections to the material, which in turn give you more cues for remembering the material later. Also, related to this: **Take breaks** – refresh yourself and you will be more focused and efficient when you come back.

6 **Test yourself.** For example, write key concepts on flash cards, and then with the book and notes closed make yourself define the concepts. Or give yourself possible essay questions to answer, for example, a question that requires you to explain an idea or process. Testing yourself has many benefits: *reinforces #1*

6a **Testing yourself tells you** what you don't remember or don't understand. It is better to find this out before a test than at the test.

6b **Testing yourself forces you** to work out your understanding of concepts in your own words. This enhances your understanding and helps memory. You are creating more cues. Also, research shows that people have better memory for information they generate on their own, than information they read passively. *Think about information & recall. Don't just review notes!*

6c **Testing yourself involves the right kind of repetition.** Repeatedly looking over material does very little to help memory. But repeatedly recalling information from your long-term memory increases your ability to recall the information again. I still remember the phone number of a childhood friend who I haven't called since I was 13. I dialed that phone number from memory so many times I will never forget it.

We Learn By Doing. Learning ideas is the same as learning a physical activity, such as a dance step or a sport. You can't just watch the activity. You have to practice doing it, and you have to practice it with your full attention (most coaches won't let their players text or listen to iPods during practice!). In the same way, you can't just passively look over material in a book or in your notes. You have to practice doing something with those ideas. *focused practice*

We Learn All the Time without Realizing It: Think about all the things you remember that you made little or no attempt to "memorize", e.g. a fun game you played, an interesting movie, a stressful experience, or how to do a task. You remember these things because you were engaged, you were interested, you made connections, you thought about the experience, or you worked out your understanding.

Active, attentive studying saves time. You can get much more learned and accomplished in much less time.

Memory

Do you remember studying elementary school spelling words? Writing them five times each, looking up definitions, repeating them to your mom, dad, or friend? Or what about memorizing the states and their capitals? Did you visualize the state, the shape, the position on the map, or have a clever trick to match the state with the capital? For most of us, these methods did work, but some of us had more difficulty remembering the information. How can we improve our memory? Just like any other task in our academic life, we must tap into our own ways of doing things. Explore the following methods to see which work best for you.

METHODS FOR IMPROVING MEMORY

Connect New Information to Prior Learning

Making a conscious effort to connect new learning to previous learning takes concentration, but it makes for lasting learning. While taking notes, either mentally or on paper, add notes that remind you of prior experiences that will help you recall the new information when necessary. Making connections can be quick and direct or can take the form of a lengthy dialogue in your mind.

Repetition: Writing, Typing, or Saying Aloud the Information

- Retype or rewrite your notes as soon as possible after class.
- Repeat key words or phrases aloud to yourself or to others.
- Practice, especially before an oral presentation, in front of a mirror.

Association of Place or Habit

Simply making a conscious effort to remember where we were when we did an activity, or when we lost our keys, helps us to associate the item with that place: *"I am hanging my keys on the hook by the door."* Simply think purposely about the action so that it will be ready for recall when you need it.

Having a routine or habit of studying in one place or working in a particular manner can often help students remember information more easily. Find a place that is comfortable for you. Schedule study time. Don't just randomly sit down and try to study or write papers. By having this habit or routine, you are giving priority to the activity; therefore, you are telling your brain that it is important.

Visualization

Consciously making a mental picture of words, photos, people, etc., can help you recall that information later.

Looking at charts, graphs, and pictures in your text can help you instantly recall details from a lecture, providing you were an active listener during the lecture.

Graphic Organizers

Outlining during class or after class organizes large amounts of information into an organized page.

It has been said that "a picture is worth a thousand words," so draw pictures to remind you of the important parts of class, an experiment, or PowerPoint.

"The reading of all good books is like a conversation with the finest minds of past centuries."

René Descartes

French mathematician

Venn diagrams not only help you take the notes, but can also organize the information by similarities and differences for future use.

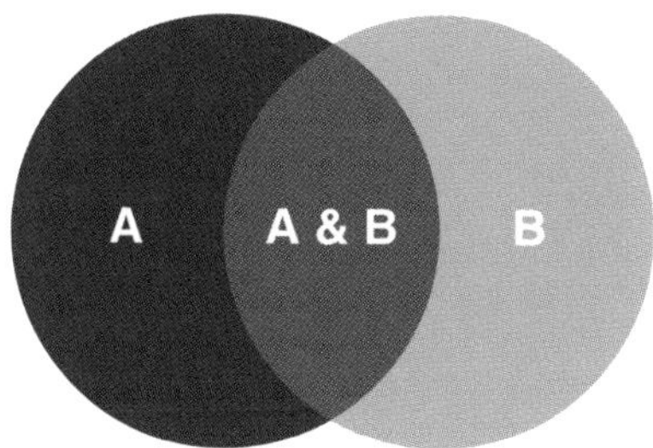

©Hayden-McNeil, LLC

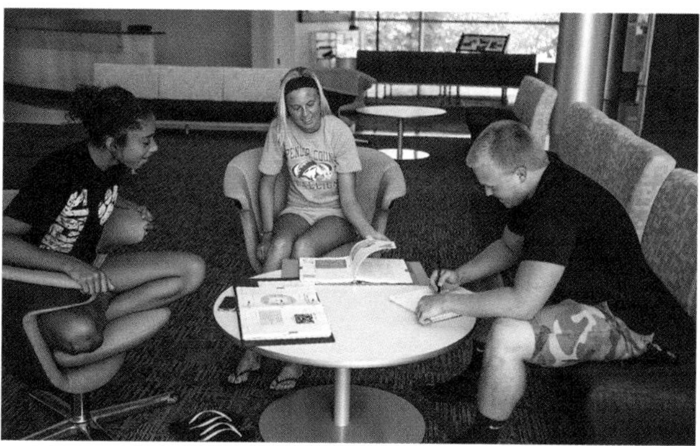

Chunk, Cluster, or Sort

Telephone numbers and social security numbers are two examples of how we are able to remember a list of numbers by breaking them into smaller parts. This method not only works for numbers, but also for information in writing and lecture. Grouping this information also gets it ready for future use in class or writing/synthesizing papers.

For example, you are given a list of random words to remember: apple, bread, notebook, pencil, carrot, soda, book, milk, water. Group them into categories like the ones below.

FOOD	SCHOOL SUPPLIES	LIQUID
Apple	Notebook	Soda
Bread	Pencil	Milk
Carrot	Book	Water

Of course, the association depends upon the need to learn the information. You must connect to the instructor's purposes for the learning.

"Teaching" the New Information

Research shows that we retain much more information if we "teach" it to someone else. So, become the teacher. With study partners, set up a classroom setting in which you and your study partners "pretend" to teach one another to study for a big exam or to prepare for a presentation. Your "students" will quickly let you know what you do not remember or need to correct.

Mnemonic Devices

Mnemonic devices are tricks that can increase your recall by abbreviating, rhyming, or associating information systems to one another. An example is PEMDAS in algebra. PEMDAS is an acronym used to help people remember the order in which you use mathematical operations:

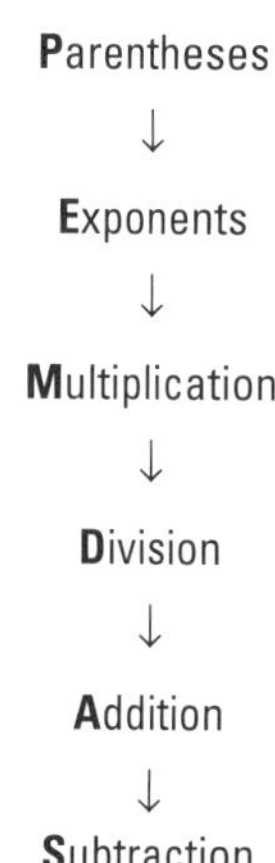

Storytelling and Word Association

Pretend that you are given a list of words to remember: girl, school, turtle, book, bus, shoe, rain, daisy, door, floor, coin. You could easily remember these if you turned them into a silly story:

The **girl** rode to **school** on the **bus**. As she exited, her **shoe** fell off. A **coin** rolled out of her pocket and hit a **turtle**. Finally off the bus, she was soaked by the **rain** and dropped her **book**. She entered the **door** of the school, but slipped and fell on the wet **floor**. She felt much better when her boyfriend gave her a **daisy**.

Mental pictures or "storyboards" like the one below help with this method.

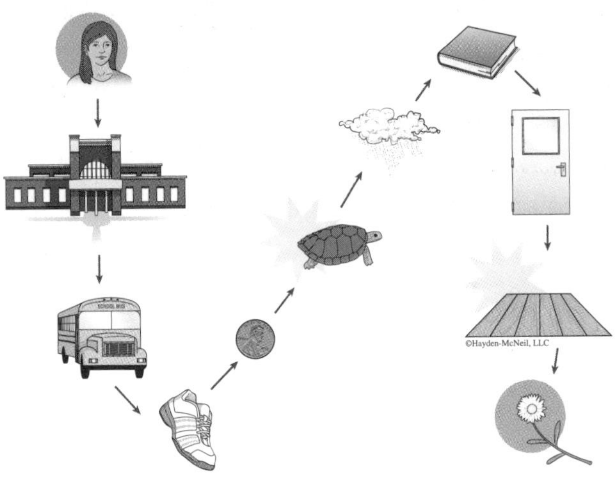

Test Time

Quiz, test, exam, midterm, and the ever-dreaded final—when you hear these words you may experience feelings of dread, panic, and even fear. Yet tests are something college students experience on a regular basis and they usually serve as a big part of the overall grade in a class. Therefore, in order to overcome those feelings and do well in your classes, it is important for you to master the art of successful testing early in your college career. Successful testing can be divided into two parts: test prep and test taking.

■ TEST PREP

Test prep begins the first day of class. When you receive your syllabus, the first thing you should do is look for exam information. Most professors list test dates and explain exam formats in the syllabus. If this information is not listed in the syllabus, the professor will probably discuss this information in class, so it is important that you attend.

Three important aspects of test prep are good habits we have already discussed: attending class, taking good notes, and reading required material. As test day approaches, it is also important to organize and outline the information that will be covered on the test. Some professors offer review sessions before exams; if possible, attend a review session, as it will provide you with valuable information about the exam. If attending a review session is not an option, make sure you attend class before the exam to get any study guides or exam assistance provided by the professor. Make sure you find out from the instructor what the format of the test will be (multiple choice, fill in the blanks, true/false, essay, etc.), as this will assist you in determining how to study.

A list of additional tips for test prep is provided on the following page, but the most important thing to remember when test time comes is this: don't wait until the night before the exam to ask yourself, "Am I ready?"

"Reading is to the mind what exercise is to the body."

Joseph Addison

English essayist, poet, and statesman

TEN TEST PREP TIPS

1. Don't spend time on what you already know.
2. Know what will be covered. Draft outlines and write essay answers to broad questions about the material.
3. Break the material into sections to study over a few days prior to the exam.
4. Focus on the key concepts, cause and effect relationships, comparison and contrast, significance, and connections within the material.
5. Look for ways to use mnemonic devices or other memory techniques.
6. Connect to what you know. Does a term remind you of someone's name? Does a date hold personal meaning?
7. Make flash cards or write out questions to quiz yourself.
8. Teach someone else the material—if you can teach it, you know it!
9. Attend test review sessions or study with other students from class.
10. Get plenty of sleep the night before, eat breakfast, and drink lots of water.

TEST TAKING

You have attended class, have stayed up-to-date on assignments, and have studied for several days before the exam. The time for your first college exam has finally arrived. The next step for successful testing is to learn how best to approach the different types of tests you may encounter. Although not all instructors test in the same manner, they do tend to incorporate one or a combination of common test types. Table 4-1 provides a list of these types along with a few helpful tips for how to approach each format when you are testing.

For information on EKU tutoring services, visit: http://www.tutoring.eku.edu

Test Anxiety: What Is It and How Do You Overcome It?

At one time or another we have all been there: that sick feeling comes over us when we look at an exam question and our mind goes completely blank, the palms of our hands become clammy, our pulse starts racing. All we want to do is bolt from the classroom. If this has ever happened to you, you have experienced test anxiety.

Table 4-1. Common Test Types.

COMMON TEST TYPES AND TIPS	
Test Type	Testing Tips
True/False You are asked to determine if a statement is true or not	• Read each statement carefully • Watch for key words that tend to show the statement is false: Always, None, Never, All, Every, Only • Watch for key words that tend to show the statement is true: Some, Most, Few, Many, Often, Sometimes • If any part of the statement is false, the entire statement will tend to be false
Multiple Choice You are asked to choose from two or more options to correctly answer the question	• Read the question and determine your answer before reading the answer choices provided • Cross off answers you know are incorrect • If more than one answer is correct, look for the choice "all of the above" • Make an educated guess if you are unsure
Essay Requires you to supply the answer to the question in paragraph form	• Read all directions closely; not all instructors require you to answer all given questions • Create an outline of your answer • Answer the question with facts and details • Write neatly; use proper grammar and correct spelling • Be concise in your answer
Short Answer/Fill-in-the-Blank Requires you to supply the answer to the question	• Read each question and make sure you understand what is being asked • Do not leave an answer blank • Look for key words in the sentence
Open Book Book and/or class notes can be used to complete the test	• Spend time preparing and familiarize yourself with the chapters and topics covered in the text • Highlight important points while preparing • Bring all allowed materials to class the day of testing

"Reading a book is like re-writing it for yourself. You bring to a novel, anything you read, all your experience of the world. You bring your history and you read it in your own terms."

Angela Carter

English novelist

■ TEST ANXIETY—WHAT IS IT?

Test anxiety is an array of physical, psychological, and emotional characteristics that students may experience, either prior to test taking or during test taking, that hinders them from organizing clear and concise thought patterns associated with the act of examination or with a particular subject of examination (Spada, Nikcevic, Moneta, & Ireson, 2006). Increased anxiety during a test or performance evaluation significantly affects focus, which results in distraction and a decrease in the ability to perform and retrieve essential data (Tobias, 1985). Studies have also shown that test anxiety has a detrimental effect on a student's grade point average, from the elementary grades all the way through to the graduate level (Chapell, Blanding, Takahashi, Silverstein, Newman, Gubi, & McCann, 2005).

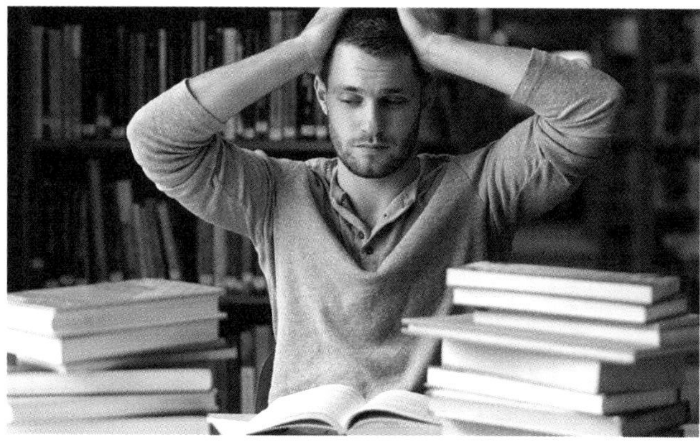

It is perfectly normal to experience some anxiety when gearing up for a test. In fact, a little anxiety actually helps increase your perception and assists in studying for that big exam. However, when that anxiety begins to take on a life of its own and creates havoc in the ability to concentrate, form memory patterns, or recall information previously committed to memory, it then becomes a hindrance instead of a help.

■ TEST ANXIETY—HOW TO DEAL WITH IT

If you find yourself becoming anxious during an exam, to the point where you cannot concentrate or recall information that you have previously studied, some simple relaxation techniques may help you in refocusing your efforts. Sit back, take a few deep breaths, and try to focus your attention on the test that is in front of you. Try to not allow yourself to become distracted by things that are going on around you. Once you have refocused your attention, you can then continue answering the questions on your exam.

There are also some test-taking strategies that you can do while taking an exam that can assist you in working through your test anxiety. First, scan the test to see how it is laid out. Are there true and false questions, multiple choice questions, matching questions, short answer, or essay questions? Once you have scanned the test, go through and answer the questions that you immediately recognize or recall. Skip over the questions of which you are not certain. Once you have answered the questions that you readily know, then you can go back and work on the ones with which you have difficulty. Also, keep an eye on the time. Know that if you have sixty minutes in which to take a test and there are fifty questions, you have a little over one minute to answer each question.

➲Need help managing test anxiety?
The EKU Counseling Center can help. Contact them at 859-622-1303 or stop by the Whitlock Building, room 571.

Several studies have also focused on how to assist students in overcoming the symptoms of test anxiety. Bembenutty (2008) found that strengthening specific study skills assists students in becoming self-regulated learners, or learners that "maintain the cognition, motivation, and behavior needed to achieve intended goals" (Schunk, Pintrich, & Meece, 2008). Some of these study skills include:

Rehearsal—the process of maintaining information in short-term memory by repeating the information over and over.

Elaboration—adjusting and expanding strategies and information by linking and associating new information with previous knowledge (Bembenutty, 2008).

It was also found that by strengthening study skills, students begin to develop a stronger sense of **self-efficacy**, which is the belief that they are capable of overcoming their anxiety associated with test taking. This, in turn, has been shown to have a direct effect on students' **intrinsic motivation**, which is the motivation from within to accomplish a given task.

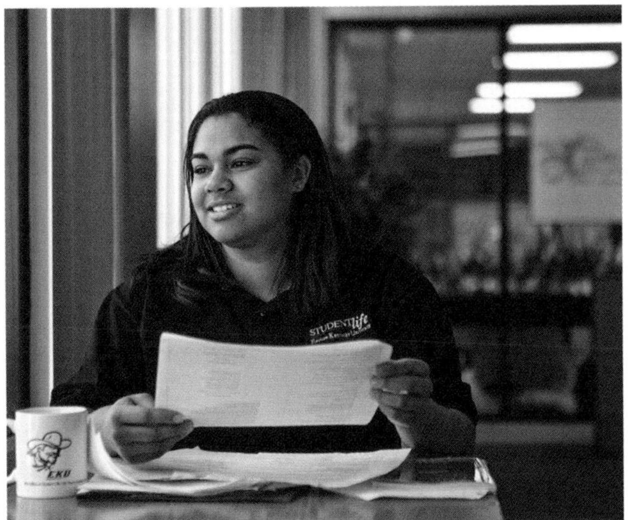

Another study by Shobe, Brewin, & Carmack (2005) relates how visualization or imagery has assisted college students in controlling the symptoms of test anxiety by helping them to relieve the stress associated with the examination. Visualization is the use of mental pictures or images that aid a person in achieving a desired emotional and cognitive outcome. For example, visualization has been readily used in enhancing sports performance, treating post-traumatic stress, overcoming speech and performance anxiety, along with use in other clinical settings to relieve anxiety disorders (p. 37).

The study also suggests that scholastic programs that equip students with increased study skills and test-retest strategies, encourage supportive communication with other students, and assist with improving the self-efficacy of the students "have been shown to significantly reduce test anxiety and improve performance" (p. 39).

By implementing these tools, you can face and overcome the challenges of test anxiety. By believing that you can achieve, developing diligent study habits, and using specific test-taking techniques, you can make a determined difference in your academic career.

Chapter Summary

The strategies and skills you learned in this chapter will not only assist you in achieving academic success at EKU, but in maintaining a productive work environment throughout your life. Active learning and listening, close reading, note taking, and test anxiety management are skills you will continue to use well beyond your time at EKU. Listening to comprehend, and not just to hear, will make you a successful student and invaluable to future employers, as well as a cherished friend to others. Reading with intention will assist with your comprehension of assigned readings in class and will also benefit you when reading for self-interest. Being a successful note taker helps you develop the skill of breaking down information and making meaning of long segments of text. The ability to manage test anxiety will improve your grades on course exams and will help you manage stress with performance assessments that occur in your chosen career. As you can see, the strategies for academic success are also the key to personal and professional success.

"I find television to be very educating. Every time somebody turns on the set, I go in the other room and read a book."

Groucho Marx

Comedian

■ KEY TERMS

Active learning: A learning model in which students are actively engaged in learning through strategies such as reading, writing, discussion, etc.

Active listening: The process of paying close attention to a speaker's words and intentionally trying to understand the meaning behind them

Annotating: Adding notes to a text or diagram to offer comments or explanations

Attending behavior: Conscious behaviors used to help you pay attention

Cornell Method: A method of note taking developed by Walter Pauk at Cornell University in the 1950s

Fundamental question: A unifying question used as a means to understand the content of a book, chapter, topic, lecture, etc.

Graphic organizer: A visual aid representing concepts and ideas which is used to clarify information and enhance understanding

Intrinsic motivation: The motivation to accomplish any given task which comes from within the individual

Mind map: A diagram used to organize thoughts, ideas, tasks, etc.

Mnemonic device: A learning technique or trick, usually verbal, which is used to aid memorization

Non-verbal response: Non-verbal part of a conversation or lecture, such as body language, gestures, and facial expressions

Open posture: A body position that indicates a readiness to receive information

Outline: A visual organizational tool enumerating various ideas from a main topic and their importance/relationship to one another

Pre-reading: The activities in which a learner engages prior to reading in order to help identify a purpose for the material being read

Reading strategies: The various processes used by a reader to draw meaning from a text

Self-efficacy: The belief that one has the ability to successfully complete a task, such as overcoming one's anxiety

Test anxiety: Physical, psychological, and emotional characteristics experienced prior to or during an examination which affect one's test performance

Venn diagram: A type of diagram developed by John Venn in which intersecting circles are used to demonstrate the relationships of sets

Verbal response: Aspect of a discussion when you articulate back to the speaker what you have heard to check understanding and accuracy

Visualization: The technique of using mental pictures or images to aid in achieving a desired emotional, cognitive, or physical achievement

NOTES

"To read a book, to think it over, and to write out notes is a useful exercise; a book which will not repay some hard thought is not worth publishing."

Maria Mitchell

American scientist

CAMPUS RESOURCES

Common Knowledge
http://www.gurus.eku.edu
Powell Student Center, Tech Commons, 859-622-2496

Crabbe Library
http://www.library.eku.edu
103 Libraries Complex, 859-622-1790

Department of English & Theatre
http://www.english.eku.edu
467 Case Annex, 859-622-5861

Developmental Education & College Readiness
http://www.developmentaleducation.eku.edu
Whitlock Building, room 327, 859-622-2306

EKU Counseling Center
http://www.counseling.eku.edu
Whitlock Building, room 571, 859-622-1303

Noel Studio for Academic Creativity
http://www.studio.eku.edu
Library 207B, 859-622-6229

Office of Services for Individuals with Disabilities
http://www.disabilities.eku.edu
859-622-2933

Tutoring Centers
http://www.tutoring.eku.edu
859-622-6778

REFERENCES

Bembenutty, H. (2008). Self-regulation of learning and text anxiety. *Psychology Journal*, *5*(3), 122–139.

BrainyQuote. (n.d.). *BrainyQuote.com*. Retrieved June 9, 2011, from http://www.brainyquote.com/

Campus Grotto. (n.d.). Cornell note taking method. *Campus Grotto: The Inside Source at College*. Retrieved March 18, 2011, from http://www.campusgrotto.com/cornell-note-taking-method.html

Chapell, M.S., Blanding, B.Z., Takahashi, M., Silverstein, M.E., Newman, B., Gubi, A., & McCann, N. (2005, May). Test anxiety and academic performance in undergraduate and graduate students. *Journal of Educational Psychology*, *97* (2), 268–274.

Mangrum-Strichart Learning Resources. (n.d.). Test anxiety. In *How-to-study.com*. Retrieved March 18, 2011, from http://www.how-to-study.com/study-skills/en/taking-tests/47/test-anxiety/index.asp

Medina, J. (2008). *Brain rules: 12 principles for surviving and thriving at work, home, and school.* Seattle, WA: Pear Press.

Ohio University, University College Communications. (UCC). (n.d.). *A concentration monitor*. Retrieved March 18, 2011, from Ohio University, UCC Website: http://studytips.admsrv.ohio.edu/studytips/docs/concentrationmonitor.pdf

Radcliffe, C. (Photographer). (n.d.). [2005–2010 EKU Photos]. In *EKU Photo Library*. Retrieved March 18, 2011, from http://www.prm.eku.edu/photolibrary/

Schunk, D. H., Pintrich, P. R., & Meece, J. L. (2008). *Motivation in education: theory, research, and application* (3rd ed.). Upper Saddle River, NJ: Merrill-Prentice Hall.

Shobe, E., Brewin, A., & Carmack, S. (2005). A simple visualization exercise for reducing test anxiety and improving performance on difficult math tests. *Journal of Worry and Affective Experience*, *1*(1), 34–52.

Spada, M., Nikcevic, A., Moneta, G., & Ireson, J. (2006). Metacognition as a mediator of the effect of test anxiety on a surface approach to studying. *Educational Psychology*, *26*(5), 615–624.

Tobias, S. (1985). Test anxiety: Interference, defective skills, and cognitive capacity. *Educational Psychologists*, *20*(3), 135–142.

NOTES

"Visualization is daydreaming with a purpose."

Bo Bennett

American businessman

5

THINK

THINK

Chapter Five

Chapter Five

THINK

After mastering the content in this chapter you will be able to:

- EXPLORE and use relevant information in order to gain knowledge and solve problems
- EVALUATE information and ideas using appropriate methods
- EXPAND and integrate ideas and information and analyze academic resources
- EXPRESS a point of view and develop it with awareness of alternatives

Fundamental Question

- What tools do I need to improve the way I think?

Essential Principles

- Parts of Thought
- Standards of Thinking
- Intellectual Traits

"Too often we...enjoy the comfort of opinion without the discomfort of thought."

John F. Kennedy

35th President of the United States of America

5

Introduction

Every day, events happen which require you to think about your decisions, and as you enter your first year of college, the likelihood of frequently facing difficult choices increases. How do you decide whether or not to study for an exam? Does that major really lead you to the career you want? Should you buy that new laptop or save money for unexpected expenses? Does that article you found for your English paper really support your thesis? What does that Facebook comment really say about you?

In scenarios such as these, as well as in other situations, we sometimes don't make the right or informed choice. Why can't we think things through more effectively so we don't make bad decisions? In college, you are going to be presented with many new challenges and choices, and the tools of being a critical thinker will help put you in the driver's seat when it comes to making better choices. To think critically is to think things through so that your thinking can drive better decisions. In other words, understanding your thought processes can improve your decisions.

In this chapter, you will consider your own experiences with critical thinking and then marry what you believe you know about it with the content of *The Aspiring Thinker's Guide to Critical Thinking* as you examine:

- What is meant by critical thinking,
- How this process can help you solve problems your first semester of college (and beyond!),
- How thinking critically can help you in seeking out answers,
- The benefits of being a fair-minded critical thinker with character!

EKU challenges you to become a more informed, critical and creative thinker who communicates effectively. As you do, you will find you make better, more informed choices that will lead you to a more successful start to college. Then, as you develop these skill sets, you will apply what you have learned from this course in every aspect of your life. You will become what you study.

"Having and using critical thinking skills enhances your college experience and will make you more marketable and successful in your future career. Most anyone can come to college, take tests, and get a degree. Becoming a critical thinker and learning to utilize those tools is what will separate you from everyone else."

Matthew Thacker
History; Physics minor

NOTES

"It is the mark of an educated mind to be able to entertain a thought without accepting it."

Aristotle

Ancient Greek philosopher

Eastern Kentucky University

THE ASPIRING THINKER'S

Guide to Critical Thinking

By Dr. Linda Elder and Dr. Richard Paul

NOTES

NOTES

Eastern Kentucky University

Introduction for Teachers and Students

Humans live in a world of thoughts. We accept some thoughts as true. We reject others as false. But the thoughts we perceive as true are sometimes false, unsound, or misleading. And the thoughts we perceive as false and trivial are sometimes true and significant. The mind doesn't naturally grasp the truth. *We don't naturally see things as they are.* We don't automatically sense what is reasonable and what unreasonable. Our thought is often biased by our agendas, interests, and values. We *typically see things as we want to.* We twist reality to fit our preconceived ideas. Distorting reality is common in human life. It is a phenomenon to which we all, at times, unfortunately fall prey.

Each of us views the world through multiple lenses, often shifting them to fit our changing feelings. In addition, much of our perspective is unconscious and uncritical and has been influenced by many forces – including social, political, economic, biological, and psychological influences. Selfishness and narrow-mindedness are deeply influential in the lives of most people.

We need a systematic way to further *sound* thinking and limit *unsound* thinking. We need to take command of our minds in order to determine in a reasonable way what thinking to accept and what to reject. Critical thinking is that process, that orientation, and in the finest cases, that way of living.

This guide focuses on the essence of critical thinking concepts. For teachers it provides a shared concept of critical thinking. For students it introduces critical thinking and provides strategies for developing one's own critical thinking. Teachers can use it to design instruction, assignments, and tests in any subject. Students can use it to improve their learning in any content area.

The skills implicit in this guide apply to all subjects. For example, critical thinkers are clear as to the purpose at hand and the question at issue. They question information, conclusions, and points of view. They strive to be clear, accurate, precise, and relevant. They seek to think beneath the surface, to be logical, and fair. They apply these skills to their reading and writing as well as to their speaking and listening. They apply them in all subjects and throughout life.

If you are a student using this guide, get in the habit of carrying it with you to every class. Consult it frequently in analyzing and synthesizing what you are learning. Aim to deeply learn the ideas you find in it - until using them becomes second nature.

"Knowing a great deal is not the same as being smart; intelligence is not information alone but also judgment, the manner in which information is collected and used."

Carl Sagan

American scientist and author

NOTES

Contents

NOTES

"The intuitive mind is a sacred gift and the rational mind is a faithful servant. We have created a society that honours the servant and has forgotten the gift."

Albert Einstein

German-born American physicist

NOTES

There are Three Main Kinds of Thinkers

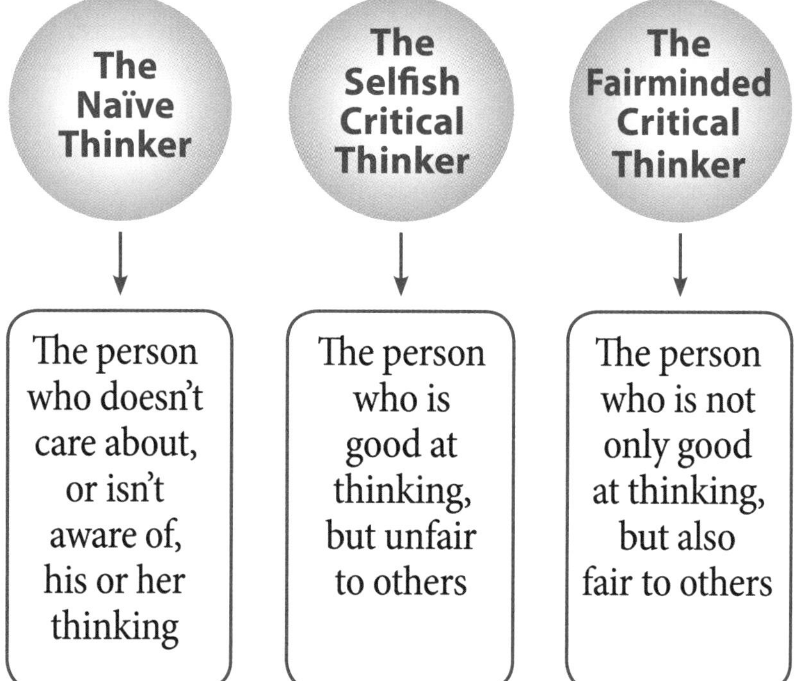
The Naïve Thinker
The Selfish Critical Thinker
The Fairminded Critical Thinker
The person who doesn't care about, or isn't aware of, his or her thinking
The person who is good at thinking, but unfair to others
The person who is not only good at thinking, but also fair to others

Each of us may sometimes be a naïve thinker, sometimes a selfish critical thinker, and sometimes a fairminded critical thinker.

We can create a better world when we work together to be fair to everyone. We will never be perfect, but we can always improve our thinking.

This guide will help you develop as a fairminded thinker.

NOTES

The Fairminded Critical Thinker

Fairminded critical thinkers work to improve their thinking whenever they can. They want things for themselves, but they aren't selfish. They want to help other people. They want to help make the world better for everyone. They are willing to give things up to help others (when it makes sense to). They don't always have the right answers, but they work to improve their thinking (and actions) over time.

Here is the voice of the fairminded critical thinker...

"I think a lot. It helps me learn. It helps me figure things out. I want to understand the thinking of other people. In fact, I even want to understand myself and why I do things. Sometimes I do things I don't understand. It's not easy trying to understand everyone and everything. Lots of people say one thing and do another. You can't always believe what people say. You can't believe a lot of what you see on TV and the internet. People often say things they don't mean because they want things and are trying to please you.

"I would like to make the world a better place. I want to make it better for everyone, not just for me and my friends. To understand other people you have to look at things as they do. You have to understand their situation and what you would feel like if you were them. You have to put yourself in their shoes. I think about people who don't have what I have, like people who are starving or homeless. I want to help create a world where everyone has enough to eat and somewhere to live.

"It isn't easy to be fair. It's a lot easier to be selfish and just think about yourself. But the world isn't a nice place to be if people are selfish."

"It is better to know some of the questions than all of the answers."

James Thurber

American writer and artist

NOTES

The Selfish Critical Thinker

Selfish critical thinkers are people who use their thinking to get what they want, without considering how their actions might affect other people. They are good at thinking, and they know it. But they are also very selfish. They may be greedy and unkind as well.

Here is the voice of the selfish critical thinker…

"I think a lot! It helps me get what I want. I believe whatever I want to believe as long as it gets me what I want. I question anyone who asks me to do what I don't want to do. I figure out how to get other people to do what I want them to do. I even figure out how to avoid thinking if I want.

"Sometimes I say 'I can't!' when I know I could but don't want to. You can get what you want from people if you know how to manipulate them. Just the other night, I talked my parents into buying me a really expensive new computer gadget I knew they couldn't really afford. But hey, they work don't they? They can always make more money. I'm their kid so they should give me what I want.

"It helps to tell people what they want to hear. Of course, sometimes what they want to hear isn't true, but that doesn't matter because you only get into trouble when you tell people what they don't want to hear. You can always trick people if you know how. Guess what, you can even trick yourself if you know how."

NOTES

The Naïve Thinker

Naïve thinkers don't see why it is important to work on their thinking. They don't want to be bothered with developing their minds.

Here is the voice of the naïve thinker…

"I don't need to think! I understand everything without thinking. I just do whatever occurs to me to do. I believe most of what I hear. I believe most of what I see on TV and what I read on the internet. I don't see why I should question the messages that come at me on TV shows and the internet. I don't think they affect me that much anyway.

"And I don't need to waste a lot of time trying to figure things out. If I need to find the answer to a problem, I just ask someone else. Other people can figure things out better than me, so why should I try to figure things out for myself? It's a lot easier to say 'I can't!' than to do a lot of work. A lot of times trying to figure things out takes too much time. And sometimes it's just too hard for me, so why bother?

"I mostly go along with whatever people are doing. It's just easier that way. I do what I'm told, keep my mouth shut, and go along with whatever my friends decide. I don't like to make waves. Thinking gets you into trouble."

"We thought that we had the answers, it was the questions we had wrong."

Bono

Irish singer, musician, and humanitarian

NOTES

Developing Intellectual Character

Fairminded critical thinkers want to develop intellectual habits or traits. These traits define how they live their lives – how they learn, how they communicate with other people, how they see the world. Here are some of the important intellectual traits or virtues. See if you can figure out what each one might mean before turning the page. When thinking about important ideas, it's always helpful to start with a dictionary.

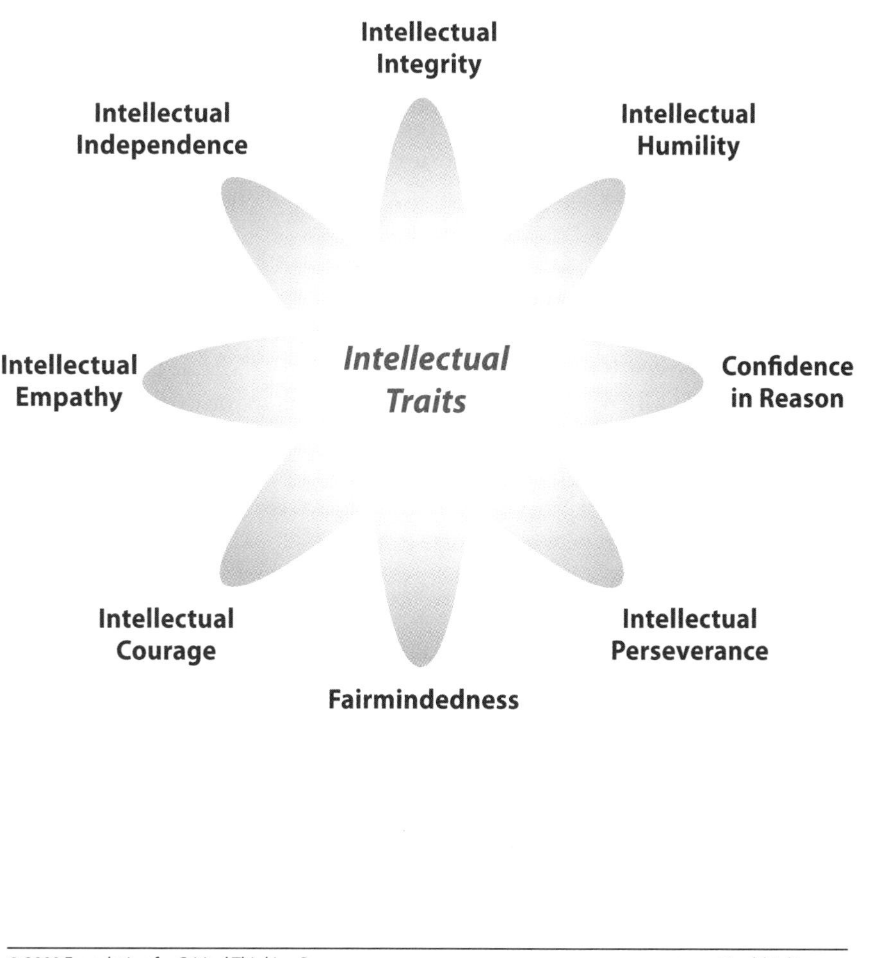

NOTES

How to Become a Fairminded Critical Thinker

Intellectual Integrity

Act towards others the way you want people to act towards you. Respect others in the same way you want to be respected. Don't expect others to act better than you are willing to act yourself. Consider the feelings of others in the same way you want your own feelings to be considered. Because you don't want others to be rude to you, avoid being rude to others. Because you don't want to be harmed by others, be careful not to harm others.

Intellectual Independence

Do your own thinking. Figure things out for yourself. It is good to listen to others to find out what they think, but you must do your own thinking to decide who and what to believe. Of course don't just believe what you want to believe. Use intellectual standards to decide; standards like accuracy, relevance, significance and fairness.

Intellectual Perseverance

Don't be a quitter. When you begin to think you can't learn something, remind yourself that *you can*. If reading is hard for you, stick to it (because it is important to learn to read well). When writing is hard, keep trying so you can learn to write better. Don't be afraid to work hard when you feel like giving up. Remember that no matter how good you are at thinking, you can always improve. And no matter how much you struggle with learning, keep trying. *Never give up!* Be the captain of your own ship. Chart your own course in life.

Intellectual Empathy

Always try to understand how other people think and feel. Whenever you disagree with someone, try to see things from that person's point of view. When you do try to see things from other people's viewpoints, you will often find that there are some things you are right about and some things other people are right about. Being able and willing to imagine how others think and feel is very important in life. If everyone did this a lot, the world would be much better for everyone. There would be a lot less pain and suffering.

"What we observe is not nature itself, but nature exposed to our methods of questioning."

Werner Heisenberg

German physicist

NOTES

Intellectual Humility

Recognize that you don't know everything. There is a lot that you don't know (and will never know). Don't say something is true *when you don't know for sure that it is.* Lots of things you *think* are true may not in fact be true. Lots of things people say are true are actually not true and lots of things you read or see on TV are not true. Always ask, "How do I know that? How do you know that?"

Intellectual Courage

Be ready to speak up for what you think is right, even if it is not popular with your friends or the people around you. Of course, sometimes speaking up can be dangerous. Use your best thinking to figure out when it makes sense to speak up and when you should just keep your thoughts to yourself. When you do speak up, try always to show respect for others. But don't ever be afraid to disagree in the privacy of your own mind. And don't be afraid to question your beliefs, to figure out what makes best sense. Develop the courage to look inside your own mind and figure out what is really going on there. Even if you have held a belief for a long time, you still need to be willing to question it, to use the tools of critical thinking to recheck it.

Confidence in Reason

The best chance we have to create a fair and just world is if we use our best thinking, all of us, together, living on the planet. When people disagree, they need to overcome disagreements by looking at the facts, at the evidence. We need to work together to come to the most defensible conclusions. Use intellectual standards in working through problems. For example, make sure you use information that is *accurate* and *relevant* to the problem you are trying to solve. Look for the complexities in deep issues. Avoid superficial answers to complicated problems as they almost never work. Think about problems from different points of view. Trust evidence, facts and reasoning. Distrust blind faith, jealousy and fear.

Fairmindedness

Try to figure out what is most fair in every situation. Think about everyone involved, not just about you. Don't put your desires and needs above those of others. You should even be willing to give things up to help other people when their needs are much greater than yours. Try to imagine what it would be like to think and feel as other people do, to be in their shoes. Don't act until you have done this. Think before you act. Don't act before you think.

NOTES

Intellectual Standards Help You Think Better

The best thinkers don't believe any and everything they hear or read. They use intellectual standards to decide what to believe. They use intellectual standards to keep their thinking on track. In this guide, we focus on some of the important ones. When you use them every day, your thinking improves.

Be clear! —	Can you state what you mean? Can you give examples?
Be accurate! —	Are you sure it's true?
Be relevant! —	Is it related to what we are thinking about?
Be logical! —	Does it all fit together?
Be fair! —	Am I considering how my behavior might make others feel?
Be reasonable! —	Have we thought through this problem thoroughly and with an open mind?

If everyone in the world regularly used intellectual standards, we could solve most of our big problems.

"An education isn't how much you have committed to memory, or even how much you know. It's being able to differentiate between what you do know and what you don't."

Anatole France

French poet, journalist, novelist, and Nobel Prize winner

NOTES

Eastern Kentucky University

Be Clear: Don't Confuse People

We are confused when we are not clear.

We are clear when we understand:

- what we are saying
- what we are hearing
- what we are reading
- what we are seeing

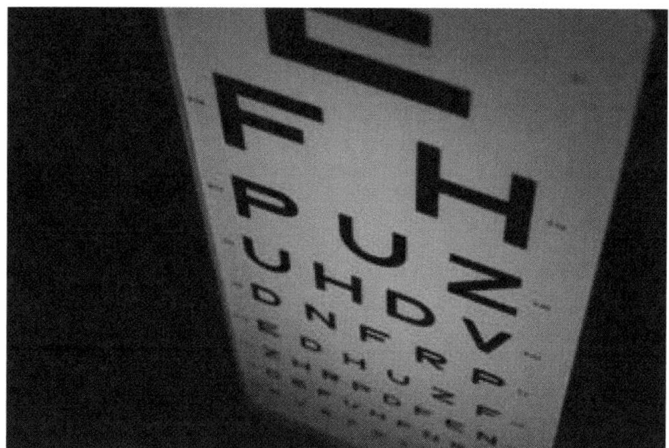

Ideas can be fuzzy or clear, like letters on an eye chart.

Things you can say and questions you can ask when you want to be clear:

- Let me tell you what I mean. Let me give you an example.
- Could you tell me what you mean?
- Could you say that in other words?
- I'm confused. Could you explain what you mean?
- Let me tell you what I think you said. Tell me if I'm right.

NOTES

Be Accurate: Make Sure it's True

Something is accurate when it is true or correct, when it is not distorted.

When we aren't sure whether something is true, we check to see if it is.

When we need to be accurate we want to hit our bull's-eye exactly. We don't want our thinking to be distorted in any way.

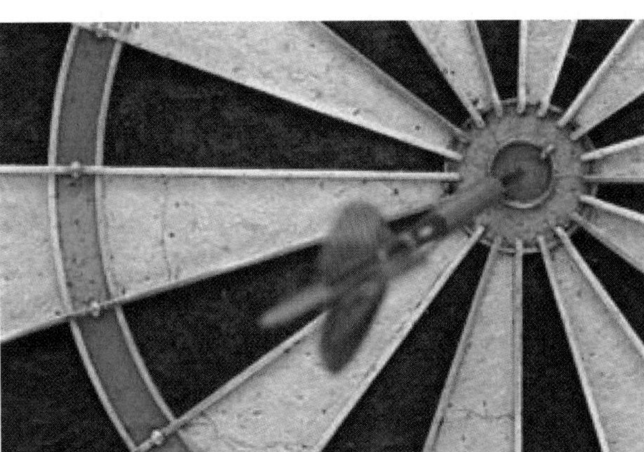

Questions you can ask to make sure you are accurate:

- How could we find out if this is really true?
- How can we check this?
- How can we test this idea to see if it is true?
- How do I know what I am saying is true?
- How do I know that what I read on the internet is true?
- How do I know that the information in this book is true?
- How do I know that what my friends say is true?
- How can I find out for myself if "X" is true?

"There is no slavery but ignorance. Liberty is the child of intelligence."

Robert G. Ingersoll

American agnostic, activist, and orator

NOTES

Be Relevant: Make Sure You Stay on Track

Something is relevant when it relates directly to:

- the problem you are trying to solve.
- the question you are trying to answer.
- whatever you are talking about or writing about.

All instruments in a cockpit are *relevant* to flying the airplane, but they are not relevant to riding a bicycle.

Questions you can ask when you are not sure whether something is relevant:

- How does what you say relate to the problem?
- How does this information relate to the question we are asking?
- What will help us solve the problem?
- How does what you say relate to what we are talking about?
- How does this relate to our purpose?

NOTES

Be Logical: Make Sure Everything Fits Together

Thinking is logical when everything fits together, when everything makes sense together.

Questions you can ask when you are not sure whether something is logical:

- This doesn't make sense to me. Can you show me how it all fits together?
- The sentences in this paragraph don't seem to belong together. How can I rewrite this paragraph so that the sentences all fit together?
- What you are saying doesn't sound logical. How did you come to your conclusions? Explain why this makes sense to you.
- The messages I am getting from this TV show don't seem sensible. Should I follow along with these ideas, or should I reject them?

"Babies naturally explore new things and test everything in their environment. You should keep this curiosity alive. Curiosity is the fuel that keeps your intellectual engine running."

Dr. John Medina in *Brain Rules*

American developmental molecular biologist

NOTES

Be Fair: Make Sure You Consider Others

When we consider the feelings of others before we do something we are being fair.

There are many problems in the world because lots of times people aren't fair to others.

It is important to be fair, both to ourselves and to others.

Questions you can ask when you are not sure whether you, or someone else, is being fair:

- Am I being selfish right now?
- Is he or she being selfish right now?
- Am I considering the thinking of others?
- Am I considering the feelings of others?
- Are we being fair to everyone in this situation?

NOTES

Eastern Kentucky University

Some Important Intellectual Standards

Remember that good thinkers decide what to believe using intellectual standards. Here are brief definitions of some of the most important ones:

Clarity:
understandable, nothing is confusing about it

Accuracy:
correct, true, not distorted

Precision:
containing the details needed to solve a problem

Relevance:
relating to the matter at hand, directly connected

Depth:
containing complexities that need to be thought through

Breadth:
involving more than one point of view

Logic:
the parts make sense together, no contradictions

Significance:
focusing on the important, not trivial

Fairness:
considering the thoughts and views of relevant others, not selfish

"Babies are the model of how we learn—not by passive reaction to the environment but by active testing through observation, hypothesis, experiment, and conclusion."

Dr. John Medina in *Brain Rules*

American developmental molecular biologist

NOTES

A Checklist of Questions You Can Ask to Target Intellectual Standards

Clarity	Could you elaborate further? Could you give me an example? Could you draw a picture of what you mean?
Accuracy	How could we check on that? How could we find out if that is true? Are we sure we aren't distorting the truth?
Precision	Could you be more specific? Could you give me more details? Could you be more exact?
Relevance	How does what you say relate to the problem? How does that bear on the question? How does that help us with the issue?
Depth	What makes this a difficult problem? What are some of the complexities of this question? What are some of the difficulties we need to deal with?
Breadth	Do we need to look at this from another perspective? Do we need to consider another point of view? Do we need to look at this in other ways?
Logic	Does all this make sense together? Are we looking at this reasonably? Does what you say follow from the evidence?
Significance	Is this the most important problem to consider? Is this the central idea to focus on? Which of these facts are most important?
Fairness	Am I considering all the relevant viewpoints? Am I being selfish? Am I being fair to myself and others?

NOTES

Think About Fairness

Fair people want to be fair thinkers. But they realize this isn't easy.

Here are some ways that people are unfair:

1) Being cruel
2) Being disrespectful
3) Being inconsiderate
4) Being rude
5) Being unkind
6) Being selfish
7) Being mean
8) Being hurtful

Fair thinkers know it isn't always easy to be fair to others. They question their behavior. They ask "How fair, how just, am I being?" Good thinkers see that lots of problems happen when we are unfair to others. And they realize that no one is perfect, that we are all sometimes unfair. They think about their thinking. They even write about their thinking and their behavior. Sometimes they keep a journal. In the journal, they write about problems in their behavior and then try to figure out why they did what they did. For example, they try to figure out what they were thinking that led them to unfair behavior.

On the next page is a journal sheet. You can make copies of it and put your copies in a notebook. Then you can write about your thinking and behavior using these sheets. This will help you see your behavior in the "mirror" of your writing.

Write one journal entry each week using these sheets and see if this helps you become more fair.

"The important thing is to not stop questioning."

Albert Einstein

American scientist and Nobel Prize winner

NOTES

Journal Entry Focusing on Unfair Thinking and Behavior

To protect your right to privacy, write only about problems you are willing to share with whoever reads your journal. Focus on problems in which you caused someone else to suffer, problems that resulted from your being cruel or selfish or rude, etc.

I was unfair when I behaved in the following way…

At the time, I didn't realize I was unfair because I thought…

I now realize I was unfair because…

To avoid being unfair in this way in the future I will…

NOTES

Eastern Kentucky University

We Take Our Thinking Apart to Find Problems in Our Thinking – and Solve Them

Here are the parts:

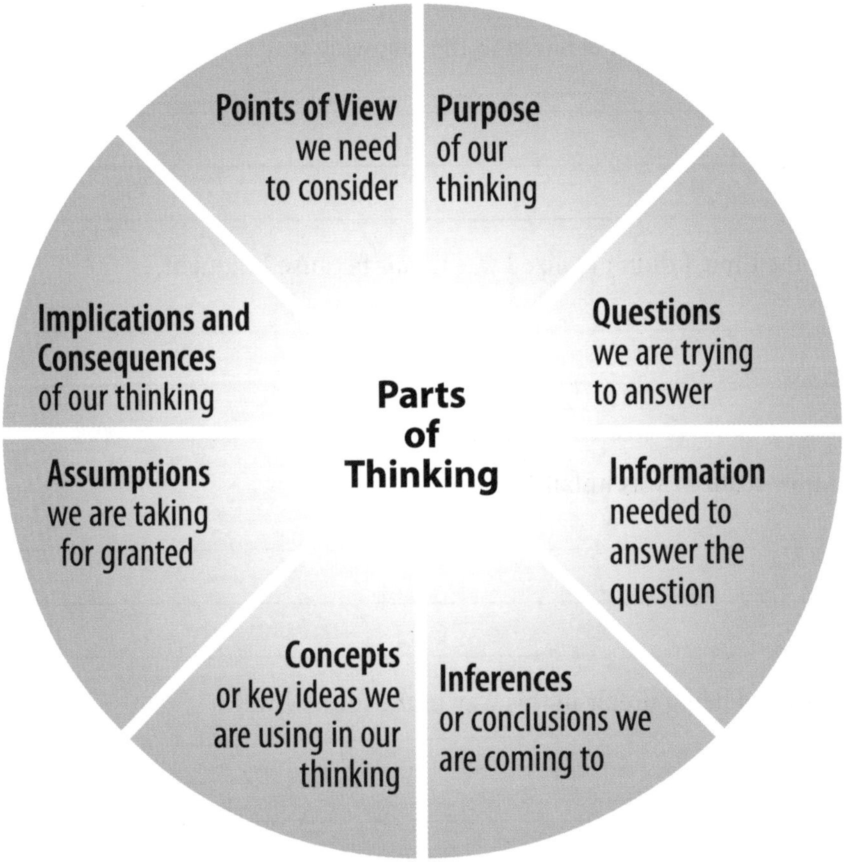
Points of View we need to consider
Purpose of our thinking
Questions we are trying to answer
Information needed to answer the question
Inferences or conclusions we are coming to
Concepts or key ideas we are using in our thinking
Assumptions we are taking for granted
Implications and Consequences of our thinking
Parts of Thinking

"He who asks a question is a fool for five minutes; he who does not ask a question remains a fool forever."

Chinese Proverb

Anonymous

NOTES

Think About Purpose

Your purpose is what you are trying to achieve or make happen.

Good athletes stay focused on their goals. Good thinkers do too.

Questions you can ask to target purpose:

- What is our purpose in doing what we are doing?
- What is my purpose in doing what I am doing?
- What is your purpose?
- What is the purpose of this assignment?
- What is the purpose of the main character in this story?
- What is my teacher trying to accomplish?
- What is my friend's purpose?
- What is the purpose of this textbook?
- Should we change our purpose?
- Is my purpose fair to everyone?

NOTES

State the Question

The question lays out the problem and helps us understand what we need to do to solve it.

Good thinkers state the question at issue as clearly as possible.

Good thinkers spend time figuring out the questions they need to ask.

Questions you can ask about the question:

- What question am I trying to answer?
- Is my question clear?
- Should I be asking a different question?
- What question are you asking me?
- What are the main questions in this chapter?

"You don't see something until you have the right metaphor to let you perceive it."

Thomas Kuhn

American physicist and philosopher

NOTES

Gather the Information

The information is the facts, evidence, or experiences you use to figure things out.

We are bombarded by information every day — from the internet, TV, radio, friends, relatives, school.... Watch out! Lots of information is not accurate.

Questions you can ask about information:

- What information do I need to answer this question?
- Do I need to gather more information?
- Is this information relevant to my purpose?
- Is this information accurate? How do I know it is?

NOTES

Check Your Inferences

Inferences are conclusions you come to. It's what the mind does in figuring something out. You make inferences every day. (Jane is my friend, so I infer I can trust her.)

Realize that every time you make an inference, you might make a different, more logical one.

An inference is a step of the mind which happens when the mind says " 'X' is true, therefore 'Y' is true."

For example, "It is raining outside," therefore "I should take an umbrella today" (see pp. 29-31).

Questions you can ask to check your inferences:

- What conclusions am I coming to?
- Are there other conclusions I should consider?
- Is my inference logical?
- Is this other person's inference logical?

"We cannot solve our problems with the same thinking we used when we created them."

Albert Einstein

American scientist and Nobel Prize winner

NOTES

Question Your Assumptions

Assumptions are beliefs you take for granted.
(" I assume we have enough gas in the car for our trip.")
Usually we don't question them, but we should.

Assumptions are usually unconscious in the mind. We don't know they are there. But we use them to figure things out.

We need to dig them up, examine them, and see if they make sense or not.

Questions you can ask about assumptions:

- What am I taking for granted?
- Am I assuming something I shouldn't?
- What assumption is leading me to this conclusion?
- What is this other person assuming?
- What do teachers often assume about students?
- What do students often assume about learning?

NOTES

Clarify Your Concepts

Concepts are ideas you use in thinking to understand what is going on and to figure out how to act in a situation.

Good thinkers are aware of the key ideas they are using in their thinking.

What is your concept of "healthy foods?" What is your concept of "unhealthy foods?"

Questions you can ask to clarify concepts:

- What is the main idea in this story?
- What idea comes into my mind when I hear the word 'school,' 'Christmas,' 'friend,' 'government,' 'peace,' _______?
- What idea am I using in my thinking? Is this idea causing problems for me or for others?
- I think your idea is a good one, but could you explain it a little more?

"For me the greatest beauty always lies in the greatest clarity."

Gotthold Ephraim Lessing

German writer and philosopher

NOTES

Understand Your Point of View

(and the point of view of others)

Point of view is what you are looking at and the way it looks to you.

Keep in mind that people have different points of view, especially when they disagree.

You have a point of view.

But can you understand other people's viewpoints?

Questions you can ask about point of view:

- How am I looking at this situation?
- What am I looking at? And how am I seeing it?
- Is there another reasonable way to look at this situation?
- Does my point of view seem to be the only correct one? (Watch out if it does.)
- Do I try to enter and appreciate the point of view of others?

NOTES

"Without critical thinking, it would be hard for any person to make a logical decision. Critical thinking requires one to think of every possible outcome in order to make the best decision. Using critical thinking will broaden your mind and allow you to see situations that you wouldn't normally notice."

Jeremy Ray
Psychology

Think Through the Implications

Do you think through possible consequences before you act?

An implication is that to which our thinking is leading us.

When you say things, you imply certain other things. For example, if you make a promise, you imply that you will keep it.

Consequences are the result of something that occurred earlier.

For example, if you are rude to someone, he might be rude back. If he is, it would be a consequence of your being rude first.

Questions you can ask about implications:

- If I decide to do "X," what things might happen?
- If I decide not to do "X," what things might happen?
- When the main character in the story made an important decision, what happened as a result? What were the consequences?
- What are the implications of trusting people I don't know?
- What are some implications of not acting to stop global warming?
- What are some implications of refusing to do my homework?

"If there is any one secret of success, it lies in the ability to get the other person's point of view and see things from that person's angle as well as from your own."

Henry Ford

American industrialist and founder of Ford Motor Company

NOTES

Eastern Kentucky University

Clarifying Inferences and Assumptions

It is important to be able to tell the difference between inferences and assumptions. People often mix up these two different parts of thinking. When you can tell the difference, you start to notice both of them. And as you do, you can check on whether they are justified.

Remember that assumptions are beliefs you take for granted. People don't usually question their assumptions. But they should.

Look at this picture to see how inferences and assumptions work in thinking:

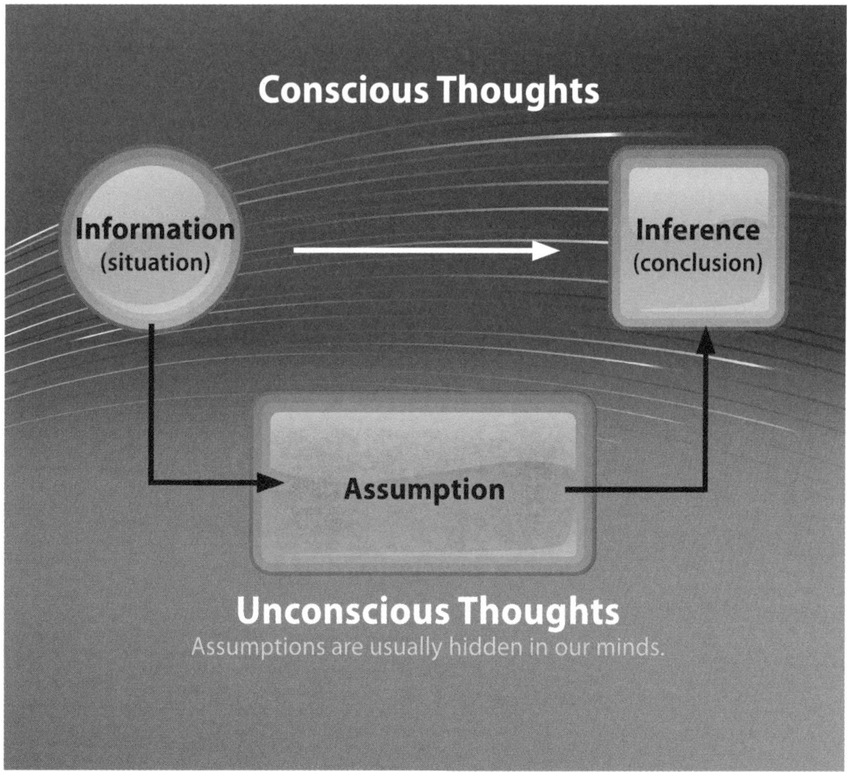

NOTES

Here are some examples which show how, in every situation, you make inferences. These inferences come largely from your assumptions and the information you have.

Information (situation):	One of my friends walks by without saying hello to me.
Possible inference:	My friend is angry with me.
Assumption that led to the inference:	Whenever my friend walks by without saying hello to me she is angry with me.

Information (situation):	I hear a kitten mewing in the bushes.
Possible inference:	The cat is lost.
Assumption that led to the inference:	Whenever you hear a kitten mewing in the bushes, it is lost.

"Assumptions are the termites of relationships."

Henry Winkler

American actor

NOTES

Finding Your Inferences and Assumptions

You can find your inferences and assumptions using the following strategy. First, figure out the information. Then figure out one inference a person might make when faced with that information. Then go "backwards" to figure out the assumption that led to the inference.

Information (Situation)	Possible inference a person might make	Assumption that leads to the inference
1. The computer freezes while you are in a program.	1. If I restart the computer the program will work.	1. Whenever the computer freezes, restarting it will solve the problem.
2. You see a man sitting on a curb with a paper bag in his hand.	2. The man must be a bum.	2. All men sitting on curbs with paper bags in their hands are bums.
3. One student in class always finishes her tests before everyone else.	3. This student must be smart.	3. Students who finish their tests first are smart.
4. A class assignment doesn't count toward your grade.	4. I don't need to work too hard on this assignment.	4. I only need to work hard on assignments that count toward my grade.

NOTES

Now think up your own situations. For each one, figure out one inference that someone might make in that situation. The possible inference doesn't have to be logical for this activity. The purpose of this activity is to check whether you understand the difference between assumptions, information, and inferences.

Information (Situation)	Possible inference a person might make	Assumption that leads to the inference
1.	1.	1.
2.	2.	2.
3.	3.	3.
4.	4.	4.

Be aware that inferences follow from assumptions and information. If your assumptions are faulty, or your information inaccurate, your inferences will be faulty as well.

Whenever you come to a conclusion, you make an inference. Everyone makes many inferences every day.

Start to notice them, and see if you can figure out the assumptions that lead to those inferences. Then you will begin to see some problems in your thinking.

The best thinkers are always on the lookout for problems in their thinking. Making your assumptions explicit is one strategy you can use over and over again to find problems in your thinking and deal with them.

"Problems are not stop signs, they are guidelines."

Robert H. Schuller

Motivational speaker and author

NOTES

Critical Thinkers Seek Better Ways of Doing Things

There's always a better way and I can find it.

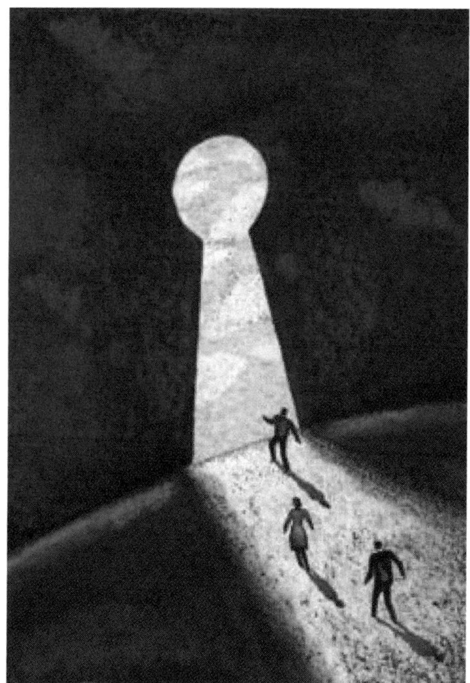

I can figure out anything I need to figure out.

Critical Thinkers Believe in The Power of Their Minds

NOTES

Analyzing Problems

Think of an important problem. Then analyze the problem by targeting some of the parts of thinking. Use notebook paper to write out your answers.

The problem is this...

(Write out the problem clearly and precisely, with details. Write the problem in different ways until you get it perfectly clear in your mind.)

This is an important problem because...

The key question that needs to be answered to solve this problem is...

(Every problem has questions connected to it. Here we want you to write out the most important question you need to answer to solve the problem. State it clearly and precisely. Being specific is very important.)

The main purpose in addressing the problem is...

The following information is needed to answer this question...

(Here you are looking for the facts that help you solve the problem.)

Some important assumptions I am using in my thinking are...

(Figure out what you are taking for granted. Make sure these assumptions are reasonable.)

CREATIVE THINKING TIP

Generate a number of potential solutions to a problem before settling on one.

Practice brainstorming. One simple truth is that creativity, like solving quadratic equations, is hard work. Genius is "one percent inspiration and 99% perspiration," said Edison. The more hard work you do in generating possible solutions, the greater your chances of finding one that works.

"Our opinions become fixed at the point where we stop thinking."

Ernest Renan

French philosopher and writer

NOTES

The key ideas (concepts) guiding my thinking as I deal with this problem are… I would describe this idea in the following way…

(For example, if the issue is pollution and how to reduce it, one key idea is "pollution." Your definition of pollution would be your description of it.)

The points of view relevant to this problem are… I would elaborate these viewpoints in the following way…

(For example, in dealing with the issue of pollution you would have to consider the points of view of: 1) animals affected by pollution, 2) people affected by pollution, 3) people who are causing the pollution and what they might say, 4) people who are working to reduce pollution.)

If this problem gets solved, some important implications are…

(Here you are trying to figure out some important things that should happen if the problem gets solved.)

If this problem does not get solved, some important implications are…

(Here you are trying to figure out some important things that will probably happen if the problem does not get solved.)

After thinking through the parts of thinking above, I think the best solution to the problem is…

NOTES

Analyzing Characters in a Story

You can use the parts of thinking to understand the thinking of a character in a story. Complete these statements, using notebook paper.

The name of the story is ______________________________.

The character I am focused on is __________________________.

The most important problem the character faces in the story is…

The main purpose of the character in the story is…

(If the purpose of the character changes over time, or if the character has more than one purpose, write out all of the important purposes of the character, and state whether the purpose changes during the story, and if so how.)

The most important information the character uses in his or her thinking in the story is…

(Look for the facts or experiences the character uses in making important decisions.)

The main concepts or ideas the character uses in his or her thinking are… I would elaborate these ideas in the following way…

(Try to figure out the ideas that drive the character to do what she or he does. For example, the main idea might be something like "greed" or "hunger" or "love" or "friendship.")

The main assumptions the character makes (the things he or she takes for granted) are…

(Look for the beliefs the character takes for granted or assumes to be true. These are beliefs that are not questioned by the character.)

"No problem can withstand the assault of sustained thinking."
Voltaire
French writer and philosopher

NOTES

The main conclusions (or inferences) the character comes to are…

(Look for the most important conclusions the character comes to, the conclusions that lead to important action. Sometimes these conclusions lead the character to make mistakes or cause problems for other people.)

The main consequences (implications) of the character's behavior are…

(Characters make decisions and then act on those decisions. Look for the important things that happen after they act. These are the significant consequences.)

NOTES

Analyzing Chapters in a Textbook

Every textbook, and every chapter in every textbook, has a logic that can be figured out. One important way to do this is by looking at the parts of the author's thinking.

Here is a template to follow:

1) **The main purpose of this chapter is...**
(Here you are trying to state, as accurately as possible, the author's purpose in writing the chapter. What was the author trying to accomplish?)

2) **The key question at the heart of the chapter is ...**
(Your goal is to figure out the main question that was in the mind of the author when he/she wrote the chapter. What was the key question she or he addresses?)

3) **The most important information in this chapter is ...**
(You want to identify the key information the author is using in the chapter to support his/her main arguments. Look for facts, experiences, and/or data the author is using to support his/her conclusions.)

4) **The main inferences in this chapter are...**
(Figure out the most important conclusions the author comes to and presents in the chapter.)

"Good thinkers always prime the pump of ideas. They always look for things to get the thinking process started, because what you put in always impacts what comes out."
John C. Maxwell
American author and motivational speaker

NOTES

5) The key concept(s) we need to understand in this chapter is (are)...
By these concepts the author means ...
(Look for the most important ideas at the heart of the author's reasoning. These might be concepts like "science" or "power" or "poverty" or "civics.")

6) The main assumption(s) underlying the author's thinking is (are)...
(Ask yourself: What is the author taking for granted in this chapter [that might be questioned]? The assumptions are beliefs the author does not think he/she has to defend. Assumptions are usually not stated and therefore can be hard to figure out.)

7a) If people take seriously what this author is saying, some important implications are...
(What consequences are likely to follow if people take the author's ideas seriously?)

7b) If we fail to accept what the author is saying, some important implications are...
(What consequences are likely to follow if people ignore the author's thinking in this chapter?)

NOTES

Analyzing Experiments

You can analyze your thinking about a scientific experiment before doing it, by completing these statements:

I would describe the experiment in the following way...

The main goal of the experiment is...

The hypothesis(es) we seek to test in this experiment is/are...

The key question the experiment seeks to answer is...

The controls involved in this experiment are...

The key concept(s) or theory(ies) behind the experiment is(are)...

The experiment is based on the following assumptions...

The data that will be collected in the experiment are...

The potential implications of the experiment are... (Here you are looking for the important consequences that might follow from information gained during the experiment.)

"Man can alter his life by altering his thinking."
William James
American philosopher

NOTES

Analyzing the Data Collected (After Experiments)

After the experiment is finished, look at the data collected and figure out what it means, what it is telling you. Complete these statements:

The data collected during the experiment was ...

The inferences (or conclusions) that most logically follow from the data are ...
(The inferences are the conclusions you come to after looking at the data.)

These inferences are/are not debatable, given the data gathered in this study and the other evidence relevant to this issue.

The hypothesis for this experiment was/was not support by the experiment results. Explain...

The assumptions made prior to this experiment should/should not be changed given the data gathered in this experiment. Changes to assumptions (if any) should be as follows...

The most significant implications of this experiment are...

Recommendations for future research in this area are...

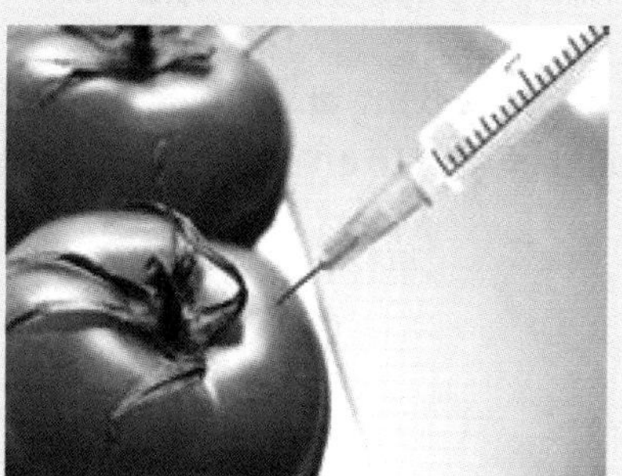

NOTES

Analyzing Subjects or Disciplines

When we understand the parts of thinking, we realize that all subjects we study in school have a logic we can figure out. We can use the following questions to do so:

What is the main purpose or goal of studying this subject? What are people in this field trying to accomplish?

What kinds of questions do they ask? What kinds of problems do they try to solve?

What sorts of information or data do they gather?

What types of inferences or judgments do they typically make? (Judgments about…)

How do they go about gathering information they use to figure things out in this subject?

What are the most basic ideas, concepts or theories in this field?

What do professionals in this field take for granted or assume?

How should studying this field affect my view of the world?

What consequences might follow from study in this discipline? How are the products of this field used in everyday life?

After studying any subject thoughtfully for a whole semester, you should be able to answer these questions about that subject.

"When the mind is thinking it is talking to itself."

Plato

Ancient philosopher

NOTES

Asking Questions in Class Which Target the Parts of Thinking

During class, you can ask questions that focus on the parts of thinking to deepen your understanding of topics or issues being discussed.

For example, on any given day you might ask one or more of the following questions:

- What is our main **purpose** today? What are we trying to accomplish in this class period?
- What **questions** are we asking today?
- What **information** do we need to gather if we want to answer these questions? How can we get this information?
- What is the most basic idea, **concept** or theory we need to understand to answer these questions?
- What **points of view** are relevant to answering these questions?
- What can we safely **assume** as we reason through this problem?
- Should we question any of the **inferences** that have been made by people studying in this field?
- What are some important **consequences** of what we are studying?

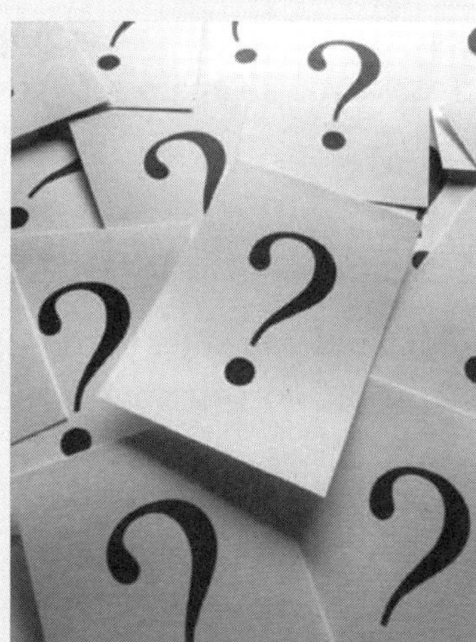

NOTES

Clarifying Your Own Ideas, Clarifying What Others Say

To clarify your thinking, you can do some very basic things:

1. **State** one point at a time.
2. **Elaborate** on what you mean.
3. Give **examples** that connect your thoughts to life experiences.
4. Use **analogies** and **metaphors** to help people connect your ideas to things they already understand. (Consider this analogy: Critical thinking is like an onion. It has many layers. Just when you think you have basically figured it out, you realize there is another layer, and then another, and another and another and on and on.)

SEEi ⟶ State, Elaborate, Exemplify, Illustrate

Here is one format you can use to make sure you are clear when speaking or writing your thoughts:

I think... (**state** your main point)
In other words... (**elaborate** on your main point in several sentences)
For example... (give an **example** of your main point)
To give you an analogy... (give an **illustration** of your main point)

There are four questions that can be used to clarify what people are saying to you:

1. Could you state your basic point in one simple sentence?
2. Could you elaborate your basic point more fully (in other words)?
3. Could you give me an example of your point from your experience?
4. Could you give me an analogy or metaphor to help me see what you mean?

"Clear thinking requires courage rather than intelligence."
Thomas Szasz
Famed psychiatrist and social critic

NOTES

Thinking Through Conflicting Ideas

It is important to be able to think about and write clearly on ideas that conflict with one another. After all, lots of ideas do. Here is a structure you can use. Write your answers on your own paper.

1. **Find two important potentially conflicting ideas. These ideas may be in a textbook or in different books or just two ideas you are concerned with.** For example, you might be concerned with ideas like:
    - individual freedom vs. laws that limit individual freedom
    - human rights vs. protecting the earth
    - love vs. control
    - animal rights vs. human desires
    - mainstream views vs. dissenting views
    - education vs. indoctrination
    - reasonable cooperation vs. blind loyalty
2. **Think through one important conflict between the ideas you have selected.**
3. **Clearly state one important point about that idea.** This is your thesis.
4. **Elaborate your thesis** (in several sentences).
5. **Give an example of your thesis** (some negative consequences that some people or animals actually experience because of this problem).
6. **Write out at least one reasonable objection to your position** (from a different point of view).
7. **Respond to that objection** (pointing out and giving credit to any strengths in this position).
8. **Construct a dialogue between some one defending your view and someone who (intelligently) opposes it.**

NOTES

"Critical thinking is vital for college success. Almost every course asks the fundamental questions of why something does this, or how A compares to B. Critical thinking establishes a thought process and a way of answering every one of these questions."

Cameron Turner
Computer Information Systems Networking

Eastern Kentucky University

Thinking Through Important Ideas

Every subject has key concepts or main ideas. Use the following guides for figuring out the essence of key concepts. Write your answers on your own paper.

1. **State the meaning of the concept in one simple sentence.**
2. **State the significance of the idea.** (This idea is important because…)
3. **Give an example of the concept** (as it applies to real life).
4. **Connect the idea to other important ideas in the subject.**
5. **Give examples for number 4 above.**

Here is a pattern for practicing the guidelines above:

1. X is…In other words…
2. X is important because…
3. For example…
4. This idea is connected to the following ideas within the subject…
5. Some examples that show the relationship between this idea and other important ideas are…

"You can kill a man, but you can't kill an idea."
Medgar Evers
American civil rights activist

NOTES

Reflecting Upon Important Ideas Learned

At the end of each lesson, it is a good idea to reflect upon important ideas you have learned and to connect ideas with other ideas you have learned. This will help you build your knowledge and remember important ideas. You can use this reflection sheet in all your classes to deepen your knowledge over time.

Complete these statements:

1. The purpose of the activity was... ____________________

2. The most important conclusions (inferences) I have come to in doing this activity are... ____________________

3. The most important idea (concept) I learned in this activity was... ____

4. This idea is important because (implications)... ____________________

5. This idea connects with other important ideas I have already learned including... ____________________

   I would articulate the connections between these ideas as follows... ____________________

6. Some questions I have now that I didn't have before are... __________

7. I can get answers to these questions by doing the following... ______

NOTES

Eastern Kentucky University

The Thinker's Guide Library

The Thinker's Guide series provides convenient, inexpensive, portable references that students and faculty can use to improve the quality of studying, learning, and teaching. Their modest cost enables Instructors to require them of all students (in addition to a textbook). Their compactness enables students to keep them at hand whenever they are working in or out of class. Their succinctness serves as a continual reminder of the most basic principles of critical thinking.

For Students & Faculty

Analytic Thinking—This guide focuses on the intellectual skills that enable one to analyze anything one might think about — questions, problems, disciplines, subjects, etc. It provides the common denominator between all forms of analysis. **#595m**

Asking Essential Questions—Introduces the art of asking essential questions. It is best used in conjunction with the Miniature Guide to Critical Thinking and the How to Study mini-guide. **#580m**

How to Study & Learn—A variety of strategies—both simple and complex—for becoming not just a better student, but also a master student. **#530m**

How to Read a Paragraph—This guide provides theory and activities necessary for deep comprehension. Imminently practical for students. **#525m**

How to Write a Paragraph—Focuses on the art of substantive writing. How to say something worth saying about something worth saying something about. **#535m**

The Human Mind—Designed to give the reader insight into the basic functions of the human mind and to how knowledge of these functions (and their interrelations) can enable one to use one's intellect and emotions more effectively. **#570m**

Foundations of Ethical Reasoning—Provides insights into the nature of ethical reasoning, why it is so often flawed, and how to avoid those flaws. It lays out the function of ethics, its main impediments, and its social counterfeits. **#585m**

How to Detect Media Bias and Propaganda—Designed to help readers come to recognize bias in their nation's news and to recognize propaganda so that they can reasonably determine what media messages need to be supplemented, counter-balanced or thrown out entirely. It focuses on the internal logic of the news as well as societal influences on the media. **#575m**

Scientific Thinking—The essence of scientific thinking concepts and tools. It focuses on the intellectual skills inherent in the well-cultivated scientific thinker. **#590m**

Fallacies: The Art of Mental Trickery and Manipulation—Introduces the concept of fallacies and details 44 foul ways to win an argument. **#533m**

Engineering Reasoning—Contains the essence of engineering reasoning concepts and tools. For faculty it provides a shared concept and vocabulary. For students it is a thinking supplement to any textbook for any engineering course. **#573m**

Critical Thinking for Children—Designed for K–6 classroom use. Focuses on explaining basic critical thinking principles to young children using cartoon characters. **#540m**

"All achievements, all earned riches, have their beginning in an idea."

Napoleon Hill

American author

Eastern Kentucky University

Glossary of Critical Thinking Terms & Concepts — Offers a compendium of more than 170 critical thinking terms for faculty and students. **#534m**

For Faculty

Active and Cooperative Learning—Provides 27 simple ideas for the improvement of instruction. It lays the foundation for the ideas found in the mini-guide How to Improve Student Learning. **#550m**

How to Improve Student Learning—Provides 30 practical ideas for the improvement of instruction based on critical thinking concepts and tools. It cultivates student learning encouraged in the How to Study and Learn mini-guide. **#560m**

Critical and Creative Thinking—Focuses on the interrelationship between critical and creative thinking through the essential role of both in learning. **#565m**

Critical Thinking Reading and Writing Test—Assesses the ability of students to use reading and writing as tools for acquiring knowledge. Provides grading rubrics and outlines five levels of close reading and substantive writing. **#563m**

Socratic Questioning—Focuses on the mechanics of Socratic dialogue, on the conceptual tools that critical thinking brings to Socratic dialogue, and on the importance of questioning in cultivating the disciplined mind. **#553m**

Critical Thinking Competency Standards— Provides a framework for assessing students' critical thinking abilities. **#555m**

Intellectual Standards— Explores the criteria for assessing reasoning; illuminates the importance of meeting intellectual standards in every subject and discipline. **#593m**

Educational Fads— Analyzes and critiques educational trends and fads from a critical thinking perspective, providing the essential idea of each one, its proper educational use, and its likely misuse. **#583m**

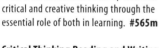

"Aspiring Thinker's Guide to Critical Thinking" Mini-Guide Price List:
(+ shipping and handling)

Item #554m
1–24 copies $6.00 each
25–199 copies $5.00 each
200–499 copies $4.00 each
500+ copies $3.50 each
Prices subject to change.

For pricing of other guides, please visit our web site at **www.criticalthinking.org**

For More Information
(To order guides or to inquire about other resources)

Phone: 707-878-9100
Fax: 707-878-9111
E-mail: cct@criticalthinking.org
Web site: www.criticalthinking.org
Mail: Foundation for Critical Thinking
P.O. Box 220
Dillon Beach, CA 94929

NOTES

CREATIVE THINKING TIP

Try to go with the flow.
While playing sports, have you ever had those times when the basket looks so big that you can't help but put the basketball in it, or the pitched ball is so large you can't miss hitting it? Those periods of time are called "flow" and they happen when we are totally in touch with our subconscious or in perfect rhythm. Flow can occur while writing or talking. It's most likely to occur when your concentration is intense upon something you truly enjoy doing and you have followed some of the Creative Thinking Tips.

NOTES

Eastern Kentucky University

The Foundation for Critical Thinking
PO Box 220
Dillon Beach, CA 94929

Foundation for Critical Thinking

The Foundation for Critical Thinking seeks to promote essential change in education and society through the cultivation of fair-minded critical thinking, thinking predisposed toward intellectual empathy, humility, perseverance, integrity, and responsibility. A rich intellectual environment is possible only with critical thinking at the foundation of education. Why? Because only when students learn to think through the content they are learning in a deep and substantive way can they apply what they are learning in their lives. Moreover, in a world of accelerating change, intensifying complexity, and increasing interdependence, critical thinking is now a requirement for economic and social survival. Contact us to learn about our publications, videos, workshops, conferences, and professional development programs.

About the Authors:

Dr. Linda Elder is an educational psychologist who has taught both psychology and critical thinking at the college level. She is the President of the Foundation for Critical Thinking and the Executive Director of the Center for Critical Thinking. Dr. Elder has a special interest in the relation of thought and emotion, the cognitive and the affective, and has developed an original theory of the stages of critical thinking development. She has coauthored four books on critical thinking, as well as twenty thinkers' guides. She is a dynamic presenter with extensive experience in leading seminars on critical thinking.

Dr. Richard Paul is a major leader in the international critical thinking movement. He is Director of Research at the Center for Critical Thinking, and the Chair of the National Council for Excellence in Critical Thinking, author of over 200 articles and seven books on critical thinking. Dr. Paul has given hundreds of workshops on critical thinking and made a series of eight critical thinking video programs for PBS. His views on critical thinking have been canvassed in *New York Times, Education Week, The Chronicle of Higher Education, American Teacher, Educational Leadership, Newsweek, U.S. News and World Report,* and *Reader's Digest.*

ISBN 978-0-944583-41-8
Item #554m

"If everyone is thinking alike, then somebody isn't thinking."

George S. Patton

United States Army General

Critical and Creative Thinking at EKU

While this orientation class may be your first introduction to the Elder and Paul Critical and Creative Thinking Framework, it is unlikely to be the last time you will be part of such conversations. Professors and instructors across campus are incorporating these critical thinking concepts and strategies into their classes in a variety of disciplines. You will have many opportunities to consider and practice such things as applying the Elements of Thought or evaluating information using the Intellectual Standards.

CREATIVE THINKING TIP

Express yourself through pictures, metaphors, and stories.
Most children create some kind of paracosm or fantasy universe. Writers like William Faulkner retained this ability into adulthood as he developed an entire fictional county in Mississippi he called Yoknapatawpha, and George Lucas translated his elaborate childhood fantasies into six *Star Wars* movies.

One technique in particular that you will find useful regardless of the courses you take is that of SEE-I— the method of thinking things through described in the **Aspiring Thinker's Guide**. SEE-I can be used in every class in which you are called upon to write, speak, or find information—in other words, all of them! You will find this technique helpful in forming your thoughts, writing essays, testing your understanding, and explaining things to others.

State the concept or idea in a sentence or two.

Elaborate on that concept by providing more information to help clarify its meaning.

Exemplify the concept by providing examples of what the concept is and what it is not.

Illustrate the concept by using it in a context other than its original concept.

SEE-I: A CLOSER LOOK

SEE-I is a method that is used to help students understand tough concepts and to also let instructors know when students are having trouble with various concepts.

As you first begin to try out SEE-I, your efforts will be fairly simple and uncomplicated, focused mostly on finding sufficient information to "Elaborate" or figuring out the difference between "Exemplify" and "Illustrate." Everyone who learns this technique experiences these growing pains! However, the more you exercise these intellectual muscles, the more effective your attempts at SEE-I will become.

In addition to the work you are about to do in class, we thought it might be helpful to offer a few examples of how different EKU faculty instruct their students in using SEE-I. Included here are basic models, and some instruction that "raises the bar" on writing good statements using this technique. As your comfort in using SEE-I increases, this deeper look into the components of SEE-I will be very useful in growing your own skills.

SEE-I: The Scientific Method

S The scientific method is a technique for structuring the process of research so that one can perform their analyses in the most objective way.

E The scientific method is used across many disciplines and involves a process of hypothesis testing and data analysis.

E An example of the scientific method involves asking a research question, developing background research, creating hypotheses, testing hypotheses, analyzing data and drawing conclusions, and publishing the results. The scientific method is not asking your friends' opinions about the cause of crime and blindly believing those opinions.

I The scientific method is to a researcher what a recipe is to a chef; both approach their task with a plan that they carefully follow to complete the finished product.

SEE-I: Crime and Society

S A crime is an act of commission or omission that is in violation of a statute either prohibiting or prescribing some action and is punishable by law.

E Crimes are often classified as felonies, whose punishment usually involves one or more years of incarceration, or misdemeanors, whose violation involves less than one year of incarceration.

E Murder is a crime; killing a person in self-defense is not.

I Crime is to society what a snake bite is to a human being; both are painful, both can be prevented with proper measures of protection, and both can escalate to kill their victim if treatment is not given.

Chapter Summary

How will you apply these new-found skills today, tomorrow, and the rest of your life?

Critical thinking is fundamentally about thinking things through to make informed choices. What does this mean? It means that, as a college student at EKU, you have such an incredible opportunity to learn how to be a better thinker. As you use the Paul and Elder Framework, consider how to state, elaborate, exemplify, and illustrate, and strive to become a fair-minded thinker. You will use this knowledge every day. From applying for financial aid, to choosing courses, to applying for internships, to buying a new car, to choosing a life partner, critical thinking will impact you personally and academically. Now go out and think!

"Education is not preparation for life; education is life itself."

John Dewey

American philosopher

CAMPUS RESOURCES

Department of Philosophy and Religion
http://www.philosophy.eku.edu
Case Annex, room 268, 859-622-1400

Noel Studio for Academic Creativity
http://www.studio.eku.edu
Library 207B, 859-622-6229

REFERENCES

BrainyQuote. (n.d.). *BrainyQuote.com*. Retrieved June 9, 2011, from http://www.brainyquote.com/

Einstein, A. (n.d.). Albert Einstein quotes. In *ThinkExist.com*. Retrieved June 9, 2011, from http://thinkexist.com/quotation/the_intuitive_mind_is_a_sacred_gift_and_the/15585.html

Garner, B. (2010, Sept.). Problem-based learning: A strategy for enhancing the relevance connection. In *The Toolbox: Teaching and Learning Resource for Instructors, 9*(1). Retrieved April 9, 2011, from the University of South Carolina, National Resource Center for the First Year Experience and Students in Transition Web site: http://u101tech.sa.sc.edu/NRC/toolbox/output/archive/files_pdf/09_01.pdf

Medina, J. (2008). *Brain rules: 12 principles for surviving and thriving at work, home, and school.* Seattle, WA: Pear Press.

Paul, R., & Elder, L. (2009). *The aspiring thinker's guide to critical thinking*. Tomales, CA: Foundation for Critical Thinking.

NOTES

"I hated every minute of training, but I said, 'Dont quit. Suffer now and live the rest of your life as a champion.' "

Muhammad Ali

American former professional boxer

Making Connections

One of the most fundamental and powerful aspects of the first year in college is making connections. In other words, building and maintaining relationships with peers, professors, advisors, and staff represents an integral part of how you begin to be a successful college student. This relationship building is dependent on your ability to communicate effectively. The communities and situations you encounter at EKU are likely more diverse than those you encounter in your hometown, encompassing not only a wide range of cultures and ethnicities, but also beliefs and ideas. Similarly, the expectations of college-level communication are much different, requiring you to consider these varied beliefs and ideas as well as the standards for communicating in different contexts.

While it is true you will be required to do many formal presentations during your tenure at EKU, the opportunities you have to interact with people outside of the public speaking arena are essential to your academic, personal, and professional development. As you engage in these opportunities, developing a sense of who you are and where you want to be will enhance your confidence in constructing and delivering competent communication.

This chapter will briefly explain how an awareness of self and identity management are key components to the beginning of a successful college career. You will then consider some of the contexts in which you will be challenged to express yourself competently. Finally, you will examine the expectations of college-level research and communication.

Managing Your Identity

The first year of your college experience is an exciting and challenging time. One of the most exciting aspects of college is having the opportunity to manage your identity and become the person you have always wanted to be. What does it mean to manage your identity? Here is an example to illustrate this concept of **identity management** more clearly. I had a friend in high school named Timothy, but we always called him Timmy. When he and I entered our freshman year of college together, I was shocked when I heard him introduce himself to his new college classmates as Tim. My friend had decided that his childhood nickname of Timmy would no longer do for college. He was choosing to manage his identity, and one way we manage our identity is through language.

Managing your identity is not just about what name you choose to be called in college. Some scholars say "every time you lose a relationship you lose an opportunity to see yourself" (Beebe, Beebe, & Ivy, 2010, p. 37). We manage our identities and learn more about the "real" us by communicating with others. You are a new student in a new environment, or **context**. Depending on the context, you have the opportunity to present yourself in a positive light in many new situations.

How can you best use your communication skills to help you succeed in college? Beyond **self-awareness**, which means knowing who you really are and what you want to achieve in your career at EKU, you need to understand how to manage different contexts in which you might be placed in college. How can you best present yourself when you are meeting new friends? How can you put your best foot forward when you speak to your professors or other professionals in class or on campus? What does your Facebook page say about the identity you present to others? Is everything you place online about yourself truly a mirror of the *real* you? Let's examine the different contexts in which you will present yourself.

■ CONTEXT ONE: THE COLLEGE CLASSROOM

When you enter the classroom, you have the opportunity to manage your identity by putting your best foot forward. Are you going to sit in the front of the room, alert and ready for class, or are you going to slouch in the back seat in the corner, farthest from your professor? How you enter the classroom and how you sit say a lot about you. Students who sit in the front of the classroom, who do not bring their cell phones to class or who silence them for the entire class, and who listen, take notes, and engage in class discussion typically do well in class. On the other hand, students who sit in the back, arrive late to class or skip class entirely, and play on their cell phones throughout the class often wonder, "Why did I do so poorly in this class?" Of course, there is more to doing well academically in college than just sitting in the front row, but where you sit and how you behave in class are ways you can successfully manage your identity in college. Maybe you have always been a "front row Joe" in class, and your habits will not change in college. But if you did not do as well in high school as you would have liked, now is the time to manage your identity and behave in ways that make you appear as if you take learning seriously. And if you appear to take learning seriously, you *will* take learning seriously!

"From finding something on campus, to working on research, to helping you plan out your degree, your instructors will be there every step of the way. Even when you've graduated, they can help in your search for a career and they make excellent references."

NaKeshia Baldwin
Psychology; Criminology/Deviance and Sociology minors

■ CONTEXT TWO: INTERACTING WITH YOUR PROFESSORS

Think back to high school. Are there some teachers you remember fondly, who inspired you, motivated you, and

"Take advantage of every opportunity to practice your communication skills so that when important occasic arise, you will have the gift, the style, the sharpness, the clarity, and the emotions to affect other people."
Jim Rohn
Motivational speaker

challenged you to succeed? At EKU, we pride ourselves on having exceptional professors. Our professors are here for two reasons—they love to teach and they love their students! If you have a question about an assignment, or you want to talk further about a topic that was presented during class, office hours are a great time to approach your professor and ask for help.

TIPS FOR INTERACTING WITH YOUR PROFESSORS

- You do not need an appointment for office hours, but it never hurts to email your professor and ask if he or she is available to meet during office hours.
- When you go to meet with a professor, have a plan of what you want to ask or say. Having a plan of what you want to communicate with the professor will make you appear competent and show that you take the class seriously.
- Do not be afraid to ask questions if you are confused about something in class. Whether you are in the professor's office or asking him or her a question after class, speak up and let your voice be heard.
- Use the title of "Doctor" or "Professor" when addressing your college instructors, according to qualifications.

■ CONTEXT THREE: ONLINE COMMUNICATION AND EMAIL

Social Networking

Even though online communication is one of the easiest ways to communicate with others, this is another context where you can get into trouble in college if you do not manage your identity properly or present the best image of yourself. Suppose you tell a professor you cannot attend his or her class because you are sick, but then that professor sees on Facebook that you were at a party during his or her night class. What a nightmare! If you try to present yourself as a serious student, but your Facebook page says the opposite, what will people believe about you? Will they believe the you that you say you are in person, or will they believe the you that they see online?

From the privacy settings you select to the things you post on your "Wall," your social networking activities are as important as a résumé. You need to realize that Facebook is a mechanism that increases not only intentional communication to your "friends," but also unintentional communication to others who take an interest. A potential employer may access your information and review something you have posted, or hear of something that was posted, that could affect the decision to hire or fire you. Pictures and any other content on Facebook that would be inappropriate to show your mother or father generally are not appropriate for posting on social networking sites.

Post only information you want to share with *everyone*. Social networking sites are meant to convey information with very few restrictions. Even with the privacy options on these sites, your information is still readily available.

"More and more businesses are using social networking websites. We as college students need to realize that the information we put on our personal pages can make or break us. If we portray ourselves in a positive manner on our page, it can do us a world of good when future employers scope out our profiles."

Brittany Estridge
Political Science

Communicating Via Email

Email provides an opportunity for instructors to get to know their students and is sometimes their first glimpse at students' writing; it is where early impressions are made. When you communicate with a professor or any staff member at EKU, be sure to use an appropriate subject in the email, have a salutation, a body, and a conclusion. Write the email as if you were writing a formal letter to your employer. Use a respectful tone. It is never a good idea to email a professor and say, "Sorry I missed class yesterday.

Can you email me back and tell me what I missed?" This could rub some professors the wrong way. If you are concerned about missing content of a class, it is wise to visit the professor during office hours to discuss it. Remember to present the best identity—that of a committed college student—that you can.

TIPS FOR APPROPRIATE EMAIL COMMUNICATION

- Include your class and purpose of the email in the subject line.
- Formally address your professor.
- Do not use texting language or abbreviations; write formally.
- Begin each new sentence with a capital letter.
- Use appropriate punctuation.
- Thank the recipient for his or her time.
- Sign your name, student ID number and class time to the email.
- Proofread your email before clicking send.

Communicating for an Assignment

One of the most important components of building and maintaining your identity as a committed college student is your formal, required communication: your assignments. Understanding that effective college-level communication requires you to consider to whom you are communicating (**audience**), what you are trying to communicate and why (**purpose**), and the surrounding situation (**context**). In the following sections, you'll learn how to use these elements to make choices about researching, writing, and communicating.

RESEARCH

For most college research assignments, your professors will ask you to make a claim about a topic and you will have to include information from other sources to support that claim. In order to achieve your purpose, you'll need to find sources that your audience finds appropriate and credible.

The key to finding the most appropriate and credible information for your work is to start at the library web page. The library web page contains links to our online catalog (the tool for finding books, videos, and other materials) and to databases (the tools used for finding journal, newspaper, and magazine articles). These resources are available to any student at EKU and many can be accessed on your computer or phone from anywhere in the world—as long as you have Internet access.

Visit EKU Libraries online to access research resources: http://www.library.eku.edu. EKU reference librarians can also be reached via text, IM, email, or phone.

Because library databases are so different from the search engines (like Google) you use to find information on the web, they can be a little intimidating. But don't worry—getting help from a librarian is easy. You can call or stop by one of our libraries or use the "Ask Us" option on the library's website to talk to a librarian.

ACTIVITY

Answer the following questions by exploring the library web page: http://library.eku.edu/

1. Which link lists the ways to ask a librarian for help? What are the different ways?
2. What is the number for texting a librarian?
3. What is the link to the library tutorials?
4. List the names of two library tutorials.

➲For more information on finding sources, see http://studio.eku.edu/research-and-information-fluency

"We have two ears and one mouth so that we can listen twice as much as we speak."

Epictetus

Greek philosopher associated with the Stoics

LIBSTART

The library offers a lot more than just information. All GSD students will participate in a **LibStart** session: an interactive tour of the library where you'll learn more about our resources, services, and spaces.

Why evaluate?

Locating information, whether in print or electronic format, is only the first step in the research process. The next step is to evaluate the quality and the usefulness of what you find in relation to your purpose, audience, and context—your rhetorical situation.

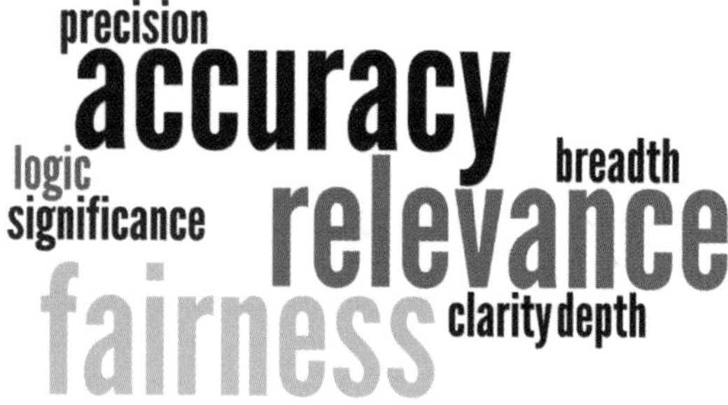

Information is everywhere but it is not all created equal.

In Chapter 5, you learned the importance of not believing everything you see, hear, and read. But how, exactly, do you know which sources you can trust, which sources are useful, and which sources are biased? Just as you can use the Intellectual Standards to improve your thinking, you can use them to evaluate and choose sources. In this section and the accompanying online exercise, you will learn how to apply three criteria for evaluating information: accuracy, relevance, and fairness.

Visit http://libguides.eku.edu/GSD101, click on the "Tutorials" tab, and watch the videos to learn more about evaluating information.

Are your sources accurate?

Questions to ask:

- Are statements backed up by evidence?
- Are sources clearly cited in such a way the reader can locate them?
- Can you verify claims presented as evidence elsewhere?
- Is the content grammatically correct?
- Are there spelling or typographical errors?

What to look for when determining accuracy:

- For web pages, look for links to outside sources, and pay particular attention to whether the link leads you to an error page or is otherwise nonfunctioning—this indicates the author/creator is not being careful when linking, is negligent in updating links, or, even worse, is attempting to "fake" links to outside sources.
- If the author/creator links to outside sources, visit those sources:
  - Is the author/creator of the original source misrepresenting the linked material (which would make the original less accurate)?
  - Does the linked source material stand up to a critical evaluation?
- The top-level domain of the URL indicates the type of organization responsible for the website, which can give you clues about accuracy. For example, in the URL **library.eku.edu**, the top-level domain is .edu. *In general*, .gov and .edu pages are more accurate than .com and .net pages. Below are the most common top-level domains:

  .edu = educational institution

  .org = non-profit organization

  .gov = government

  .net = network/utilities

  .mil = military

  .com = commercial

- For books, journals, or magazines, look for footnotes, endnotes, or links/references/mention to/of outside sources.
  - Scholarly articles and books are extensively documented with quality sources.
  - Popular information sources (and much information found on the open web) rarely cite sources in full; however, more reliable popular sources should provide enough information (like the original source title and/or author) to track down sources.

Are your sources relevant?

Questions to ask:

- Who is the intended audience for the source?
- Will information directed to the intended audience meet your needs?
- Does the information help answer your research question?
- Does the purpose of the source (e.g., research, statistical, organizational) meet your needs?

SCHOLARLY VS. POPULAR

Scholarly sources, also called peer-reviewed sources, are written by experts and undergo a rigorous review process before publication. The language is academic and can be very technical. Popular sources often are written by journalists or freelance writers. The review process is much less stringent than that for scholarly sources. The language is non-technical, as popular sources are written for a general audience.

Visit http://libguides.eku.edu/articleshelp, click on the "Types of Articles" tab, and watch the videos to learn more about scholarly and popular articles.

What to look for when determining relevancy:
In library databases, look at an article's title, its attached subjects, and the article abstract. An abstract is a short (usually one paragraph) summary of an article. You can quickly read an abstract to determine relevancy to your topic and research question.

In the library's online catalog, look at a book's table of contents, summary, and attached subjects. Sometimes a single chapter of a book will be relevant to your research.

Are your sources fair?

Questions to ask:

- Who is the author/organization responsible for the information?
- Does the author/organization responsible have an agenda?
- Are any agendas or possible conflicts of interest (e.g., monetary gain from conducting/publishing the research) clearly communicated?
- Are various points of view considered, or just those of the author?
- Is the source free of advertising?
- If advertising is included, is the advertising clearly separated from the content and identifiable as such?

What to look for when determining fairness:

- Look for any information about the author or sponsoring organization, including their affiliations and causes they support.
  - Websites: look for an "About Us" or similar page.
  - Articles (scholarly or popular): look near the author(s)' name(s) and affiliations; this information is often included on the first/title page or at the end of the article, near any references
  - Books: look on the inside flap of book jackets or the back cover
- Are arguments well-reasoned? Is the tone calm and logical, or inflammatory/offensive?

"Communication—the human connection—is the key to personal and career success."
Paul Meyer
French writer

- Are there any conflicts of interest? That is, does the author/sponsoring organization have a vested interest (financial or otherwise) in the issue at hand?

➲ Now that you have learned about accuracy, fairness, and relevancy, try evaluating the resources listed at this location: http://libguides.eku.edu/GSDlibraryassignment

■ WRITING

Once you have conducted your research and are ready to begin writing, it's important to again consider the rhetorical situation for which you're writing. Knowing your audience, context, and purpose will now help you make decisions about organization, format and style, and language.

While each rhetorical situation will require a unique approach, there are several characteristics of writing that are always valued at the college level.

Thesis Statements: Topic, Opinion, Evidence/Approach

In academic writing, you are almost always expected to offer an opinion on a topic (unless you're writing a lab report, summary, or other piece of objective writing). Many first-time college students confuse having an opinion with being biased. An opinion is your informed claim about a topic or issue and considers all of the research. A biased opinion disregards the research. Most professors will ask you to state your position or opinion clearly in a thesis statement.

A thesis statement typically includes three elements: the topic, your opinion, and the evidence or approach you will use to support your opinion. For instance, imagine that you are asked to write an essay in which you compare, contrast, and evaluate two authors' arguments on one subject. A breakdown of the elements of your thesis might look like this:

> *Topic*: Malcolm X and Martin Luther King Jr.'s arguments about education and civil liberty
>
> *Opinion*: Malcolm X's argument was more realistic/achievable for the audience and time period.
>
> *Evidence or approach*: Martin Luther King Jr. promoted formal education while Malcolm X emphasized the benefits of self-education.

A **working thesis statement,** then, might look like this:

> Even though Malcolm X and Martin Luther King Jr. both argued the importance of education for civil liberty, Malcolm X's idea of self-education was a more achievable goal for black citizens in the 1960s than King's goal of formal education.

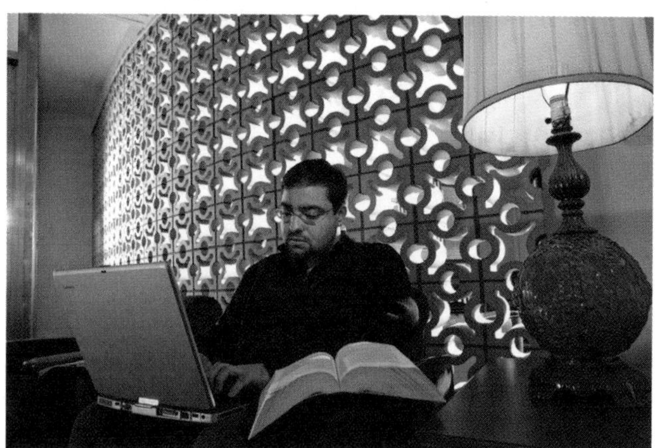

Cohesion

Once you've created a working thesis, you can begin deciding what information should be included in your paper. This sounds easier than it actually is. If you have thoroughly researched your topic, you'll likely have sources and information that are related to your topic but *are not relevant* for your audience, context, and purpose. You might be tempted to include everything you have in order to meet length requirements, but this approach usually confuses your readers or makes them lose interest. Instead, you should focus on fully developing the points that are related and be confident enough to leave out irrelevant information.

ACTIVITY

Consider the following scenario and discuss the questions listed below with a partner.

A friend has invited you on a long weekend trip out of town. You really want to go, but you'd have to leave Thursday night and you'll miss a quiz in your Friday morning class. Your instructor only allows make-up quizzes for excused absences. How do you convince him to let you make up the quiz?

You'll also have to borrow money from your parents for spending money (your friend is paying for the hotel and gas). How do you convince your parents to lend you the money for the trip?

Reflect: What was different about your two arguments? How did your audience and purpose influence what was relevant information?

Organization

After identifying your relevant information, you should think about how to logically organize it for your purpose. In high school you may have been taught to lead up to your strongest point. While this is good advice, your college-level papers will likely be more complicated. So, you'll want to understand the different organizational options you have (and might be expected to already know).

- Narrative
- Problem-Solution
- Comparison/Contrast
- Empirical Research
- Argumentative
- Research Proposal

If you're unfamiliar with these structures or not sure which one would work best for your rhetorical situation, ask for help. Talk to your professors or work with a consultant in the Noel Studio.

"It's not how much you write, it's the quality of how you write it. Professors are concerned with how well you defend your platform, whether you can think for yourself, and how well you explain your thought process instead of parroting another's views."

Andrea Danley
Dietetics

Answer the "So What?" Question

It's typically not enough for you to merely present a topic and your opinion on it—you also need to explain why both the topic and your opinion are important. If you've proposed a solution to a problem, for example, one way to answer the "so what" is to outline the benefits that would result from your solution. Three typical ways to frame your answers to the "so what" question are:

1. A call to action
2. Implications for future research
3. Identifying the benefits/outcomes of a proposed solution

Answering the "so what" helps your audience understand why the topic is important to them and makes your overall purpose explicit.

Use of Sources

Integration

There are several different ways that you will integrate sources into your own writing, and you should understand the multiple roles that each of your sources might play. Sources can:

- *Establish background*: you can use sources to introduce a topic, explain why it's important, and offer any information your audience would need to understand your main point.

"A writer writes not because he is educated but because he is driven by the need to communicate. Behind the need to communicate is the need to share. Behind the need to share is the need to be understood."

Leo Rosten

Polish-born American comic novelist

- *Explain or support your own claims:* sources can help (and should be used) to validate your opinion.
- *Challenge your claims:* you should use sources to present differing perspectives on a topic and show how and why other people might disagree with you.

Varied and appropriate sources help establish your credibility because you're not just relying on a "because I said so" approach.

After you understand how your sources fit into the content of your writing, you should make sure that you consider how they fit in stylistically—they should be integrated both logically and grammatically to create a seamless flow. Here are four rules for integrating sources:

1. *Introduce the source:* never let a source stand on its own. Use introductory or signal phrases to credit the source and indicate to your audience that you are using a source (e.g., "According to," "Smith questions," "Jones claims," etc.).
2. *Use the source:* quote, paraphrase, or summarize the necessary information for your audience. Use only the information that is crucial and logical for the claim you are making at that point in your paper.
3. *Cite the source:* citing the information is crucial and the conventions vary according to the style guide you are using. The importance of citing information is explained in the next section.
4. *Explain the information:* explain how the specific information from the source relates to your own argument. This step is crucial for coherent and sophisticated college-level writing but many students skip it, making the information seem weird and unconnected.

Citation and Documentation Styles

Any time you use another person's words or ideas, you must acknowledge that other person. Did you summarize or paraphrase? Quote directly? Just use a general idea from the work? It doesn't matter how you find it (online through a Google search, in a library database, in a magazine or book, etc.) or exactly how you use it—you must acknowledge that you used the source. Failure to do so is **plagiarism** and is a violation of EKU's Academic Integrity policy. In academic work, we acknowledge the ideas of others by citing sources.

To learn more about EKU's Academic Integrity Policy, please visit: http://www.studentrights.eku.edu/academic-integrity

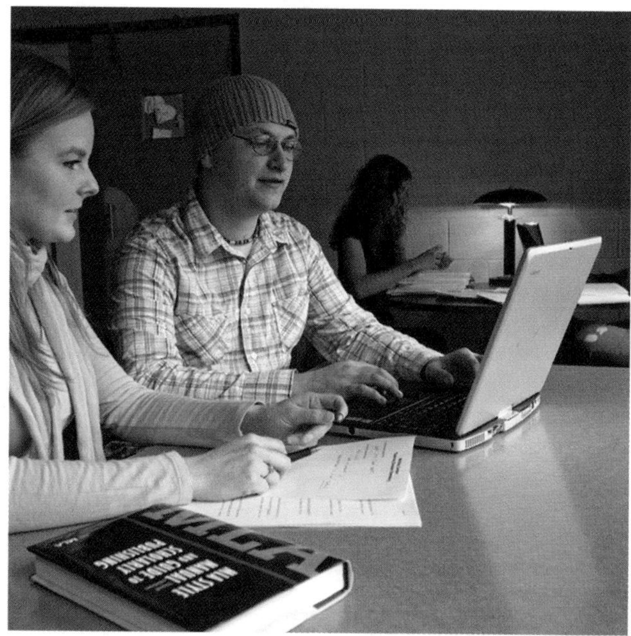

There are numerous **documentation styles** for citing sources and the style you use will be determined by your instructor and/or the discipline in which you are writing. Though there are many different citation styles (e.g., APA, MLA, Chicago, CSE), they all have some basic principles in common. While there are a few exceptions to this rule, each citation typically consists of two parts: a marker within the text (whether an in-text citation, endnote, or footnote) that points to a bibliographic citation in an alphabetical list (sometimes called a Works Cited list or Bibliography) at the end of the work. Formatting and the exact details of these citations will vary by style, but they will usually contain the source author, title, and publication information (e.g., the title of the *journal* an *article* was published in, as well as the *date* and *place* of publication). It is best practice to always have a style guide or handbook nearby while you are drafting or revising.

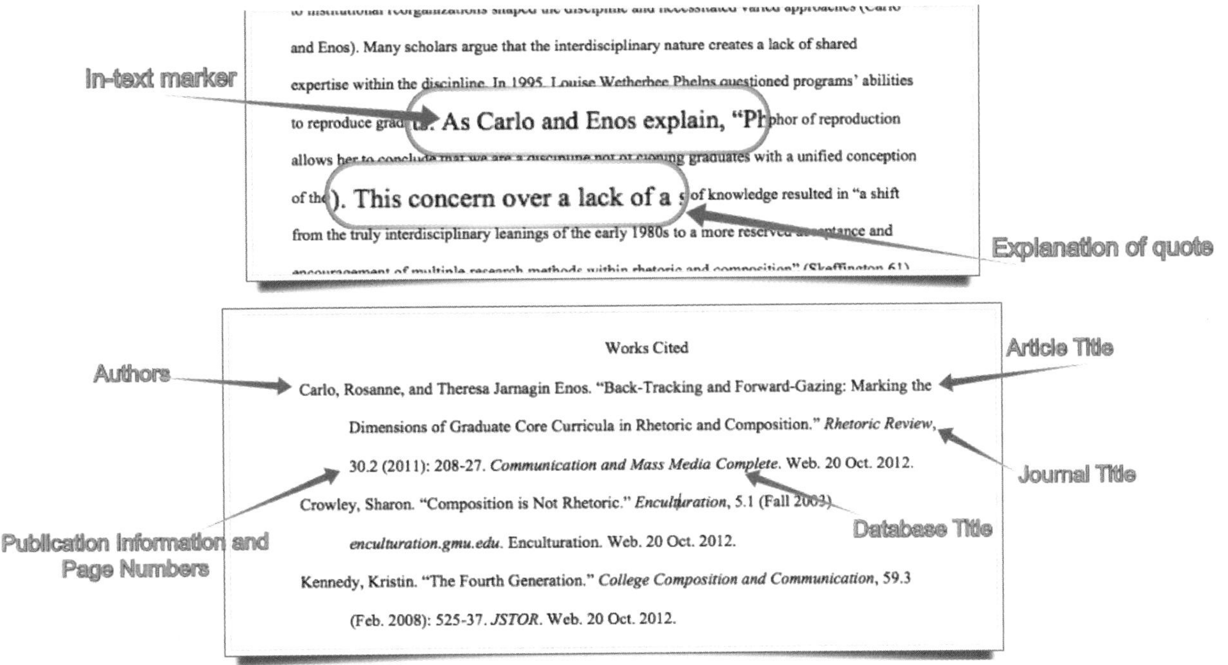

PLAGIARISM 101

The deliberate act of claiming another's work as your own is intentional plagiarism.

Examples of Intentional Plagiarism:

- Buying an essay from an online writing service
- Asking a friend to write your paper
- Cutting and pasting text from sources without any acknowledgement

Obviously, a calculated attempt to pass off another writer's work as your own can significantly damage your academic integrity. Such incidents can be reported by your instructor to the EKU Academic Integrity Office.

A second type of plagiarism with which many students are unfamiliar is unintentional plagiarism. Unintentional plagiarism is usually in the form of faulty source citations.

Examples of Unintentional Plagiarism:

- Putting a passage in quotation marks but omitting the name of the source
- Neglecting to put quotation marks around direct quotes
- Paraphrasing incorrectly because your rewording is too close to the source's original wording. (Even if you give credit to the source, an inaccurate paraphrase is still considered plagiarism.)
- Failure to clearly cite sources for information that is apparently not your own

Most instructors know that this sort of plagiarism is often a result of inattention to detail or lack of knowledge about citation styles. However, regardless of whether it is intentional or unintentional, you do not want to be accused of ANY type of plagiarism. This is crucial in order to maintain your academic integrity. To ensure that you are using sources properly, always seek out assistance from your instructors and take advantage of campus resources designed to help students with writing and research.

"The art of communication is the language of leadership."

James Humes

American presidential speech writer

DOCUMENTATION STYLES

- MLA (Modern Language Association): used primarily in the field of Humanities. Examples include English, philosophy, and the arts. For help, consult the *MLA Handbook for Writers of Research Papers.*
- APA (American Psychological Association): used primarily in the field of Social Sciences. Examples include anthropology, psychology, and sociology. For help, consult the *Publication Manual of the American Psychological Association.*
- Chicago: consists of two distinct systems. The *Notes-Bibliography System* is preferred by those in history, literature, and the arts. The *Author-Date System* is favored by those in the sciences. For help, consult the *Chicago Manual of Style* (CMS). Students may also use Kate L. Turabian's *Manual for Writers of Research Papers, Theses, and Dissertations*, which offers slight modifications to the CMS system for student writers.
- CSE (Council of Science Editors): used in the fields of Physical Sciences, Mathematics, and Life Sciences. Examples include chemistry, physics, geometry, and biology. For help, consult *Scientific Style and Format: The CSE Manual for Authors, Editors and Publishers*. Because the CSE Manual does not provide guidelines for student papers, it is best to check with your instructor.

Non-Written Communication

What if your project does not require you to write a paper? What if instead of a written document, your product is a speech, a research poster, or a website? Understanding the rhetorical situation—your audience, context, and purpose—will assist you in becoming an effective communicator, regardless of the format or mode you use to communicate your message. Further, much of what is true for writing will be true for all types of communication. In the following sections, we'll focus on one of the most common non-written communication situations you'll encounter in your college career: presentations.

■ PRESENTATIONS

You might not realize it, but you navigate rhetorical situations in conversation hundreds of times a day. Every single conversation you are involved in throughout your day, from a call home to hanging out with friends in your dorm or apartment, is comprised of an audience, a context, and a purpose. You might not consciously and deliberately think through each of these rhetorical situations, but that doesn't make them any less present—they've just become instinctual or "second nature" for you.

The more formal speaking situations you are involved in as a college student—and perhaps later as a professional—are less likely to be second nature for you and will require more thoughtful planning. For example, the familiar language you use with your group of friends or in conversations with your family might not be appropriate for in-class discussions; likewise, you probably wouldn't casually slip the Latin species and genus names you learned about in your biology class into a conversation with your parents about the family pet. Class speeches or presentations require you to consider the rhetorical situation much the same as academic writing does. Just as an awareness of audience, context, and purpose will help you make decisions about organization, format and style, and language when writing an essay, understanding the rhetorical situation will help you make decisions about proper attire, tone, visual aids, and other aspects of your speech or presentation.

➲As a part of EKU General Education Requirements, all students must take:
CMS 100—Introduction to Human Communication,
CMS 210—Public Speaking or
EES 250—Social Intelligence Skills

■ CONSIDERING YOUR AUDIENCE

For many projects, the first audience you'll want to consider is your instructor; however, the audience for most college speeches or presentations will extend beyond the instructor. For example, often you will be asked to present information—both formally and informally—to

your classmates. As you plan your speech, you should definitely consider your instructor's expectations, but you also may want to consider ways you can effectively inform and engage the class. Ask yourself questions about your audience, such as:

- If your presentation is about a career, will your audience be familiar with the **jargon** used in the field? If not, you'll want to use more commonly known synonyms or provide a definition for your audience.
- Are there any interesting tools used in the career? If so, consider engaging your audience by providing examples of the tools and allowing your audience to explore and play with the tools.
- If you plan on using a funny viral video, first consider the gender, cultural backgrounds, age distribution, and other such demographical characteristics of your audience—will they all be familiar and comfortable with the video and/or the style of humor? If not, you might want to reconsider using it, or, perhaps, provide the audience with background and contextual information so that they better understand how it relates to your topic.

■ DEFINING YOUR PURPOSE

While your primary purpose may be to get a good grade, you should also consider the end result of the communication product. Think instead about the purpose of the communication by asking yourself questions like:

- Is the purpose of your presentation to merely inform your audience? Or are you trying to persuade your audience to believe or agree with your line of thinking?
- What do you want your audience to understand or know?
- How do you want your audience to feel?
- Do you want your audience to take action on an issue?

Answering these questions will help you decide how to present your information, from organization to relevant stories, facts and statistics, and visual aids you might include.

■ DETERMINING AND UNDERSTANDING YOUR CONTEXT

In addition to asking yourself *why* you are presenting the information you are presenting—your purpose—consider the *where*, *when* and *how* of your presentation:

- At what time of day will you be presenting, and how might that affect your audience? Will they be thinking about lunch because your class meets right before noon, or will they still be groggy during an early morning class?
- What size is the room in which you will present?
- Do you have access to technology and/or the internet?
- Is there a way to project a slideshow or video to a large screen?

Think of ways to make your presentation work in the specific situation or environment. If you have the ability to project to a large screen, consider developing a visual aid—like a slideshow or video—that works in that environment. If the room is too "low tech" for that, consider providing handouts for your audience. Are you afraid your audience will be tired or distracted? Consider incorporating a quick activity, interesting story, or an interesting and relevant video clip to get them involved or grab their attention.

Aside from assignment requirements, instructor expectations, and consideration of the rhetorical situation (audience, context, and purpose), there are a few common guidelines that will be applicable to nearly any formal speaking assignment you might encounter in college. In fact, you shouldn't be surprised to learn that effective speeches and presentations will share common characteristics with writing.

> "The ability to express an idea is well nigh as important as the idea itself."
>
> Bernard Baruch
>
> Economic advisor to President Franklin D. Roosevelt

"In college you have to speak time and time again. It gets you comfortable with your audience and gives you practice. It forces you to get better at public speaking."

Will Stout
English Teaching

DEVELOPING THESIS STATEMENTS AND ORGANIZING YOUR PRESENTATION

Most every mode of formal communication—from a narrative essay to an empirical research paper—will have some form of thesis statement. Speeches and presentations are no exception. The way you put together and deliver the thesis statement will vary depending on the type of speech or presentation. We identify a few of the most common types of speeches and presentations below. If you are unfamiliar with or unsure of how to best structure a thesis statement for any of these types, ask your instructor or consider scheduling a consultation with a Noel Studio consultant:

- Informative
- Entertaining
- Demonstrative/instructional
- Persuasive

The type of speech or presentation will also impact organization. The organizational pattern you choose will vary slightly depending on the type of speech or presentation and the rhetorical situation (audience, context, and purpose), but a good rule is to stick to a simple, easy-to-follow pattern and present your information in the way that will be most relevant to your audience, context, and purpose.

Don't forget to provide transitions between your introduction, main points, and conclusions so your audience can follow along as you present. Remember: your audience will not be able to reread something they didn't quite understand the first time around!

SUPPORTING YOUR PRESENTATION WITH SOURCES

Integration

Finally, regardless of the type of presentation, you will likely need to refer to sources outside your own mind to support your speech or presentation. How you use those sources will depend on the assignment requirements, type of speech or presentation, and the rhetorical situation (audience, context, and purpose). Many of the suggestions offered earlier in this chapter concerning incorporating sources into your writing will be relevant for speeches and presentations, too. Individual professors also will have their own unique requirements and expectations when assigning a speech or presentation. Always refer to your assignment prompt or directions, never be afraid to ask for clarification from your professor, and consider scheduling an appointment with the Noel Studio if you need help using your sources.

Citation (and Documentation)

Just as in writing, citing your sources and giving credit where credit is due is expected when giving a speech or presentation; citing your sources also makes you a more credible speaker. When incorporating oral citations into your speech, keep it quick, simple, and clear, providing just enough information to tell your audience who and what you are citing. Mentioning the author's name, the title of the source, what the source is, and a date should do the trick in most cases. For example:

- Try something like this for a website: "The USDA's website reported that in fiscal year 2009 more than 9 million people per month received supplemental nutrition through the WIC program."
- Try something like this for a book or journal: "Ken Robinson defines creativity in his 2010 book *Unlocking Creativity* as 'generating outcomes that are original and have value.'"

In general, adherence to a particular citation style is not necessary for oral citations in your speech or presentation; however, if you provide written documentation of your sources to your audience or instructor, whether in a slide presentation or on a handout, you should follow the citation style recommended or preferred by your instructor.

TIPS FOR PRESENTING

- Don't forget to practice!
  - If at all possible, practice with an audience, even if it's an audience of one.
  - If you'll be standing when you present, practice while standing.
  - Practice while wearing the clothes you'll wear the day you present.
  - Practice using any visuals, manipulatives, or other presentation aids you plan to incorporate into your presentation.
  - Be sure to practice meeting—and staying within!—your time requirements.
- Smile if appropriate. You will feel better and so will your audience.
- If you want to appear knowledgeable and engaged in your topic, make sure your posture and hand movements convey confidence and appropriate enthusiasm or interest in your topic.
- Practice your gestures and other movements, too.
- If you are appropriate and the setting allows for movement, consider walking a bit as you present—you don't have to stand stationary at the front of the room!
- Maintain eye contact with your audience, but try to shift your eye contact around the room, front-to-back and left-to-right.
- Consider the rhetorical situation (audience, context, and purpose) and dress appropriately. Your first impression begins before you open your mouth.

If you need help selecting a topic or drafting an outline or speaking notes, or if you'd like to do a practice run, consider scheduling an appointment with a consultant and/or booking a presentation practice room in the Noel Studio.

"The liberty of speaking and writing guards our other liberties."

Thomas Jefferson

3rd President of the United States of America, author of the Declaration of Independence

Noel Studio for Academic Creativity

The Noel Studio for Academic Creativity offers free, individualized support with communication projects and products for any EKU undergraduate or graduate.

In the Noel Studio, students work with a trained consultant to establish goals for the session; for example:

- Choosing a topic
- Organizing thoughts and ideas
- Researching, drafting, and revising
- Improving grammar, punctuation, and clarity
- Developing persuasive appeals
- Arranging effective collaboration and group dynamics in presentations
- Citing sources properly
- Developing effective speech communication practices
- Thinking critically and creatively about a topic or communication piece
- Asking questions
- Understanding media options and uses

Any currently enrolled student at EKU can visit the Noel Studio for assistance with any communication project. The Noel Studio is not designed to fix communication "problems." Instead, consultants support students as they hone their communication skills. Seeking feedback from an informed and objective audience is an important part of successful communication. Whether a student is writing a research paper or lab report, preparing for a collaborative speech, or developing a digital narrative, Noel Studio consultants are here to help.

The Noel Studio includes larger breakout spaces and smaller presentation practice rooms that members of the EKU community are welcome to reserve. Presentation practice rooms and breakout spaces can be reserved for a wide variety of purposes, including:

- Practicing and recording presentations
- Refining visual components
- Collaborating with peers
- Refining digital products and projects
- Exploring nonverbal communication and group dynamics

Chapter Summary

In this chapter, you learned that the most important aspect of communicating at the college level is understanding your rhetorical situation. Knowing your audience, context, and purpose helps you identify the information you need and determine how to effectively express your opinions and ideas. While this chapter has focused on researching, writing, and speaking, you should consider how understanding the rhetorical situation can also inform your choices when communicating in other modes such as visual (e.g., research posters, comic strips), digital (websites, YouTube videos), or even mobile (apps). Even if you have never been asked to design communication in these different modes in the past, you might be asked to later on in your college or professional careers.

NOTES

“We keep moving forward, opening new doors, and doing new things, because we’re curious and curiosity keeps leading us down new paths.”

Walt Disney

American film producer, founder of The Walt Disney Company

■ KEYTERMS

Audience: The person, people, or group for whom your communication is directed

Context: The circumstances, setting, and environment in which an event, statement, or idea occurs and which lends to understanding that occurrence

Documentation styles: Discipline-specific guidelines for using and citing sources

Identity management: The communication strategies people use to influence how others view them (Adler, Rosenfeld, & Procter, 2007)

Information literacy: The ability to access, evaluate, organize, and use information from a variety of sources (ACRL, 2000)

Jargon: Language that is specific to a particular field; it includes technical terminology (legal, computer, and medical terminology are examples of jargon)

Plagiarism: Using someone else's work and representing it as one's own original work

Popular sources: Sources intended for a general audience and not necessarily prepared or reviewed by subject experts

Purpose: Both the message and the reason for communicating to a given audience within a particular context

Rhetorical situation: The combined elements of audience, context, and purpose that create the need for and influence the writer or speaker's communication

Self-awareness: Knowing who you really are and what you would like to achieve

Scholarly sources: Sources written by experts, evaluated by peer experts, and intended for a scholarly/academic audience

Working thesis statement: A draft statement of the primary claim. The working thesis is typically revised before completing and submitting or presenting the final piece of communication

NOTES

"The single biggest problem in communication is the illusion that it has taken place."

George Bernard Shaw

Irish literary critic, playwright, and essayist; 1925 Nobel Prize for Literature

CAMPUS RESOURCES

Blackboard Online Learning
http://www.learn.eku.edu
859-622-3000

Crabbe Library
http://www.library.eku.edu
103 Libraries Complex, 859-622-1790

Department of Communication
http://www.communication.eku.edu
Combs Building, room 317, 859-622-1871

Department of English & Theatre
http://www.english.eku.edu
Case Annex, room 467, 859-622-5861

EKU Computer Labs
http://www.it.eku.edu/computerlabs
859-622-3000

Student Email Support
http://www.it.eku.edu/support/mymail-students
859-622-3000

Noel Studio for Academic Creativity
http://www.studio.eku.edu
Library 207B, 859-622-6229

Office of Student Rights & Responsibilities
http://www.studentrights.eku.edu
Turley House 1, 859-622-1500

REFERENCES

Adler, R.B., Rosenfeld, L.B., & Procter II, R.F. (2007). *Interplay: The process of interpersonal communication* (10th ed.). New York, NY: Oxford University Press.

Association of College and Research Libraries (ACRL). (2000, January 18). *Information literacy competency standards of higher education.* Chicago, IL: American Library Association. Retrieved March 18, 2011, from ACRL website: http://www.ala.org/ala/mgrps/divs/acrl/standards/standards.pdf

Beebe, S. A., Beebe, S. J., & Ivy, D.K. (2010). *Communication: Principles for a lifetime* (4th ed.). Boston, MA: Allyn & Bacon.

BrainyQuote. (n.d.). *BrainyQuote.com.* Retrieved June 9, 2011, from http://www.brainyquote.com/

Medina, J. (2008). *Brain rules: 12 principles for surviving and thriving at work, home, and school.* Seattle, WA: Pear Press.

NOTES

"Speak when you are angry—and you'll make the best speech you'll ever regret."

Dr. Laurence J. Peter

American "hierarchiologist," educator, and writer

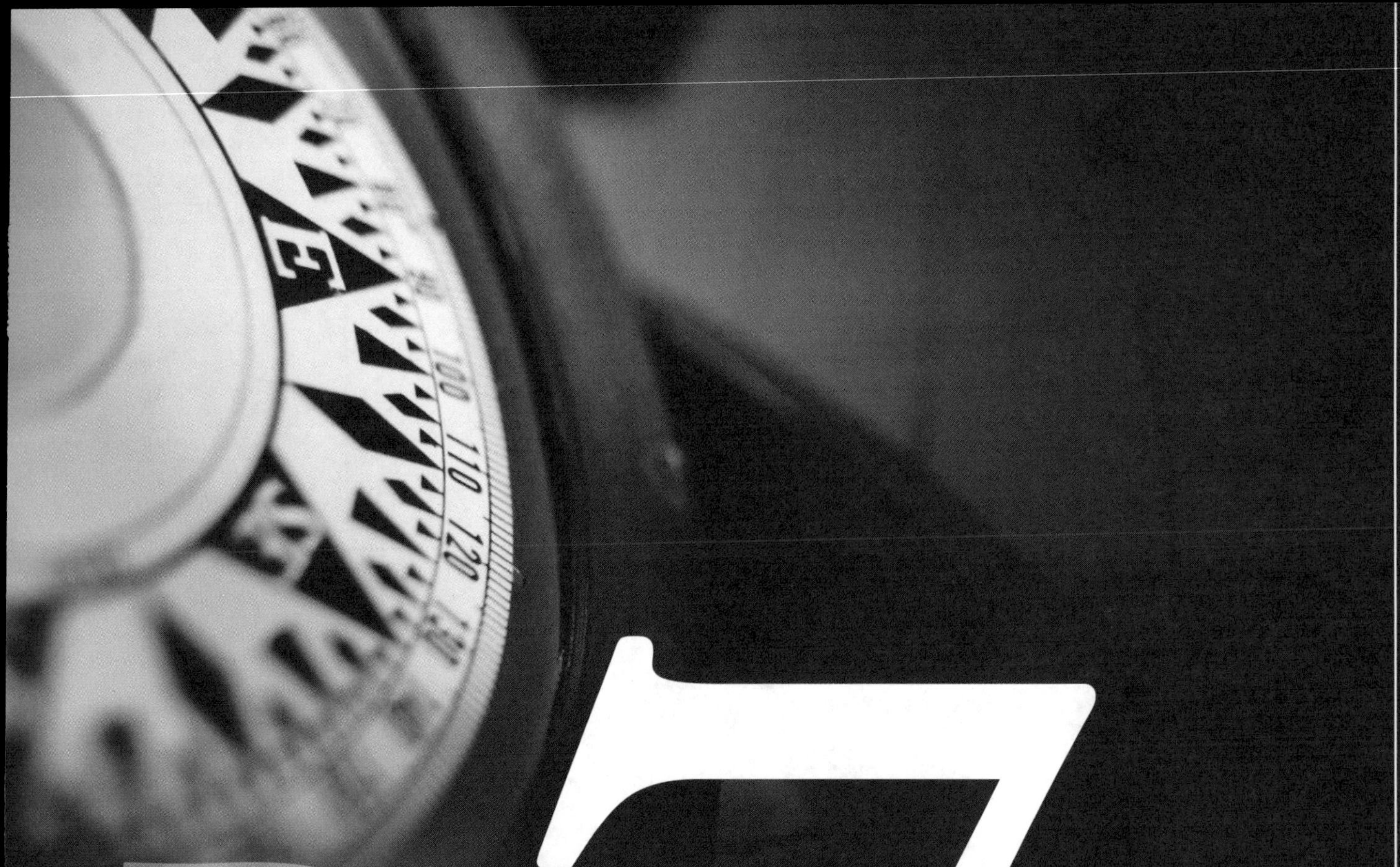

7

PLAN

PLAN

Chapter Seven

Chapter Seven

After mastering the content in this chapter you will:

- Be able to identify your values, interests, skills, and personality characteristics
- Be able to explore careers
- Comprehend elements of a college major
- Be able to navigate DegreeWorks
- Be able to set appropriate goals, prioritize tasks, and revise, as necessary

Fundamental Question

- How do I plan my EKU experiences to most effectively prepare for my future career?

Essential Principles

- Goal Setting
- Academic Performance
- Resources
- Career Choice
- Networking

"It is hard to fail but it is worse never to have tried to succeed."

Theodore Roosevelt

President, United States of America

Exploration and Decision Making

As an incoming EKU college student, you are faced with the task of making important decisions which will impact your future long after you graduate. You must choose what classes to take, what campus organizations and activities to become involved in, and perhaps most importantly, what major to select. The major you choose will require you to match your interests, skills, personality and values to a suitable career field. Selecting the "right" major and career field is a personal choice that can jump-start your journey to a challenging and rewarding future.

■ PREPARING FOR YOUR FUTURE

Choosing a career path first begins with taking a look at who you are as a person. Most people are happiest in a career that allows them to express elements of who they are. As you consider who you are in relation to choosing a career path, the following are important first steps to take:

1. Become aware of the characteristics that make you who you are.
2. Identify the components of yourself which are MOST important to you to include in a career.

If you choose a career that fits who you are, you will tend to be more motivated to take the necessary steps to achieve your career goal. Also, if you choose a career based on your key components, the choice will more likely result in a career about which you are passionate.

Increasing Clarity

What are some of the qualities about yourself that you need to be aware of as you consider your career path?

One of the most important characteristics to identify is your interests or what it is that you like. Take a moment to reflect upon your experiences at home, work, school, and leisure. What are your favorite school subjects? What are your favorite hobbies or pastimes?

What are things you really enjoy that you would like to incorporate into a career?

Other important aspects of yourself to consider are your strengths and the skills you have developed thus far. What is it that you do well? The strengths and skills that you have developed can come from your experiences at school or from jobs you have had. You may have developed other skills from people you know: teachers, employers, mentors, friends, coaches, siblings, parents, or others. Can you think of some of your strengths or skills you would like to include in a career?

Personality is another dimension to take into account. Think of personality as what makes a person tick. Take a moment to consider your personality. Are you an outgoing people person or are you quiet and introspective? Are you an outdoor person who likes being physically active? Are you artistic and/or musical? Are you a leader? Are you organized? What are the personality features that stand out for you? Which of your personality features would you like to express in a career?

Knowing your **values** can also be important when choosing your future career path. Values are principles that are important to you that guide your decisions. Examples of values are family, living in a desirable location, helping others, prestige, wealth, personal satisfaction, and job security. What are the values or guiding principles you consider important to you that you want to take into account in planning your career path?

In summary, knowing which of your interests, skills, personality characteristics, and values you would like to express in a career is a very important part of choosing a career path that will result in happiness and satisfaction.

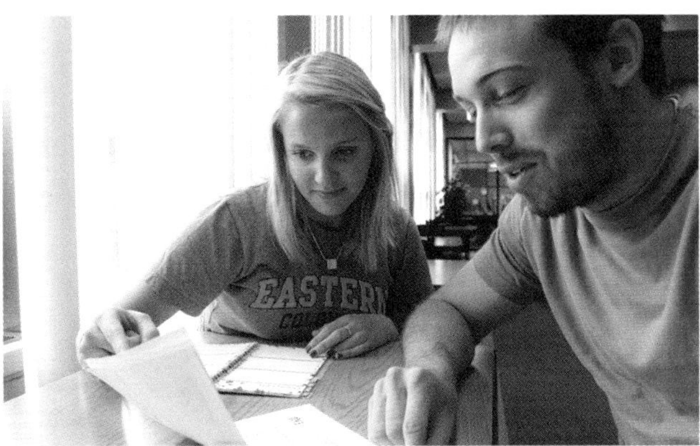

Building Confidence—Exploring Career Options

When researching your career options, there are a few things you can do that will help you match possible careers with your interests, skills, personality, and values.

Begin by learning as much as you can about the careers you are considering.

- Review the tasks and activities unique to each career profile so you know what knowledge, skills, and abilities are required to be successful in that field.
- Learn about the type of work environments that are common in these fields. What settings would you find yourself in on a regular basis?
- Find out the educational or training requirements for each career field you are researching and learn what types of degrees are needed to stay competitive.
- Develop accurate salary expectations and compare these to average state and national wages by using reliable and accurate resources on hourly or annual salary statistics, such as the wage data collected by each state through the Occupational Employment Statistics (OES) survey, conducted by the Bureau of Labor Statistics (BLS) at the U.S. Department of Labor.
- Find out if the careers you are most interested in will be in demand where you prefer to live and work after you graduate. Research the employment outlook using the data provided by the Bureau of Labor Statistics to match your career options with projected trends in the job market.
- Keep your options open by evaluating related occupations and comparing and contrasting the options to find which career matches best with who you are.

Once you have researched the various careers in which you are interested, it is time to take that information and do some serious consideration. Focus on how each career option fits you. Reflect on what you have discovered about the specific career profiles that interest you and ask yourself:

- Do the knowledge, skills, and abilities required fit with my academic strengths?
- Am I willing to obtain a master's, PhD, or other specialized training if necessary?
- Do the demands of this career match with what is important to me (family time, salary expectations)?
- What challenges might be presented in the job market (competition, location)?
- What else do I need to know or consider before identifying my career objective?

"I'd rather fail at doing something I love than succeed at doing something I hate."

George Burns

American humorist

Careful analysis and reflection of who you are and your targeted career options will build your confidence and help clarify your choices as you decide on an academic major and career field.

■ MAKING CONNECTIONS—PULLING IT ALL TOGETHER

To keep you motivated towards graduation, your college education should give you the proper balance of challenge and stimulation, both in the classroom and through internships, co-op opportunities, clinicals, and practical experiences. This may seem like an overwhelming task but, fortunately, there are several offices on our campus that can assist you with planning for your career and help you to make those very important career connections. The Counseling Center, Academic Advising, and the Center for Career and Cooperative Education have tools and resources that can guide you through this important and sometimes stressful process of exploring career decisions and clarifying your choice of a major. Following are some of the services these offices can provide.

Counseling Center

To help you navigate the career decision-making process, a course, GCS 199—Career Counseling Seminar, is offered by the EKU Counseling Center. This one-hour credit course can help you to:

- Identify your interests, skills, personality characteristics, and values.
- Discover careers that fit these qualities.
- Research careers of interest to you.
- Learn how to effectively select a major and career that fits YOU!

The Counseling Center staff can also provide the opportunity for you to:

- Work through the stress of beginning the career decision-making process.
- Handle pressure from others including parents who want to impose a career preference on you.
- Tackle any concerns you might have that get in the way of your educational or career goals; for example, self-doubt, lack of motivation, fear of failure and/or fear of success, etc.

Academic Advising

The Academic Advising staff promotes student success by working with you to:

- Select general education requirements.
- Explain requirements for majors.
- Clarify career and life goals.
- Develop practical academic plans.
- Reach your full academic potential.
- Provide information, resources, and contacts with consideration given to ALL majors on campus.

Center for Career and Cooperative Education

Career Development and Exploration

The Center for Career and Co-op offers a variety of career resources for you to:

- Explore career options that fit your personality/skills/interests/values.
- Identify your strengths and the skills you can offer potential employers.
- Find information on your major related to career paths, supply and demand, destinations of past graduates, salaries, and potential employers.
- Explore your interests and gain detailed information on a wide variety of occupations by using online career planning tools.

Cooperative Education and Internships

So, now you have an idea of what major you would like to pursue, or perhaps you have already declared that major but still have some doubts about your choice. Now is a great time to explore your choices by participating in job shadowing, volunteer work, part-time jobs related to your major and, as soon as you are eligible, clinicals, field work, and/or cooperative education and internships.

Cooperative education and internships promote student success by providing supervised career-related experiences that will help you to:

- Test drive your choice of major to further define your career goals.
- Gain academic credit in your field.
- Add to your professional development by applying classroom learning to your chosen field.
- Understand that a degree alone is not enough—in this job market, you must have experience.

■ MAKING CONNECTIONS—BUILDING YOUR NETWORK

Networking is important in building professional connections that will serve you throughout your time at EKU and beyond. Did you know that today more than 70% of career opportunities come as a direct result of networking? Your network is not only comprised of family, friends, employers, etc., but should now include your EKU "team" of advisors, professors, orientation instructors, as well as the staff of the offices included in this section. These professionals will be able to assist you in strategies to help you build, maintain, and grow your network to achieve career and personal success.

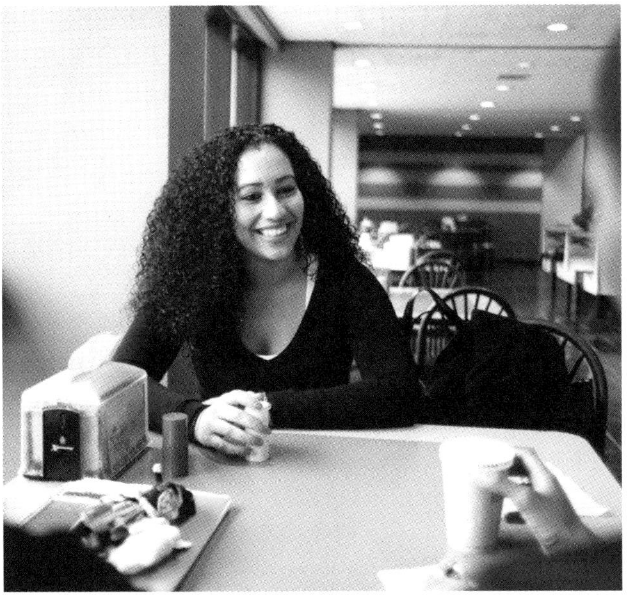

■ BE ENGAGED IN YOUR ACADEMIC ENDEAVORS

Majors and Degrees

A **major** is a compilation of courses that gives you knowledge in a field of study. Majors are offered by departments within a college. EKU is comprised of the following five colleges:

- College of Arts and Sciences
- College of Business and Technology
- College of Education
- College of Health Sciences
- College of Justice and Safety

> **MAJOR EXPO**
>
> Have your questions about majors and careers answered! Each fall and spring, EKU hosts a Major Expo where you can talk to faculty and advisors representing the various departments and majors on campus. To learn more, visit: http://www.advising.eku.edu/majors_expo.

EKU offers over 160 degree programs. Students can earn four types of degrees at EKU:

- Associate—*undergraduate degree*
- Bachelor—*undergraduate degree*
- Master—*graduate degree*
- Doctoral—*graduate degree*

An **associate degree** is an undergraduate academic degree awarded upon completion of a course of study requiring a minimum of 60 credit hours. You should ask your advisor about your major, degree requirements, and academic planning.

A **bachelor's degree** is an undergraduate academic degree awarded upon completion of a course of study requiring a minimum of 120 credit hours. A bachelor's degree is based on a comprehensive program that includes:

"Education is not the filling of a pail, but the lighting of a fire."

William Butler Yeats

Irish poet

General Education Courses Courses foundational to a liberal arts education	**Academic Major** **Bachelor's Degree** 120 hours minimum **Associate Degree** 60–76 hours (depending on major; refer to catalog)	Major Courses Courses specific to major
Supporting Courses Provided by department outside major		**Electives** Courses can be either within or outside major

General Education Requirements

Major Requirements

- Concentration (DegreeWorks)/Options (Catalog)
- Supporting Course Requirements

Electives

- General elective courses
- Co-op credit

Possible additional requirements

- University requirements such as orientation
- Developmental courses
- Professional education
- College requirements
- Minor requirements (some minors are required for degree)

Specifics about course requirements for majors at EKU as well as a description of each course offered can be found in the Undergraduate Catalog. To view the requirements you have yet to fulfill for your chosen degree, visit DegreeWorks on your EKUDirect account.

How do you decide which major is for you? And how do you plan your schedule of courses to earn your chosen degree? Academic Advising is an invaluable tool that will help you make these important decisions.

Undergraduate Catalog
http://www.undergradstudies.eku.edu/catalog
EKUDirect
http://www.it.eku.edu/ekudirect

■ ACADEMIC ADVISING

The purpose of academic advising is to help you clarify your career and life goals, develop meaningful academic plans, and optimize your academic potential. Advisors will help you select courses that will enable you to reach your career goals in the most efficient manner. Your advisor may suggest or recommend courses, but will not present you with a list of courses you must take. The ultimate decision for choosing your courses each semester is up to you, based on consultation with your advisor during your planning meeting each semester. Each semester you must work with your advisor to review your progress and plan for the timely completion of your degree program. Your advisor will give you your **registration access code** at the conclusion of your meeting. Without this code you will not be able to register online.

You will find that the advising process takes various forms across the EKU campus depending on the college and department in which you declare your major. Several colleges have a central advising office where you will meet with advisors for either the first two years or all four years to plan your program. Some students are advised by faculty who teach major courses in a degree program and also advise students who are majors in that degree.

The Academic Advising Center is the main advising center for undeclared students. There are some faculty members who advise undeclared majors, but until you choose a major, it is likely that you will find your advisor in the Academic Advising Center. The advising office is also the place to visit when you want to declare a major or change your major.

Your Advisor

Your advisor will help you discover where you are and where you need to go. He or she will help you navigate throughout your college experience and will ensure you are utilizing the resources and tools you need to successfully reach your goals.

The college system can be intimidating and complex, with lots of policies and procedures. Your advisor can help you interpret and understand what is expected of you. They are available via phone, email, or in person, to answer your questions.

Students Being Advised Are Expected To:

- Schedule regular appointments or make regular contact with your advisor during each semester. Remember, you may not get an appointment the same day you call to schedule. Call early—plan ahead!
- Arrive prepared for each appointment with questions or material for discussion
- Be an active learner by participating fully in the advising experience
- Ask questions if you do not understand an issue or have a specific concern
- Keep a personal record of your progress toward meeting your goals by keeping the planner feature of DegreeWorks up to date, including the list of classes you intend to take the next semester
- Organize official documents so that you can access them when needed
- Complete all assignments or recommendations
- Gather all relevant decision-making information
- Clarify personal values and goals and provide accurate information regarding your interests and abilities
- Become knowledgeable about University, college, and departmental programs, policies, and procedures
- Accept responsibility for your decisions

For advising and registration dates, visit: http://colonelscompass.eku.edu/registration-advising-dates

Academic Advisors Are Expected To:

- Understand and effectively communicate the curriculum, graduation requirements, and University and college policies and procedures
- Encourage and guide you as you define and develop realistic goals
- Encourage and support you as you gain the skills to develop clear, attainable educational plans
- Provide you with information about and strategies for utilizing the available resources and services on campus
- Help you understand the purposes and goals of higher education and its effects on your life and personal goals
- Be available to meet with you for advising during office hours
- Be reachable via telephone, email, or web access
- Assist you in gaining decision-making skills and in assuming responsibility for your educational plans and achievements
- Maintain confidentiality according to FERPA guidelines

"He who would learn to fly one day must first learn to stand and walk and run and climb and dance; one cannot fly into flying."

Friedrich Nietzsche
German philosopher

■ NAVIGATE DEGREEWORKS

"**DegreeWorks** is a web-based tool for you to monitor your academic progress towards degree completion. DegreeWorks also allows you and your advisor to plan future academic coursework" (EKU DegreeWorks, n.d.).

What Are the Benefits of DegreeWorks?

- Access important information via the web 24/7
- Learn the degree requirements and identify the courses you must complete to earn your degree
- Learn, before you change your major officially, how the courses you have completed meet the new major requirements or impact your time to graduation
- See how courses you want to take will apply to your degree requirements
- Learn about courses, including descriptions and pre-requisites
- Estimate how many semesters it will take you to graduate

The DegreeWorks worksheet, or **degree audit**, combines EKU's degree requirements and the coursework you have completed into an easy-to-read worksheet that helps you see how completed courses count toward degree requirements, and see what courses and requirements are still needed. The DegreeWorks audit provides the following information:

Student Information—This section includes information such as academic advisor, degree, major, classification, overall GPA, and ACT scores, etc.

Degree Information—This section of the audit contains information concerning your degree requirements. It shows the academic year for catalog requirements, hours required, hours applied, academic standing, and GPA. It also shows the overall requirements to complete the degree you are seeking (i.e., general education, university, major, minor, etc.).

General Education Requirements—This section indicates the courses that will fulfill the general education requirements for the degree. As requirements are fulfilled, the box next to each requirement is checked off.

Major and Minor Requirements—Each major and minor will be displayed in a section providing you the courses needed to fulfill the program requirements.

Additional Information—The audit also shows you electives, insufficient courses (those which do not count for credit, or in which you failed or withdrew), and in-progress courses. At the bottom of the audit is a legend and a disclaimer (EKU DegreeWorks, n.d.).

"DegreeWorks ia a great tool to utilize as a student. It helps monitor the progress in completing one's degree. I can check my grades, look up previous credits and future classes, along with calculating my GPA. It's also useful when meeting with your advisors about scheduling."

Sarah Franklin
Business Administration

Creating a Plan

The **DegreeWorks Planner** can be used to develop an academic plan for each semester all the way up to graduation. It is your responsibility to create a plan, and you have the ability to create as many plans as you wish. You are required to have one active and locked plan in DegreeWorks. Only your advisor has the ability to lock and delete plans. Once your advisor approves your course of action, he/she will lock your plan. You will not be able to edit a locked plan. However, you can create a new plan.

YOUR TOOLBOX

- Undergraduate Catalog
- DegreeWorks
- Curriculum Guides
- General Education Worksheet

What If?

"The **'What If' Function** in DegreeWorks allows you to hypothetically change your major, minor, or concentration. Your new 'What If' audit will show you what coursework is required for this major, minor, or concentration; what courses you have taken that satisfy requirements; and what courses are still left for you to take" (EKU DegreeWorks, n.d.).

The "What If" function is a very valuable tool when exploring or seeking to change a major. You should contact the department of the area you are exploring to review the program requirements and help develop a new academic plan.

➲IMPORTANT: If you change your major, you are automatically changed to the current catalog year and will be subject to the current catalog requirements.

DegreeWorks
For more information on DegreeWorks, go to http://www.registrar.eku.edu/degreeworks

Goal Setting

MAKING A PLAN FOR YOUR FUTURE

Goal setting is vital to creating your road to success. The process of determining goals must be well thought out and customized to fit you as an individual. Establishing goals allows you to create an outline, or plan, to help you achieve what you want in life. Goals provide a framework for decisions, an opportunity for incremental achievements, and a system for personal reflection.

HOW TO SET GOALS

Evaluate Priorities

Sometimes you may have many goals in mind and it is often difficult to determine which goals are most important and what you should do first. To effectively establish goals you must first evaluate your priorities.

Ask yourself a few questions to get started:

- What is important to you?
- What do you value?
- What do you want from your education?

These questions will help you organize your thoughts and enable you to prioritize your desired outcomes.

Remember—You must prioritize your tasks for each day. Ask yourself: What needs to be handled at the given moment? What is important and urgent? For example, going to class should take priority over meeting your friends for lunch. Completing homework should take priority over spending time with friends in the evening.

Research

When establishing goals it is important to know what is required for reaching the goals. Research will provide you with the in-depth knowledge needed to better understand what you are striving to accomplish and help you make important decisions when establishing goals. Learning details and information about what you want to accomplish will help you have a better understanding of the task at hand. For example, if you want to be accepted into the Nursing Program, you must first successfully complete chemistry.

"Mentoring is a brain to pick, an ear to listen, and a push in the right direction."
John C. Crosby
American politician

This is important for you to know so you can understand all of the requirements associated with reaching your goal.

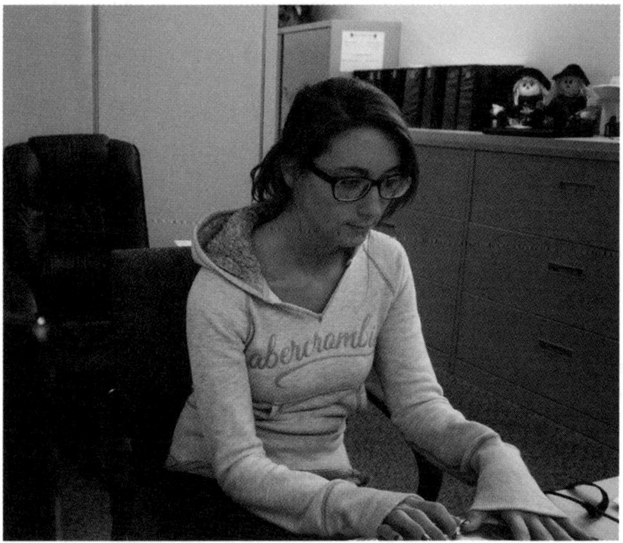

Categorize Goals

When creating goals, you must divide them into short-term and long-term. **Short-term goals** involve plans that can be completed within a short amount of time. Short-term goals are stepping stones towards your **long-term goals**.

A long-term goal is completed over an extended period of time, a year or longer. Long-term goals are a plan for where you want to be and who you want to become. Some examples of short-term and long-term goals follow.

Short-term goals:

- Earn an "A" in my orientation course this semester
- Turn in all assignments on time this semester
- This semester I will read the chapters before class

Long-term goals:

- Graduate from Eastern Kentucky University
- Find a job within my field, one month after graduation
- Purchase a home

Writing SMART: SMART Goal-Setting Method

The **SMART goal method** is used in developing purposeful and clear goals. Using this method will help you accomplish your goals.

Specific—goals that are clear and detailed. When you have specific goals you are able to see your overall purpose for the goal, exact steps to take to achieve the goal, and how long it will take to successfully accomplish it. For example, saying, "This semester I will not be late for my classes" is more specific than stating, "I will never be late for class."

Measurable—criteria you set for yourself to measure your goals. This will help keep you on track and allow you to see how you are progressing towards your goals. Measurable goals will contain elements of frequency, amount, or intensity. The goal stated above is measurable because you can track your progress throughout the semester.

Attainable—goals are within reach and can be successfully accomplished. Since arriving to class on time is primarily based on actions you control, this would be an attainable goal.

Realistic—a goal you will be able to fulfill. A realistic goal is one that you have the ability and know-how to accomplish. For example, if you schedule 8 am classes and typically are not a morning person, arriving on time to class may not be a realistic goal. In this situation you would want to consider altering your class schedule.

Timely—each goal that you set must be completed in a timely manner. You must have a time frame for when you want to have your goal completed. By stating you will not be late for class for a semester, you have given yourself a time frame to measure and achieve your goal (Doran, 1981).

Review

Review the goals you have written and ask yourself the same questions with which you began. What is important to you? What do you value? What do you want from your education? Will the goals you have established help you reach your expectations?

Evaluation

After writing your short- and long-term goals, it is important that you evaluate your progress regularly. Short-term goals need to be evaluated often, considering the length of time to accomplish the goal. For example, you must evaluate your progress toward receiving an "A" in math class within the first few weeks of class. If you determine you are not on track, you will have time to make adjustments, such as visiting the tutoring center.

Dealing with Roadblocks

Having a clear concrete plan is not a shield against roadblocks. Life will throw many obstacles your way, but you have to be creative and think critically about how to deal with them. When a roadblock appears, you must review your goals and see what revisions are needed. Keep in mind that revisions are necessary for success. It is okay if your original goals change; it does not mean that you have failed. As you progress through life, your views, ideas, and needs may change. As this evolution occurs, your goals will also evolve.

Rewarding Yourself

Your short-term goals are stepping stones towards your long-term goals. It is important to reward yourself after accomplishing short- and long-term goals. For example: It is the end of the fall semester and one goal that you had set was to earn an "A" in your English class. You have earned your "A," so now you are going to reward yourself by purchasing a new outfit.

CREATIVE THINKING TIP

Orient yourself towards developing goals.
The more clearly you can state your objectives in life, the easier their attainment will be. "Aha moments" come when the mind is primed to solve a problem. Ever go to bed thinking about how to fix something and wake up suddenly with a good idea what to do? Without planting a seed, your mind has nothing with which to work.

Chapter Summary

College is the time to prepare for your future. As you think about a career field, explore your personality, values, and personal strengths; also explore careers that match who you are and what you want. Several services at Eastern Kentucky University are available to help you along this journey, including the Counseling Center, Academic Advising, and the Center for Career & Cooperative Education. These resources can help you identify your goals and suggest ways to help you accomplish them.

As you pursue your goals, keep your GPA in mind. Strive for a minimum of 2.0, and remember that falling below this mark jeopardizes your success at EKU. Again, a 2.0 is the *minimum* you should accept. Some programs require a higher GPA for acceptance. Recognitions and awards await those with high GPAs, including the Dean's List, Dean's Awards, and President's Award. Challenge yourself to earn one or all of these each semester!

Finally, get to know your academic advisor. Their job is to help keep you on track so that you can graduate and achieve your goals. They can also share academic and employment opportunities with you and help you build your social network. Between regular meetings with your advisor make use of DegreeWorks so that you can stay informed regarding your progress throughout the school year. Knowing what courses you have taken and have yet to take, you can assess your progress and establish appropriate goals.

"Goals provide the energy source that powers our lives. One of the best ways we can get the mos from the energy we have is to focus it. That is what goals can do for us; concentrate our energy.
Denis Waitley
American motivational speaker and author

■ KEY TERMS

Associate degree: Degree awarded for studies in an undergraduate major generally lasting two years

Bachelor's degree: Degree awarded for studies in an undergraduate major generally lasting four years; a baccalaureate degree

Degree audit: A worksheet on DegreeWorks which details completed, in-progress, and future coursework for a student as well as listing completed and outstanding requirements for degree completion (EKU DegreeWorks, n.d.)

DegreeWorks: A web-based tool which lets students monitor their progress toward degree completion and plan future courses with their advisors (EKU DegreeWorks, n.d.)

DegreeWorks planner: A tool in DegreeWorks which allows students to create a proposed schedule of courses for future semesters

Electives: Courses that are not part of major, minor, or general education requirements, but are still required to graduate; generally chosen based on personal interest

Long-term goal: An objective that a person works to achieve within a period of months or years

Major: Compilation of courses that gives a student knowledge in a specified field of study

Personality: The sum of a person's individual qualities and traits which form their unique character

Registration Access Code (RAC number): Numerical code required to register for classes. All students receive a new RAC number from their advisor each semester

Short-term goal: An objective that a person works to achieve within a period of days or weeks

SMART goal method: A goal-setting method used to develop purposeful and clear goals as objectives are measured by the criteria indicated by the SMART acronym: specific, measurable, attainable, realistic, and timely

Values: Personal rules or beliefs, such as what is good or useful or desirable, by which individuals make decisions each day

"What If" function: A feature of DegreeWorks which allows students to hypothetically change their majors to explore the necessary requirements for degree completion in that major

NOTES

"If you don't know where you're going, every road will get you nowhere."

Henry Kissinger

American statesman

■ CAMPUS RESOURCES

Academic Advising Office
http://www.advising.eku.edu
Whitlock Building, room 347, 859-622-2276

Advising—Arts & Sciences
http://cas.eku.edu/students-and-advising
Roark Building, room 105, 859-622-1405

Advising—Business & Technology
http://cbt.eku.edu/college-advising-office
Business & Technology Center, room 257, 859-622-1086

Advising—Education
Combs Building, room 423, 859-622-1828

Advising—Health Sciences
http://www.health.eku.edu/college-health-sciences-advising-2
Rowlett Building, room 203, 859-622-1523

Advising—Justice & Safety
http://www.justice.eku.edu/academic-advising
Stratton Building, room 354D, 859-622-7216

Center for Career and Cooperative Education
http://www.career-coop.eku.edu
Whitlock Building, room 468, 859-622-1296

EKU Counseling Center
http://www.counseling.eku.edu
Whitlock Building, room 571, 859-622-1303

O*Net Online
http://www.onetonline.org/

Occupation Outlook Handbook
http://www.bls.gov/ooh/

■ REFERENCES

BrainyQuote. (n.d.). *BrainyQuote.com*. Retrieved June 9, 2011, from http://www.brainyquote.com/

EKU DegreeWorks (n.d.). Frequently asked questions. In *EKU DegreeWorks*. Retrieved March 18, 2011, from http:// www.registrar.eku.edu/degreeworks/faqs/

Doran, G.T. (1981, Nov.). There's a S.M.A.R.T. way to write management's goals and objectives. *Management Review*, *70*(11), 35–36.

RESOURCES & REFERENCES

NOTES

"Life is not a having and a getting, but a being and a becoming."

Matthew Arnold

English poet and critic

8

CAPITALIZE

Chapter Eight

Chapter Eight

CAPITALIZE

After mastering the content in this chapter you will:

- Be able to plan and develop a budget
- Be able to revise a budget (manage budget and funds)
- Be able to evaluate financial sources
- Understand financial aid terms
- Be able to explain the difference between a loan and a grant
- Understand the consequences of debt

Fundamental Question

- How can I become financially responsible?

Essential Principles

- Cost of College
- Personal Finances
- Financial Resources
- Debt Management

"Money is only a tool. It will take you wherever you wish, but it will not replace you as the driver."

Ayn Rand

Russian writer

Who's in Control: You or the Money?

It's the weekend and you're broke. Welcome to college life. Oh sure, you could just go home for the weekend. At least you'd get your laundry done, but what fun would that be? After all, part of the reason you came to college was to hang out with friends and have a little fun, a chance to be independent and make your own decisions. Unfortunately, with that independence comes the responsibility of paying your own way. If you're not paying attention to your finances, there will be a lot of broke weekends.

The good news is you can have the college lifestyle you want; it just requires planning. The key is to control your money, not to let it control you. If you have a part-time job and your last paycheck was gone four days after you got it, or if you blew through your financial aid refund within a month of getting it, you have a problem. There is nothing worse than calling mom and dad four weeks into the semester and telling them you are out of money. If this has happened to you, chances are your money is the one in control, not the other way around.

With some basic knowledge and a little planning, you won't be sitting at home on Friday nights, and you may even have enough left over for spring break. The first step for managing your money is to understand it. Where is it coming from? How much do you have? How often do you get it and how long do you have to make it last? The second step is spending it, or rather knowing how to spend it without getting yourself into trouble.

In this chapter we will take an in-depth look at your money—where it's coming from, what it's paying for, and how to spend it wisely but still have fun. The financial choices you make now will affect you for years to come. Too many mistakes now and it will cost you later,

even after you graduate. With a little planning and a little discipline, you can avoid broke weekends, have the college experience you want, and start your post-graduate life on the right foot.

■ COST OF ATTENDANCE

You've moved into your residence hall room, met the roommate, scoped out the hotties, and managed to find your way to your first class—but do you know what it is costing you to be a college student? College is an investment. U.S. Census Bureau statistics show that over a lifetime a college graduate will earn close to a million dollars more than someone who didn't go to college.

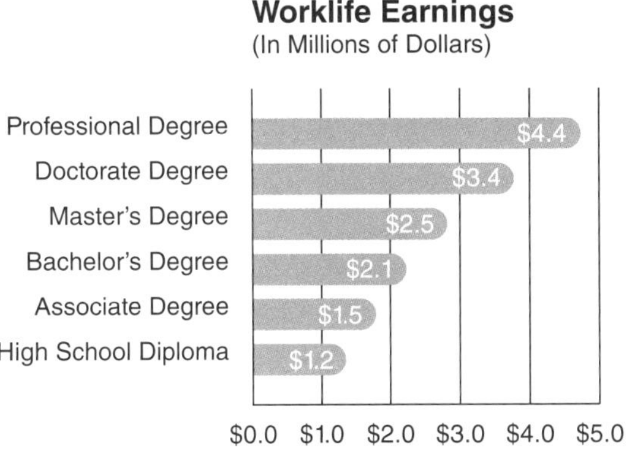

So now you are here, you are making the investment, but what exactly is your money paying for?

Cost of attendance is the overall cost a student will pay each year to attend school. It includes tuition, books, housing, meals, and personal expenses.

Tuition

Tuition is the cost you pay for educational instruction. In other words, the amount of money you have to pay to sit in the classroom and learn the subject matter. Tuition will most likely be the largest single expense you will encounter while earning your degree.

Textbooks

You'll also have to buy textbooks. College textbooks are not cheap! Books can be purchased at the University bookstore or at off-campus bookstores, online, and at used bookstores. You can even rent textbooks at the EKU Bookstore, too. One of the newest ways to acquire textbooks is by digital download; just click a few buttons and voilà, the book appears in your computer. It's a great alternative to lugging heavy books all over campus! By taking the time to shop around and evaluate your options, you can save a significant amount of money.

> **BOOK BUYING TIP**
>
> Talk to other students! You may find someone who is taking a course you plan to take next semester. Ask them if you can buy the copy of the book they are using. Find out the buy-back price of the book and offer them $5 or $10 more. They will get more money and you get a super deal. Plus you will have all the notes they made in the margins! It's a win-win proposition!

Housing Allowances

There are a number of places you can choose to live while you are in college. Most students live in a residence hall, but some live at home or in off-campus housing such as an apartment. Living on campus is the first choice for many students, particularly for the first couple of years.

Nontraditional students, many upper-classmen, and most graduate students choose to live in off-campus housing. They typically rent an apartment or house. Before deciding to live off campus, be sure to look at the big picture. It is not just the monthly rent you have to come up with. You will have other up-front costs as well. Landlords usually require a security deposit to cover any financial losses they may incur if you or your roommates damage the property. You might also have to pay deposits or fees to utility companies to have your services turned on. Unless you want your living room furniture to consist of a couple of lawn chairs and your bed to be an air mattress, you may need to buy furniture too. All of these things mean you'll need extra cash.

> "The only way not to think about money is to have a great deal of it."
>
> Edith Wharton
>
> American author

➲Renter's Insurance

Renter's insurance is a must if you have an apartment or house. It will cover your possessions in case of a fire or break-in. Renter's insurance is inexpensive, costing between $15 to $25 per month.

If you want to move off campus, set a target date, do your research, and save, save, save. Once the time comes you will be ready and your dinner table won't be an upside-down trash can with a piece of plywood on top.

Board

Board is a fancy term for food. You have to eat. The University offers several different meal packages that you can choose to purchase. These packages consist of a combination of cafeteria meals and an allowance for meals at other eating establishments on campus. Choose the package that best fits into your budget but don't buy one that has more meals than you think you can use in a semester.

After your freshman year you can continue to purchase a meal plan or you can choose to pay for your meals as you go. If you eat in your residence hall room or eat off campus more than you eat in the cafeteria, you may be better off not buying a meal plan.

Personal Expenses

Personal expenses can cover a lot of ground. They include anything you pay for out of pocket such as shampoo, toothpaste, laundry detergent, dining off campus, and any monthly bills you are responsible for paying, like car insurance or cell phone bills. Personal expenses are where most students get into trouble. It is the easiest place to overspend if you don't have a budget, but more on that later.

Now that you have an idea about what you'll need money for, you will be able to calculate your cost of attendance. At the beginning of each semester make a list of your personal costs for tuition, books, dorm/housing, meals, and personal expenses. Once you know the big picture it will be easier to stick to a budget.

Online Course Expenses

Online courses are billed at a higher tuition rate and are charged in addition to regular course tuition. All online courses are charged by the credit hour and do not factor in to a full-time rate. http://www.eku.edu/onlinelearning/courses

Paying for It All

Now that you have an idea of the cost of going to college you'll have to figure out how to pay for it. This is a good time to sit down and talk to your family. Find out exactly what they are paying for, what you're expected to pay for, and what you'll need financial aid to pay for. This is a family decision and is different for every student. It's not uncommon for freshman students to leave the financial decisions up to their parents. Not a good idea. Some decisions, like student loans, affect your financial future. You need to be a part of the planning process!

■ FINANCIAL AID

Outside of personal and family contributions, **financial aid** is another way students can pay for college. It includes scholarships (which were discussed in Chapter 3), federal financial aid, or private funding. Federal financial aid includes grants, student loans, parent loans, and federal work-study.

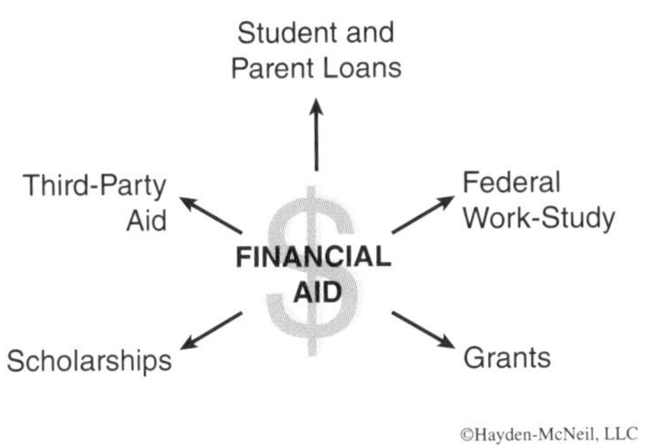

Federal Financial Aid

Federal financial aid is available to all college students. It consists of grants, loans, and student employment. The amount and types of aid you are offered are based on your family's financial need. All students, regardless of need, are eligible for student loans. Federal aid requires an application called the **Free Application for Federal Student Aid**, or **FAFSA**. A new application is required for each year you're in college. You need to complete your FAFSA as soon after January 1st of any given year as possible. Talk to your parents about filing their taxes early. If you wait, you could miss out on some of the available aid. Funding is not unlimited, and some funds do run out!

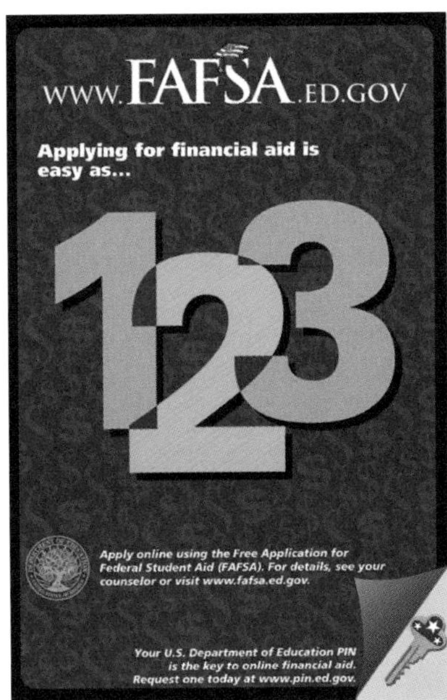

For the Free Application for Federal Student Aid (FAFSA), visit: http://www.fafsa.ed.gov

Grants

A **grant** is "free" money. In other words, it is money that does not have to be paid back. There are a number of grants available but the most common, and the largest, is the Pell grant. With the exception of the Pell, most grants have limited funding available and can only be offered until the money runs out. That is why it is so important to apply for financial aid early!

Loans

Federal student **loans** are government-supported, low-interest loans called **direct loans**. They have to be paid back after you graduate or leave school. The government sets an annual maximum that a student can borrow. Freshmen have the lowest annual maximum, seniors the highest.

Student loans are either subsidized or unsubsidized. **Subsidized loans** are interest-free until the loan goes into repayment. That means that while you are in school you will not have to make any payments or pay any interest. After you graduate you have six months before any payments are due. **Unsubsidized loans** will accrue interest from the time you take out the loan. While you do not have to make any payments on the loan or the interest while you are in school, you are being charged interest every month and it is being added to the amount you owe.

A **parent PLUS loan** is available to dependent students who don't have enough money to meet their cost of attendance after all of their other aid has been offered. This is a loan for the parent and the parent is responsible for paying it back.

"To fulfill a dream, to be allowed to sweat over lonely labor, to be given a chance to create, is the meat and potatoes of life. The money is the gravy."

Bette Davis

American actress

"If you're not careful, student loans hide things. You might get into something you aren't familiar with and end up owing money while still knee-deep in Gen-Ed requirements. Figure all this out BEFORE you sign the dotted line."

Dana Ecton
Communication Disorders

Private Student Loans

There are a few loan companies that offer private student loans. These loans are not made through the federal government and require the borrower to apply directly through the lending institution offering the loan. Private loans can be helpful for independent students who need to fill the gap between federal aid and cost of attendance and for dependent students whose parents do not want to take out the parent loan. Private student loans are credit dependent. Students without enough credit history to qualify on their own will need a **co-signer** who can pass the credit check. A co-signer is someone who guarantees that if you **default** on the loan that they will pay it back on your behalf.

"Loans can be tricky but very helpful if you know how to handle them correctly. I suggest only borrowing what you absolutely need—don't forget that loan money has to be paid back."

George Rothwell
Middle Grade Education

Federal Work-Study

Student employment is a great way to earn money for personal expenses. The federal work-study program pays the student an hourly wage for working on campus. It is important to note that federal work-study money goes directly to the student and not to the amount the student owes the University for tuition and other charges. The program is designed to help students with the personal expenses component of their cost of attendance budget.

Other Sources of Financial Assistance

There are a number of organizations that offer tuition and other assistance for students attending college. There are several government agencies, called **third-party agencies**, who offer aid based on specific circumstances. The two most common are Vocational Rehabilitation, which provides assistance to students with physical and learning disabilities, and Workforce Investment Act (WIA), which provides assistance to dislocated workers.

Veterans and active duty members of the U.S. Armed Forces are eligible for benefits through the Veterans Benefits Administration. Spouses and children may also be eligible. EKU's Student Outreach and Transition Office (SOTO) houses the office of Veterans Affairs which is dedicated to helping veterans and members of the military coordinate their benefits. Students considering a career in the military may be eligible for scholarships through EKU's ROTC program.

For more information about benefits for veterans and active service members and their spouses and children, visit: http://www.vba.va.gov/VBA/ or http://soto.eku.edu/veterans

Additionally, payment plans are offered through the Student Accounting Services office. Payment plans provide students the opportunity to spread the amount owed to pay off their bill over the span of a semester. The balance due after all other aid has been applied can be divided into four monthly payments, one due each month of the semester. The balance must be paid in full before the semester ends.

It's important to understand that financial aid is not unlimited. You can lose your financial aid if your GPA drops below a 2.0 or if you withdraw from or fail too many classes. You are also limited on how many overall hours you can earn without completing a degree. That means that you have to stay on track to graduate in a certain period of time. Some aid and most scholarships are limited to eight semesters—the time it takes the average student to earn their degree. Other aid is cut off after you have earned a certain number of overall hours but haven't yet earned your degree.

If you're planning ahead, you can only receive grants as an undergraduate student. Once you have earned your degree, you can still get federal loans, but no grants. If you are planning on earning your master's degree, it pays to plan ahead so that you can maximize your undergraduate aid. With good budgeting you may even be able to set aside some of your undergraduate money to pay for grad school!

Now that you know what school is going to cost and how you are going to pay for it, you have the starting point for setting up your personal budget. Once you have determined how much money you have coming in and then subtracted out the money you owe to the University, the rest is yours for personal expenses.

Common Financial Aid Questions

Q: What determines how much financial aid I will get?
After you have completed your FAFSA, you will be given a number called the Expected Family Contribution (EFC). The EFC measures your family's financial strength based on income, assets, family size, and the number of people attending college. It does not take into consideration things like personal debt or expenses. It is not how much you are expected to pay out of pocket to the University. What it does do is determine your financial need and what types of aid you are eligible for. Students with lower EFCs are eligible for grants, while students with higher EFCs are only eligible for loans.

Q: What determines dependent vs. independent status?
For financial aid purposes students are considered either a dependent or an independent student. Dependent students have to use parent information on the FAFSA; independent students do not. Students under 24 years of age are considered dependent unless they meet one of the following exceptions:

- You are married
- You have a bachelor's degree and are working on a master's or doctorate
- You are active duty in the armed forces for purposes other than training
- You are a veteran of the armed forces
- You have children; you must be the primary financial support for the child and not be living at home with your parents
- You have a legal dependent who has been assigned to you by the court

"Never spend your money before you have earned it."
Thomas Jefferson
3rd President of the United States of America

- You are an orphan, or you were in foster care or a ward of the court (non-criminal) at any time after age 13
- You have been granted legal emancipation from your parents by the courts
- You are an unaccompanied, homeless youth whose status can be documented by a high school liaison or by a shelter director
- You are in a legal guardianship

You are not independent simply because you are under 24, live independently, and pay your own expenses. Also, it does not matter who claims you on taxes. If you claim yourself, you are still a dependent student for financial aid purposes.

Q: I have to send my tax returns to the school. Why?
Some applications are selected for a review process called verification. The federal government requires that one third of all applications be reviewed by school officials for accuracy. If you are selected, you will need to submit documentation to the school regarding both your and your family's income. If you are selected, don't wait until the last minute to turn in your documentation. Verification is a time-consuming process. If you wait until the last minute, your aid may not be ready at the beginning of the fall semester!

Managing Your Personal Expenses

Now comes the hard part! Your bill is paid and you have money coming in for personal expenses. Your goal is not to run out of money before the semester ends, which is easier said than done! A **budget** is one of the best tools for making sure you stay on top of your money, and starting one is simple. Before you begin, decide if you want to do a monthly budget or a two-week budget. Choose a time frame that best suits your needs. A monthly budget is the most common, but if you find that you run out of money before you run out of month, a shorter time frame may help. If you will be using only your financial aid refund for personal expenses, you will be better off putting the money into a savings account first and then transferring a portion of it to your checking account once a month.

STEP ONE: DETERMINE YOUR INCOME

Determining your **income** may be as simple as dividing your financial aid refund by 4 or 8, but most students will have money coming in from different sources. You need to total the amount from all sources. If you need to estimate some of your income, estimate low. That way anything over the amount you estimate can go into your savings account.

Let's look at an example.

> *You have decided to base your budget on how much money you will need for one month. You received a financial aid refund of $1,000 for the semester and have a part-time student job that will give you a paycheck every two weeks of approximately $150. To determine how much money you will receive each month you will need to divide your refund by 4 since there are 4 months in the semester. In order to make your refund last all semester, you will only be able to spend $250 a month in addition to the amount you will receive from the paychecks from your student job. Since you will get paid twice a month, you can add $300 to the $250 you will have from your refund. You have $550 to work with during the month.*

STEP TWO: EVALUATE YOUR EXPENSES

Once you know your income, you need to evaluate your **expenses**. Expenses can be grouped into two categories: fixed and variable. **Fixed expenses** are the easy ones to budget for. They occur at the same time each month and are always for the same amount. Fixed expenses can include things like car payments, car insurance, or cell phone bills. **Variable expenses** are harder to plan for because they aren't the same amount each month or they may not occur on a regular schedule. These can include expenses like clothing, entertainment, and gasoline.

Before you begin building your budget you need to look at one very important factor. Is your income more than your expenses? Or is it less? If you are bringing in more money than you need you are in good shape. All you'll have to do

is resist the urge to spend it on items not in your budget. However, if your expenses are greater than your income you'll have to make some adjustments by either reducing expenses or earning additional money. Since earning additional money isn't always an option, look first to see if there are expenses that can be reduced or eliminated.

To figure out if you're overspending, write down everything you spend for a week. This means everything! Think that small expenses like a cup of coffee or a trip to the vending machine don't count? They do! Once you have it all on paper, you will be surprised to see the impact that small purchases have on how fast you run out of money. Items like fast food, vending machines, high-end coffee drinks, bottled water, and music downloads can be budget killers.

Table 8-1. Sample expense chart.

SAMPLE EXPENSE EVALUATION CHART				
Date	Amount	What For?	Necessary Expense?	Is There an Alternative?

If you are on a tight budget you may have to change some behaviors and make some sacrifices. A few simple changes could make all of the difference between enjoying college life and sitting home alone every weekend. Once you've written down your expenses give them a good hard look and then ask yourself some questions.

1. Is this expense necessary?
2. Can it be eliminated?
3. If not, is there a cheaper alternative?

You'll discover that a few simple changes can make all the difference.

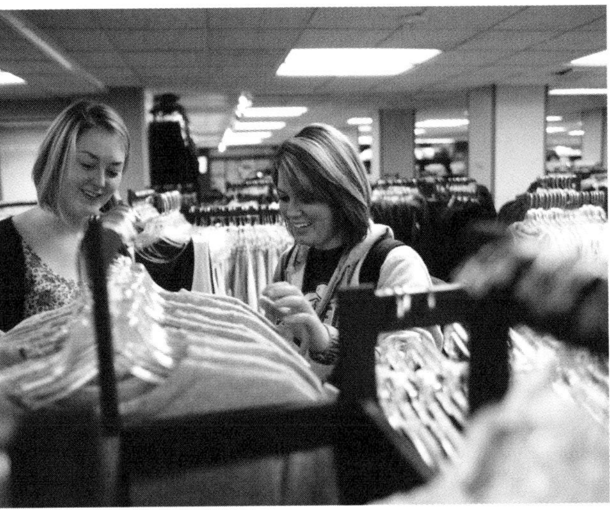

To continue with our example, you've tracked your expenses and found that you were spending $620 a month, $70 more than your $550 income.

When analyzing your expenses, you discover something you hadn't noticed. You have a one-hour break between your first class of the morning and your second class. To pass the time, you hang out at the coffee shop. Since you're not a morning person and you tend to skip breakfast, you generally grab a cup of coffee and a muffin between classes. You spend approximately $5 every day.

Is this expense necessary? Not really. Can it be eliminated? Yes, if you skip breakfast entirely. However, you are really hungry by the end of your first class and you need some breakfast. So, is there a cheaper alternative? You can carry a breakfast bar and a travel mug of coffee with you or eat before you leave your dorm room in the morning.

If you eliminate the expense entirely you will save $25 a week, $100 a month, and $400 a semester! If you bring your own coffee and breakfast at a cost of $2 a day, then you can still save $60 a month. By packing your own breakfast and skipping a few trips to the vending machine, you can easily eliminate $70 from your budget.

"Rule No.1: Never lose money. Rule No.2: Never forget rule No.1."

Warren Buffett

American businessman

■ STEP THREE: BUILD YOUR BUDGET

Now that you've calculated your income and analyzed your expenses, it's time to build your budget. It's easier to manage your expenses if you divide them into categories. The categories you choose will be based on the type of expenses you have. If you live on campus, you may need only a few categories, consisting mainly of personal expenses such as entertainment, dining, or clothing. If you live off campus, you will need to add utilities, groceries, and other expenses into the mix.

You're almost done with your budget, but now it's time to put it on paper. List your categories and then list your expenses under the appropriate categories. Once you've allocated all of your expenses, add up each category individually. The totals are the amount of money you spent while you were tracking your expenses. Use those totals as the basis for your budget next month.

Continuing with our example, you have chosen entertainment, eating out (movies and sporting events), cell phone, dorm food and snacks, personal hygiene (shampoo, laundry detergent, toothpaste, etc.), and savings as your categories.

Table 8-2. Sample expense chart.

DATE	ENTERTAINMENT	EATING OUT	CELL PHONE	FOOD/SNACKS	PERSONAL HYGIENE	SAVINGS
Totals						

Now you have a budget. The tricky part is sticking to it! If you find that you are running out of money before the month is over, go back to step two and reanalyze your expenses. You may need to look at your budget every couple of months to make sure you are staying on track. Income changes over time and so do expenses. Plus, bad spending habits can creep in if you're not paying attention. Monitoring your budget will keep you out of trouble!

Saving Money

Many college students think that they may not need to save money or that it's not really necessary. The reality is that there will be expenses in college that sneak up and surprise you. Your car could break down or your roommate might end up with an extra ticket for your favorite band's upcoming concert. There is also spring break to think about. You might decide you want to study abroad. If you are in a major that requires an internship or student teaching, you won't get paid for them in most circumstances. You'll still have expenses, so you'll need savings to pay them.

To ensure you have savings, make it a category in your budget. If you know you need to save for a future expense, determine how long you will have before you need the money and save enough each month to meet your savings goal. You can also add to your savings in small ways like putting birthday and other cash gifts into your savings account. Resist the instant gratification of a trip to the mall! You might just wish you had that money later when all of your friends are lying on the beach during spring break and you're painting the living room with your mom.

Borrowing Money

Credit is a contractual agreement where a borrower receives something of value (money or goods) now and agrees to pay for it in installments or at a later date, with **interest**. Interest is a fee charged for the use of financial resources. If you have taken out a student loan, it is a type of credit called an **installment loan**. The federal government gives you money that you, in turn, use to pay for school. After you graduate, you have to pay the loan back, plus interest. Installment loans are a type of credit where

you borrow a fixed amount and pay it back by making payments of a predetermined amount on a regular basis.

There is another type of credit you will encounter while in college. It's called **revolving credit** and is usually in the form of a credit card. With this type of credit, borrowers are given a **line of credit**. A line of credit is a specific amount of money that a lender has made available for a borrower that can be used at the borrower's discretion. For example: A student has a $1,000 limit on his credit card. He can spend any portion of the $1,000 in any amount, as long as it is not more than $1,000.

Credit cards require a **minimum monthly payment**, usually based on the outstanding balance. The borrower can pay more if he chooses but is always required to pay at least the minimum. The payment includes a monthly interest charge on the entire outstanding balance. Interest charged on a revolving balance adds up quickly. Credit cards with high balances and low minimum monthly payments can keep a borrower in debt for 30 years or more. And that is only if the borrower has stopped borrowing. If he hasn't it will keep him in debt for life!

As a student, the promise of only having to pay $15 dollars a month to finance something you want can be tempting but let's look at the big picture. Interest rates charged on credit cards given to students can be high because you haven't established a financial history yet. The credit card company is willing to give you a chance but they are going to charge you a higher interest rate to balance the risk that they don't know for sure if you will pay them back. If you borrow $1,500 at a 16.8% interest rate, and make only the minimum monthly payments without using the card for any future charges, it will take you 23 1/2 years to pay off the credit card!

Credit cards can be an important tool to help cover emergency expenses and help students build a credit history, but they can also lead to trouble. Always keep in mind that credit card companies are in business to make money off of you. They didn't offer you a credit card because they wanted to help out a starving college student. They gave you that card to make a profit! It's up to you to use credit wisely.

"Credit cards are an easy way to find yourself in a world of trouble and a lot of debt. Just be careful! Know how to manage your money."

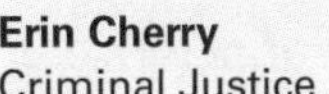

As a general rule, credit cards should never be used for everyday expenses. If you can eat it, drink it, or wear it you should pay for it out of your regular budget. Save the credit card for emergencies or expenses that are not recurring. When you do use your card, pay it off quickly. Ignore the minimum monthly payment. If you pay double the minimum, you will pay off the card approximately 60% faster. If you triple the payment, you will pay off the card 85% faster. Using the previous example, if you increase the payment from $15 to $45, the card will be paid off in just 3 years. You'll save 20 years of interest!

There are other dangers lurking in the credit card world. Credit card companies don't just charge interest; they charge other fees as well. Many cards charge an annual

"A wise person should have money in their head, but not in their heart."
Jonathan Swift
Irish writer

fee. This is a fee you pay just for the privilege of carrying a card around in your wallet. You'll pay it whether or not you owe a balance, and you'll pay it every year. You will also be charged a late fee if your payment is late. Late fees can be $45 or more and your lender won't stop there. Your interest rate will increase as well. Remember the risk factor? If you pay late, even the lender will consider you high risk and raise your rate to hedge their bets in case you default.

It's important to read the disclosure statements that come with your credit cards. The disclosure statement is a document that explains all of the terms and fees the lender has established for use in managing your account. It will include a list of all of the fees and penalties they can charge you. With most cards, your interest rate will change from year to year. The disclosure statement will also include information on what basis the company calculates your interest rate. Don't accept a credit card until you have read the disclosure.

Credit Reports

Did you know that everything you do financially is being recorded? There are three agencies that keep track of how you spend and borrow money. They compile all of that data into a document called a **credit report**. A credit report has two parts: your **credit history** and your **credit score**. Your history lists what accounts you have or have had as well as your payment record. If you have ever made a late payment, it's on your credit report. A credit score is like a grade and it can range from 300 to 850. The higher the number, the better your credit. In order to be considered as having good credit, you will need a score of 700 or higher.

Anyone with a financial interest in you can request your credit report, not just lenders. Landlords, utility companies, insurance companies, even potential employers have an interest in knowing how well you have managed your money.

To obtain a FREE copy of your credit report, visit: http://www.annualcreditreport.com

Want to get a great job when you graduate? It is not uncommon for an employer to review your credit history as part of your background check before they hire you. If you have a poor credit history a company might think twice about hiring you. Landlords and utility companies care too. They want to be paid on time, and if your credit report shows you have a history of late payments, they may not want to rent to you or they may charge you additional deposits. Even insurance companies will charge you more if you have bad credit. Overall, you can expect to pay more for everything if you have a poor credit history.

Believe it or not, reviewing your credit report can actually help you improve your credit. You are entitled to one free credit report each year, and it's a good idea to get in the habit of checking it now for a number of reasons. If there are any mistakes on your credit report, you can get it corrected long before it becomes a potential issue. Mistakes can be disputed and the credit reporting agency has to correct them. It's easier to fix them early than have to explain later—especially if a job or an important loan approval is hanging in the balance.

Credit scores are calculated based on the types of credit you have, the amount of credit you have available, the amount of debt you have, and the length of time you've had it. The analysis will tell you what adjustments you can make to improve your score.

Possibly the most important reason to check your credit report is that it can alert you if your identity has been stolen. **Identity theft** is one of the fastest growing crimes in the U.S. and college students are one of the most targeted groups. Identity theft occurs when an imposter uses personal information (social security, driver's license, birth date) to assume your identity, usually for financial gain. You may not know that someone has your identity until it is too late. Checking your credit report on a regular basis will allow you to spot any new accounts that you didn't open.

You are not responsible for any charges incurred if your identity is stolen. Still, it can take years to find all of the accounts and it is up to you to get everything removed from your credit. A few simple steps to protect your personal information now can save you a lot of time and heartache.

1. Shred documents with personally identifiable information like name, address, family information, and account numbers.
2. Keep all documents that you can't shred, like your birth certificate and social security card, in a locked drawer or box.
3. Don't say social security, driver's license, or account numbers out loud where they can be overheard.
4. Watch for shoulder surfers. These are people who lurk in public places trying to take pictures of your ID or credit cards as you use them. Cover PIN number keypads with your free hand when you use them.
5. Go paperless. Many bills and bank statements can be viewed online. Choose the paperless option to have your paper billing stopped.
6. Clear browser histories and saved passwords from your computer. If you get a new computer, shred the data on your old hard drive. If you don't know what that means, find your nearest computer geek and ask them how to do it.

Chapter Summary

College is a great place to begin your financial journey. The financial decisions you make now will have an impact on your life for years to come. Knowing where your money is coming from and where it is going is the foundation to a stress-free college life. Well, except for maybe during finals week. By taking the time to develop a simple budget, sticking to it, and staying out of credit card debt, you will stay on track and broke weekends will be a thing of the past.

"It is more rewarding to watch money change the world than watch it accumulate."

Gloria Steinem

Political and social activist

■ KEY TERMS

Budget: An estimate of expected income and expenses over a determined period of time

Co-signer: A person who jointly signs a loan document to guarantee repayment on behalf of the borrower if the borrower defaults

Cost of attendance: The estimated cost for a student to attend a college full-time for an entire year including tuition, books, housing, meals, and personal expenses

Credit: Contractual agreement where a borrower receives money or goods and agrees to repay these in installments at a later date with interest

Credit history: A record of an individual's past of borrowing and repaying money

Credit report: A document which details an individual's credit history and indicates their present credit score

Credit score: A numeric measurement on a scale from 300 to 850 which indicates a person's creditworthiness or capacity to repay debts

Default: Failure to repay a loan

Direct loan: Government-supported, low-interest loan that must be repaid after a student graduates or leaves school

Expenses: Costs or outflow of money

Financial aid: Money provided for students to help pay for their college expenses, usually in the form of scholarships, grants, loans, or work-study

Fixed expenses: Costs which are constant in amount and payment date from month to month

Free Application for Federal Student Aid (FAFSA): An application filed by college students annually to determine their eligibility for federal financial aid

Grant: A sum of money which is awarded by an organization for some particular use and which does not have to be paid back

Identity theft: A type of fraud in which one person uses personal information to assume the identity of someone else, usually with the intended purpose of financial gain

Income: The sum of monies received from all sources, including work pay, financial aid, etc.

Installment loan: A type of credit for which a fixed amount is initially borrowed and is then repaid by regular payments of a predetermined amount

Interest: A fee that a borrower is charged for the use of financial resources

Line of credit: A specific amount of money that a lender makes available for a borrower to be used at the borrower's discretion

Loan: Borrowed money which must be paid back with interest

Minimum monthly payment: The lowest amount that must be paid on an outstanding balance each month

Parent PLUS loan: Borrowed and repaid by a parent on behalf of a dependent student

Revolving credit: A line of credit which is renewed as the debt is paid off

Subsidized loan: Interest free until it goes into repayment

Third-party agencies: Government agencies which provide financial assistance to college students based on specific circumstances

Tuition: The specified fee students are charged to receive instruction at a school, college, or university

Unsubsidized loan: Accrues interest from the time of lending

Variable expenses: Costs which vary in amount and/or lack a regular schedule from month to month

NOTES

"There are people who have money and people who are rich."

Coco Chanel

French fashion designer

■ CAMPUS RESOURCES

ColonelOne Card Office
http://www.financialaffairs.eku.edu/ColonelOneCard
Powell Student Center, 859-622-2179

Financial Aid
http://finaid.eku.edu
Whitlock Building, room 251, 859-622-2361

Scholarship Office
http://scholarships.eku.edu
Whitlock Building, room 346, 859-622-8032

Student Employment
http://finaid.eku.edu/student-employment-services
Whitlock Building, room 251, 859-622-1760

University Housing
http://housing.eku.edu
Whitlock Building, room 552, 859-622-1515

■ REFERENCES

BrainyQuote. (n.d.). *BrainyQuote.com.* Retrieved June 9, 2011, from http://www.brainyquote.com/

Day, J.C., & Newburger, E.C. (2002, July). Figure 1: Synthetic work-life earnings estimates for full-time, year-round workers by educational attainment based on 1997–1999 work experience [graph]. In *The big payoff: educational attainment and synthetic estimates of work-life earnings* (Current Population Reports, Special Studies, P23–210). Washington, D.C.: U.S. Census Bureau, Commerce Department. Retrieved March 18, 2011, from U.S. Census Bureau website: http://www.census.gov/prod/2002pubs/p23–210.pdf

EKU Office of Student Financial Assistance. (n.d.). *Eastern Kentucky University Financial Aid.* Retrieved March 18, 2011, from http://finaid.eku.edu/

Information for Financial Aid Professionals (IFAP). (2002, January 8). Applying for financial aid is as easy as 1-2-3 [graphic]. Retrieved March 18, 2011, from IFAP website: http://www.ifap.ed.gov/eannouncements/0107FOTWebandPINSite.html

RESOURCES & REFERENCES

NOTES

"Anybody who thinks money will make you happy, hasn't got money."

David Geffen

American businessman

Chapter Six

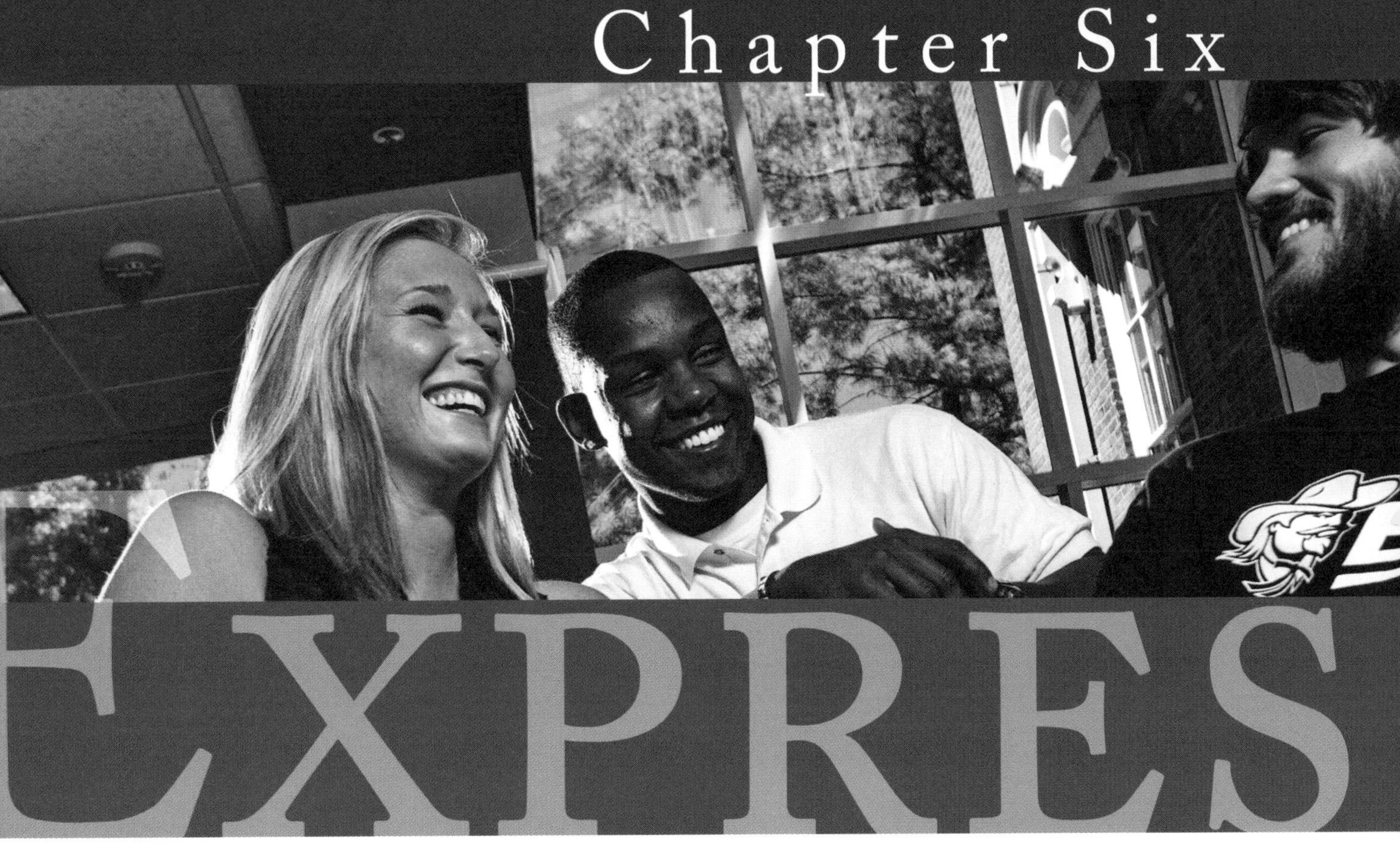

After mastering the content in this chapter you will:

- Know the characteristics of effective oral and written communication
- Understand the value of expressing oneself with clarity, accuracy, and precision
- Be able to identify strategies to construct an appropriate and effective presentation
- Appreciate the importance of doing quality research before communication occurs

Fundamental Question

- What do I need to know and do to become a competent communicator?

Essential Principles

- Connection with Others
- Research and Information Literacy Skills
- Written Communication Skills
- Non-Written Communication Skills

"Bad human communication leaves us less room to grow."

Rowan D. Williams

Anglican bishop, poet, and theologian

6

Express

Chapter Six

Thrive

Chapter Nine

Chapter Nine

THRIVE

After mastering the content in this chapter you will:

- Be able to utilize the EKU wellness resources/services
- Understand healthy nutrition principles
- Understand the benefits of physical activity
- Be able to identify strategies for improving mental health
- Be able to implement techniques to effectively manage stress
- Examine consequences associated with high-risk behaviors
- Be aware of personal safety and security at EKU

Fundamental Question

- How do I become a healthier student?

Essential Principles

- Sound Decision Making
- Stress Management
- Prevention

"Healthy citizens are the greatest asset any country can have."

Winston Churchill

English statesman, British Prime Minister

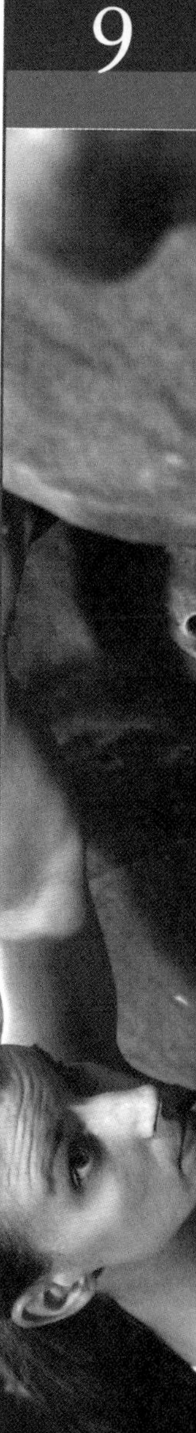

What Is Wellness?

Success in college, as in life, centers on being able to function well in your environment. The ability to do your best is the result of the mind and body working together. How you feel and think is a reflection of your overall wellness. Among other things, your health status dictates your ability to attend classes and social functions, to concentrate, to manage stress, and to maintain a balance in your daily living to accomplish academic and social goals.

Wellness is much more than just the absence of illness. Even without disease, factors such as inactivity, a poor diet, or not getting enough sleep can deprive you of feeling your best. The way you live, or your lifestyle, has a significant influence on your health.

Wellness is a dynamic characteristic of our lives; it changes daily. Wellness is also multidimensional. Visualize wellness as being made up of six dimensions or parts as listed below. We can talk about the dimensions separately, but they can never really be separated one from another; any change made to one dimension affects each of the others. The goal is to balance all the dimensions so you can live well today and assure a better quality of life as you get older.

The six dimensions of wellness are physical, emotional, intellectual, social, spiritual, and environmental.

➲ **Check out these courses promoting wellness!**

PHE 180 "Wellness Experience"
Participate in activities based on current interest.

PHE 390 "Lifetime Activity Series"
Participate in activities for lifetime enjoyment.

HEA 285 "Health Across the Lifespan"
Develop wellness strategies for healthful living today and in the future.

■ THE SIX DIMENSIONS OF WELLNESS

- Physical wellness has to do with strength, endurance, flexibility, and the ability to resist disease and/or recover from illness.
- Emotional wellness refers to the ability to properly handle emotions and feelings.
- Intellectual wellness deals with the ability to learn information and apply it to make healthy and rational decisions.
- Social wellness is the ability to form close relationships, fit into social groups, and function well in society.
- Spiritual wellness involves the belief that we all belong to something greater than ourselves and can contribute something special to the world. Spirituality includes the concepts of faith, optimism, and altruism.
- Environmental wellness means taking care of the planet by playing an active role in protecting the environment. Keeping the air, land, and water clean is an important goal.

➲Social Wellness:
EKU has over 150 Registered Student Organizations (RSOs) including Greek chapters, political organizations, and student interest clubs. For a complete list, visit http://eku.orgsync.com/

EKU is working to be environmentally conscious. You can find information on how to get involved at http://www.green.eku.edu

Each of these dimensions has its own specific definition, yet they are all interdependent as they affect one another. Your lifestyle habits can affect one dimension which causes changes in another. For example, if you do not get enough sleep, your physical wellness will be primarily affected. Yet the tiredness and other health side effects of sleep deprivation can bring about consequences such as emotional distress, a negative effect to your emotional wellness, and difficulty concentrating and learning, negative effects to your intellectual wellness.

Keep in mind these six dimensions of wellness and how they function as a unit as you read about the steps to creating a healthy lifestyle.

➲Wellness Enhancing Courses

Spiritual:
PHI 240 "Philosophy of Religion"
Study of religious language, experience, and ethics, the nature and existence of God and the problem of evil.

REL 360 "Religion and Global Ethics"
A study of recent proposals for a global ethics and the theory and practice of interreligious dialogue.

REL 301"World Religions"
Study of the basic notions found in the world's great religions.

Environmental:
BIO 317 "Conservation of Wildlife Resources"
Introduction to conservation of plants and animals.

GLY 303 "Global Environmental Obstacles"
Study of Earth's complex interconnected systems that cycle elements, water, and earth materials over time.

Steps to Creating a Healthy Lifestyle

Although there are many habits and behaviors that work together to create a healthy lifestyle, there are a few that are especially important for the new college student. These key steps will help you have a healthy lifestyle in college and after graduation.

Get Enough Sleep: Your body needs time to recharge. Your memory and thinking will be clearer with a good night's rest. Avoid pulling all-nighters before big exams; if you are constantly sleep deprived, eventually your grades and your health will suffer.

Eat a Nutritious Diet: It can be challenging to eat a nutritious diet while in college. It's okay to splurge on a burger and fries occasionally, but try to eat more fruits, vegetables, and whole grain breads and pasta rather than meats and unhealthy "comfort foods."

Be Physically Active Every Day: There are many campus resources available for students to get active. Exercise can help you maintain a healthy weight, keep your heart strong, protect against osteoporosis later in life, and improve your memory skills.

Manage Stress: Stress is a natural part of college life but it can be managed. Most important is to manage your time well. Finding a balance between work, school, and socializing will help keep your stress levels under control.

Avoid Alcohol and Drug Use: The consequences of excessive and underage drinking affect virtually all college campuses and college students, whether they choose to drink or not. Death, injury, assault, sexual abuse, unsafe sex, academic problems, health problems, suicide attempts, drunk driving, vandalism, property damage, alcohol abuse and dependence, and legal problems are all consequences associated with alcohol use.

Protect Yourself from Sexually Transmitted Infections: Sexually active adolescents (ages 10 to 19) and young adults (ages 20 to 24) are at higher risk for getting sexually transmitted infections (STIs) (CDC, DSTDP, 2010).

"Never hurry. Take plenty of exercise. Always be cheerful. Take all the sleep you need. You may expect to be well."
James Freeman Clarke
Author and theologian

In the next few pages, we will talk about each of these steps in more detail as well as the ways in which the facilities and staff at EKU can help you with the goal of achieving a healthy lifestyle.

Sleep and the College Student

Many studies show that sleep deprivation is a serious problem among college students (American Academy of Sleep Medicine, 2007; National Sleep Foundation, 2009). Sleep deprivation results in impaired coordination, accidents, and missed time at work and school. With the hectic pace of college life, many students are tempted to cut back on sleep in order to get everything done. However, doing so can often hurt rather than help academic performance and can negatively affect your physical health.

■ SLEEP AND ACADEMIC SUCCESS

Numerous studies have shown that a good night's sleep triggers changes in the brain that help to improve memory (Schlaug, Aslop, Gaab, & Stickgold, 2005). There are still some questions looming as to the specific role of sleep in forming and storing memories. However, the general consensus is that continuous, uninterrupted sleep throughout a whole night is optimal for learning and memory.

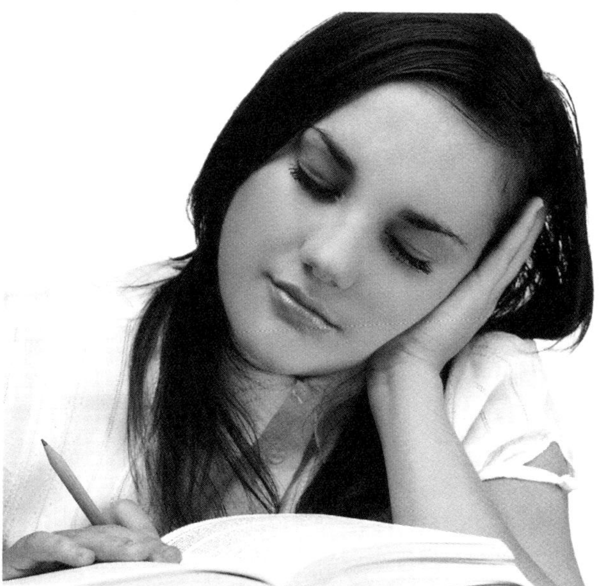

Sleep deprivation can negatively affect your cognitive functioning, accuracy, alertness, and concentration. Students with symptoms of sleep disorders are more likely to receive poor grades (American Academy of Sleep Medicine, 2007). After you go to sleep, the brain consolidates and practices what you learned during the day so that you will actually remember those lessons. That means sleep after a lesson is learned is as important as getting a good night's sleep before a test or exam. College students who pull all-nighters are more likely to have a lower GPA than students who consistently get good sleep. A common "fix" utilized by college students to address all-nighters is sleeping late on weekends. Yet, those students who apply this "fix" are still more likely to perform poorly in the classroom (American Academy of Sleep Medicine, 2007).

TIPS TO PREVENT WEIGHT GAIN

- Be physically active. Burn more calories by increasing your daily activity level. Establish an exercise routine now!
- Take care of yourself. Stress can lead to snacking or binging. Prioritizing your needs and planning ahead can help you deal with stress without overeating.
- Eat more fruits and vegetables. Per calorie, fruits and vegetables are some of the most nutritious foods you can choose. The fiber and water in fruits and vegetables help you feel full so eating these foods regularly often results in a lower calorie intake.
- Eat smaller portions. Food is everywhere at college—parties, meetings, snacks, fast food restaurants, vending machines. Develop a habit of taking smaller portions to avoid eating more calories than your body needs.
- Eat sweets and fried foods less often. Adding sugar or fat to foods adds calories without nutrients—"empty calories."

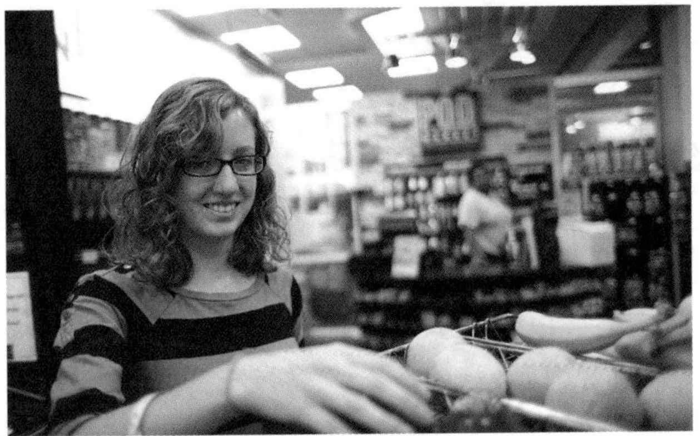

Mental Health

■ THRIVING AND SURVIVING IN COLLEGE

How a student experiences college is unique to each individual, but there is no doubt that adjusting to this new environment can present a number of challenges. It can be seen as a time of transition, in which new relationships and new expectations are formed and added stressors are common everyday experiences. For some, this will result in distress and mental health issues, while others will rise to the challenge and excel, despite the added stressors. This section focuses on how your mental health can impact your academic success at EKU and the resources available to help you.

■ WHAT IS MENTAL HEALTH?

Mental health refers to a state of well-being in which one can effectively cope with everyday stressors, have a good command of one's own strengths and abilities, maintain active and fulfilling social connections, and be productive in their everyday activities.

Maintaining good mental health is no easy task. Most college students have to juggle:

- New living arrangements
- New relationships
- An active social life
- Stress of maintaining good grades
- Holding down jobs

■ STRESS AND ANXIETY

Students who are experiencing high levels of stress are among the most common visitors to the EKU Counseling Center. Anxiety among college students is not uncommon and can result in more serious psychological issues. Much of this anxiety stems from taking and studying for exams, grade competition, and the large amount of content that needs to be mastered in a small amount of time (Abouserie, 1994). Nationwide, over 25 percent of college students say they feel overwhelmed (Sax, Lindholm, Astin, Korn, & Mahoney, 2002).

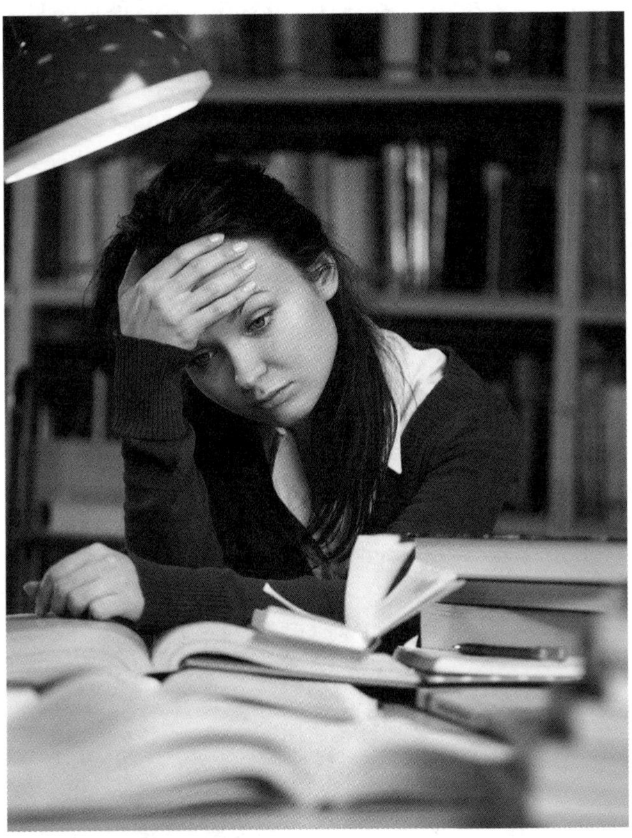

What Is Stress?

Stress is defined in different ways by different researchers. In the early years of research, it was defined as readjustment to changes in life, whether those changes are "good" or "bad" (Holmes & Rahe, 1967). Other researchers talk of stress as being any event or part of life that involves some threat to our self-esteem (Paykel & Cooper, 1992). As you can see, there are different ideas of what stress is.

"A healthy outside starts from the inside."

Robert Urich

American actor

Thus, we are left with the idea that stress is in the eye of the beholder. Though stress may be hard to define in the abstract, each of us knows it when we feel it, and what might be "stressful" for one person may not be for another.

What Are the Common Outcomes of Stress?

Although the results will be different for each individual person, there are a few effects of stress that are common for most people and are divided into three categories: biological, psychological, and behavioral. These effects tend to arise primarily from the negative type of distress and they vary according to the level of stress being shouldered.

Biological effects of stress can include:

- Headaches
- Upset stomach
- Difficulty concentrating
- Problems sleeping

In addition, people who have medical conditions like asthma, seizure disorders, heart conditions, and diabetes usually experience more frequent and more severe episodes of illness when they are experiencing high levels of stress.

Psychological effects of stress can include:

- Feelings of nervousness
- Worry and doubt
- Racing pulse
- Sweating
- Dizziness
- Panic attacks
- Difficulty making decisions
- Difficulty concentrating
- Feelings of hopelessness
- Feelings of helplessness
- Feelings of worthlessness
- Dissatisfaction with self
- Sleeping and eating disturbances
- Complaints of physical illnesses

Behavioral effects of stress can include:

- Forgetfulness
- Irritability/suspiciousness
- Rushing and subsequent mistakes
- Substance abuse

(American Institute of Stress, n.d.)

➲Online Resources to Help with Stress Management:

- http://www.dr-bob.org/vpc
- http://www.aboutstressmanagement.com
- http://www.mindtools.com/smpage.html
- http://helpguide.org/
- http://www.webmd.com/balance/stress-management

How Can I Manage Stress in My Life?

The first step in stress management is to determine which events and situations are under your control. Being in an auto accident that is not your fault is out of your control. However, if you find out the first week of class that you will have four research papers due in different classes at the end of the semester, and you wait until the last two weeks of the semester to start working on them, you have a situation which is under your control.

In addition, managing your thinking patterns related to the experience of stress can help you control the amount of distress you feel. Recognizing that, as a human, the only thing you can be perfect at is being imperfect can help you accept your own failings and experience less distress in life. When you come to the conclusion that you cannot control other people's thoughts, feelings, or behavior, it takes a real burden off your shoulders. Likewise, when you recognize that you cannot do everything that everyone wants you to, or be exactly what everyone wants you to be, you can relax and simply be yourself (Mayo Clinic staff, 2010).

➲Want to learn more about mental health?

HEA 380 "Mental Health Education"
Learn to understand mental and emotional health.

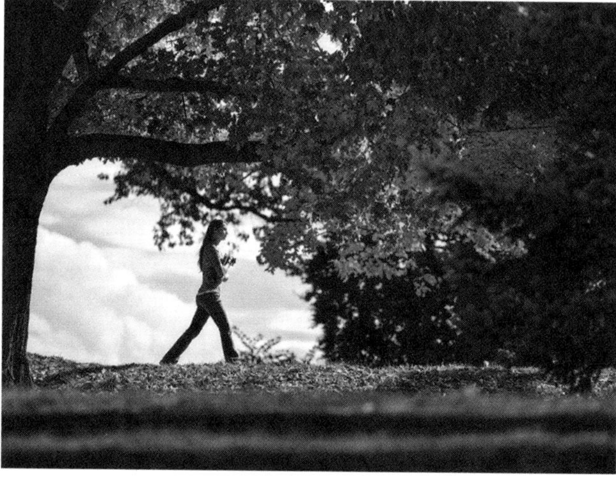

10 STRESS BUSTER TIPS

1. Eliminate unrealistic expectations: Think "I am going to do my best" rather than "I have to be perfect."
2. Change your internal language: Instead of saying "I have to..." say "I choose to..."
3. Take care of your body: Eat well, sleep enough, and exercise regularly.
4. Learn to accept what you cannot change.
5. Work off stress: If you are angry or upset try to blow off steam physically by running, biking, etc.
6. Learn relaxation techniques: Practice them regularly.
7. Keep a journal: Observe when you are stressed, the causes, your responses, and the outcomes.
8. Share your concern with someone: Talk to a friend, a parent, and/or a counselor.
9. Do something for others: Consider doing something for someone else and get your mind off yourself.
10. Develop a hobby or interest: Find something that you really enjoy and pursue it.

■ DEPRESSION

What Is Depression?

We all feel sad or discouraged from time to time. However, when such feelings occur for two weeks or more, it may be depression. Approximately two-fifths of college students report that they frequently feel overwhelmed and up to 53 percent report that they have struggled with depression since their first year in college (Furr et al., 2001).

Depressed college students suffer from feelings of emptiness and inadequacy, report more somatic concerns and illnesses, and have poorer grades than students who are not depressed (American College Health Association, 2002).

If you feel that you are suffering from anxiety and depression, know that you are not alone. Many students feel stressed and overwhelmed by all of the changes that come with going to college. There are many campus resources that are available to help you deal with stress, anxiety, and depression; EKU's Counseling Center is a great place to start. Be alert to the early warning signs of depression listed below and use the four strategies given in the following section to help manage your mental health.

Early Warning Signs of Depression

- Excessive procrastination
- Decrease in the quality of work
- Too frequent office visits (dependency)
- Listlessness, sleeping in class
- Marked changes in personal hygiene
- Impaired speech/disjointed thoughts
- Threats regarding self or others
- Marked changes in behavior

(Office of Student Life Studies, 2000)

The five most prevalent mental disorders affecting college students are:

- Alcohol use disorders (20.37%)
- Personality disorders (17.68%)
- Nicotine dependence (14.55%)
- Anxiety disorders (11.94%)
- Mood disorders (10.62%)

(Blanco, Okuda, Wright, Hasin, Grant, Liu, & Olfson, 2008)

Suggestions to Help You Cope with Anxiety and Depression

There are many campus resources available to help you deal with stress, anxiety, and depression. The following four strategies can also help you manage your mental health.

1. Stay connected to others: All human beings have a need to feel connected to others, and feeling such connections is a particularly powerful tool for maintaining mental health (Pollock, 2004).

"Depression is probably the most common mental health problem that college students face these days."

Richard Kadison, MD

Chief, Mental Health Services, Harvard

2. Engage in action empathy: Action empathy occurs when one person demonstrates their friendship to another through their behavior instead of words (Pollock, 2006). For example, spend time with your friends, actively help your friends, or back up your deserving friends when they are in a crisis. You will likely find that this behavior is reciprocated to you just when you need it most.

3. Maintain a relationship with your parents: Keeping in touch during both the good times and bad will help your family to understand your daily life and to be better informed and more capable of helping if a problem arises.

4. Develop positive coping behaviors: Coping strategies that involve taking an action to deal with the stressor, accepting the inevitability of the stressor, and reframing the stressor in a positive manner (e.g., the worst thing that can happen is…) can minimize stress and decrease possible mental health issues. On the other hand, coping strategies that involve avoiding or worrying excessively about the stressor have been found to decrease mental health (Brougham, Zail, Mendoza, & Miller, 2009).

EKU's Counseling Center

THE COLLEGE YEARS AND COUNSELING

The college years are very exciting and yet can be overwhelming. The Counseling Center staff is available to assist you with any challenges or important issues you want to address. Psychologists and counselors at the Counseling Center have training and expertise in helping college students address personal, social, and academic challenges. EKU counselors are non-judgmental and great at listening and understanding, and all counseling sessions are confidential.

WHAT ARE THE COUNSELING CENTER SERVICES?

Counseling Center services include individual counseling, group counseling (up to 8 students), career counseling, grief counseling, substance abuse services, consultation, helpful workshops, and referrals when a different service or level of service is needed. Psychiatric services are available on a limited basis in conjunction with counseling.

What Happens in Counseling?

The Counseling Center's professional staff assists students in addressing the stresses and challenges that interfere with their adjustment to university life and/or interfere with achieving their goals and potential. Students may seek counseling with concerns about a variety of issues including: stress, managing time, improving self-esteem, relationship issues, test anxiety, lack of confidence, shyness, home sickness, substance abuse, depression, anxiety, career choice, family issues, sexual assault, loss, trauma, sexual identity, adjusting to college, and many others.

➲ Workshops at the Counseling Center

Helpful tips on a variety of subjects including:

Time management	Test anxiety
Study skills	Substance abuse
Stress management	Healthy habits
Procrastination	

Watch for advertisements!

Alcohol and Other Drugs

Students often assume all college students drink heavily. This assumption is false. According to the 2010 Core Alcohol and Drug Survey conducted by the EKU Substance Abuse Committee (2010), 51% of EKU students surveyed reported not drinking alcohol. The majority of EKU students (62%) reported they had not engaged in binge drinking in the past week. Binge or heavy drinking is defined as five or more drinks at one sitting.

It is risky to assume that heavy drinking is normal and that it will not affect you in serious ways. In fact, college students who drink alcohol cite hangovers, missed classes, and poor academic performance as consequences of alcohol consumption. Other serious consequences can include injury, sexual assault, arrests (i.e., DUI or underage drinking), or an alcohol abuse disorder. Due to student alcohol consumption 599,000 students are injured, 97,000 students are sexually victimized, and 110,000 students are arrested yearly (Hingson, Heeren, Zakocs, Kopstein, & Wechsler, 2002; Hingson, Heeren, Winter, & Wechsler, 2005).

■ WHAT IS LOW-RISK VS. HIGH-RISK DRINKING?

The standards for low-risk vs. high-risk drinking are based on the number of drinks in a given time period. So the first thing we have to establish is what is considered "one drink." According to the National Institute on Alcohol Abuse and Alcoholism (2010), one "standard drink" equals one 12-ounce beer (5% alcohol), one 5-ounce glass of wine (12% alcohol), or 1.5 ounces of 80-proof liquor (40% alcohol).

One Drink Equivalents

To learn how alcohol affects you, see the following websites:

http://counseling.eku.edu/blood-alcohol-levels-and-you

http://www.ou.edu/oupd/oupd-bac-chart-02-20-2007.pdf

http://www.ou.edu/oupd/bac.htm

The NIAAA low-risk drinking limits in the following chart must be viewed with reference to this definition of "one drink."

Low-Risk Drinking Limits

According to the NIAAA (2010), to stay within the "low-risk" drinking category, you must stay within BOTH the daily AND weekly limits on the following chart.

Low-Risk Drinking Limits

Female ♀	Male ♂
Should not exceed:	Should not exceed:
3 Drinks Daily	4 Drinks Daily
OR	OR
7 Drinks Weekly	14 Drinks Weekly

To be low-risk you must stay within both the daily and weekly limits.

©Hayden-McNeil, LLC

The NIAAA (2010) states, "For healthy adults in general, drinking more than these single-day or weekly limits is considered 'at-risk' or 'heavy' drinking."

"Like any college, there are parties all the time and you can definitely go and socialize with friends. But drinking and using drugs doesn't have to be part of your life to have a good time."

Erica Stormes
Public Relations

"When you are young and healthy, it never occurs to you that in a single second your whole life could change."

Annette Funicello

American actress

About one in four people who exceed these limits already experience alcoholism or alcohol abuse, and the rest are at greater risk for developing these and other problems. Individual risks vary, and some people may have problems at even lower amounts than these. This is especially true of people who drink too quickly or who have health problems.

Remember, "low-risk" is NOT "no risk." "Based on your health and how alcohol affects you, you may need to drink less or not at all" (NIAAA, 2010).

➲**Some activities you can participate in to learn more about substance use and abuse:**

- Take E-Chug and E-Toke
- Attend an alcohol or drug awareness event
- Use Colonel Walk

Online Alcohol Information Resources

EKU Policy on Alcohol

http://transportation.ky.gov/driver-licensing/pages/dui-laws-in-kentucky.aspx

KY State Laws

- http://transportation.ky.gov/driver-licensing/pages/dui-laws-in-kentucky.aspx
- Interactive website on alcohol's effects on your body over time: http://www.collegedrinkingprevention.gov/collegestudents/anatomy/interactivebody.aspx
- Interactive website on how patterns of drinking impact risk of alcohol abuse: http://rethinkingdrinking.niaaa.nih.gov/whatcountsdrink/howmuchistoomuch.asp
- Website with excellent information about what alcohol poisoning is and what to do if someone has alcohol poisoning: http://www.collegedrinkingprevention.gov/OtherAlcoholInformation/factsAboutAlcoholPoisoning.aspx

➲**What can I do if I need help or am worried about a friend?**

- Educate yourself.
- Tell your RA, RHC, friend, instructor, and/or family.
- Contact the EKU Counseling Center: http://www.counseling.eku.edu

Sexual Health

The decisions you make today about sex can impact you for the rest of your life. Even though sex is a natural part of life and a basic human drive, there can be consequences. This section will provide you with information on how to communicate about sex and ways you can protect yourself against unwanted pregnancy and sexually transmitted infections (STIs). The choices you make about sex are personal, but being equipped with relevant and accurate information can help you make responsible decisions.

HUMAN SEXUALITY CLASSES

POL 446 "The Politics of Sex": Effect of sex on social and political institutions, public policies, and court rulings. Issues may include pornography, sexual and gender discrimination, domestic violence, reproductive rights, and gay rights.

WGS 232 "Identity and Sexuality": Explores the changing attitudes about and among men/women and their effect on choices and interpersonal relationships.

SOC 399 "Gender and Society": Emphasis on relationship between the social construction of gender and the experiences of women and men in societies.

■ COMMUNICATION AND SEX

No one should be coerced or pressured into engaging in sexual activity that he/she does not feel comfortable about. Sexual activity presents a myriad of issues and potential risks that may be both immediate and long-term. These include an unplanned pregnancy, sexually transmitted infections (STIs), HIV, or a change in the dynamics of a relationship to name just a few.

One way to reduce the risk of an exploitative or manipulative relationship is to engage in open communication with your partner. Before a couple becomes sexually active, both partners should communicate accurate information about current or previous STIs, sexual behaviors that each feels comfortable/uncomfortable engaging in, HIV status, and form(s) of contraception that would be used. Partners that fail to engage in these conversations prior to becoming sexually active may make emotionally based decisions that are not consistent with their values and beliefs. While it may be difficult to initiate conversation on topics related to sexuality, it is part of being a sexually responsible adult.

The use of alcohol or other mind-altering drugs is a major barrier to communication. Use of these substances seriously impairs the sending and receiving of both verbal and nonverbal communication. Each year countless sexual assaults/rapes are reported on college campuses. Often, the victim or perpetrator was under the influence of an intoxicant during the incident (Greenburg, Bruess, & Conklin, 2011, pp. 66–91).

➲**Some short-term effects of marijuana**:

- Slowed reflexes and poorer depth perception
- Sleepiness
- Impaired short-term memory
- Impaired ability to complete tasks requiring coordination and concentration
- Increased heart rate
- Decreased social inhibition
- Difficulty keeping track of time
- Risk of anxiety (even panic attacks)
- Paranoia

(NIDA, 2010)

■ CONTRACEPTION

Abstinence is the only one hundred percent effective method to prevent an unplanned pregnancy or the transmission of a sexually transmitted infection. Couples that decide to become sexually active, but do not want to experience pregnancy, must decide on a specific contraceptive method. This is an extremely important decision and one that requires both partners to critically examine the various methods available, specific need (pregnancy and/or STI prevention), effectiveness, cost, ease of use, availability, reversible/permanent, advantages/disadvantages, potential side effects, and the likelihood of using the method consistently and correctly each time. Some common methods of contraception are in Table 9-1.

Table 9-1. Common contraceptive methods.

COMMON CONTRACEPTIVE METHODS			
Method	Protection	Pregnancy Prevention Effectiveness (If used consistently and correctly)	Availability
Male Condoms[1]	YES	80–90%	Over the counter or from Student Health Services
Female Condoms[1]	YES	75–82%	Over the counter
Birth Control Pills[2]	NO	99%	Prescription
Contraceptive Patch[2]	NO	100%	Prescription
Depo-Provera[3]	NO	99%	Prescription
Emergency Contraception[2]	NO	75%	Over the counter or from a pharmacist

([1]ASHA, n.d.)([2]Greenburg et al., 2011, pp. 174–213)([3]Nihira, 2010)

■ SEXUALLY TRANSMITTED INFECTIONS

Sexually transmitted infections are a risk associated with sexual activity. STIs may be caused by bacteria, viruses, or parasites, and may result from contact with bodily fluids such as semen, vaginal secretions, blood, or direct skin contact with lesions, sores, or parasites. More information on some of the most common STIs is provided in Table 9-2.

"What the public expects and what is healthy for an individual are two very different things."

Esther Williams

American competitive swimmer and actress

Table 9-2. Common sexually transmitted infections.

MOST COMMON SEXUALLY TRANSMITTED INFECTIONS			
Name	How It Is Spread	Symptoms	Prevention/Treatment
HPV (Human Papillomavirus)	Direct contact with infected skin	Usually none but can cause genital warts or cancer	Prevent with Gardasil vaccine; NO CURE—medication can remove visible genital warts
Genital Herpes (Herpes Simplex Virus)	Direct contact with infected skin, even if no outbreak is present	Often none but can cause painful blisters/sores, fever, and swollen glands	NO CURE—medication may control outbreak symptoms
Chlamydia	Oral, anal, and vaginal sex or inherited from mother	Usually none but can cause painful urination, vaginal or penile discharge, fever, nausea, and abdominal pain	Antibiotics
Gonorrhea	Oral, anal, and vaginal sex or inherited from mother	Often none but can cause vaginal or penile discharge and painful urination	Antibiotics
HIV	Oral, anal, and vaginal sex, sharing tattoo or drug needles, or inherited from mother	No early symptoms or flu-like symptoms that are often unnoticed, rash, and weakened immune system	NO CURE—symptom control with AIDS medicine—lifetime treatment required

(Chart info obtained from: HHS, OPHS, 2009)

If you suspect you may have an STI, you should see your health care provider and be tested. Unfortunately, many college students incorrectly assume that it will simply go away. The problem is that with many STIs the infection may become dormant for a period of time and the student thinks he/she is OK, when in actuality, it has advanced or progressed to another phase.

■ SEXUAL HEALTH RESOURCES

A multitude of resources are available to EKU students either on campus or in the local community.

Local Resources

EKU Student Health Services provides pregnancy testing, free condoms, pregnancy counseling, and referral to OB-GYN health care providers. Contact http://www.healthservices.eku.edu, 859-622-1761. Located in the Rowlett Building, room 103.

The Madison County Health Department provides physical exams, pregnancy testing, various forms of birth control, OB-GYN referrals, and STI screening and education. Contact http://www.madisoncountyhealthdept.org or 859-623-7312.

Planned Parenthood, Bluegrass Health Center (Located in Lexington, Kentucky) offers birth control, emergency contraception, HIV testing, HPV and hepatitis vaccines, LGBT services, pregnancy testing, abortion referral, adoption referral, prenatal services, and STI testing and treatment. Contact http://www.plannedparenthood.org or 859-252-8494.

Richmond Pregnancy Help Center provides free pregnancy tests, OB-GYN referrals, and information on other local resources. Contact http://www.madisonphc.org or 859-624-3942.

Students at regional campuses should contact their local health departments.

Hotlines

In addition to these local resources, you also have the option of contacting one of the various hotline phone numbers dedicated to a specific topic. Upon contacting the hotline, you will speak with a trained professional to answer questions, provide additional information, or identify services in the local area.

- AIDS National Hotline 1-800-342-2437
- Domestic Violence Hotline 1-800-799-7233
- National Abortion Federation 1-800-772-9100
- National Resource Center on Domestic Violence 1-800-537-2238
- Gay and Lesbian National Hotline 1-888-843-4564
- Gay and Transgender Hate Crime Hotline 1-800-616-HATE
- National STD Hotline 1-800-227-8922
- Teen Dating Abuse Help 1-866-331-9474

Student Health Services

Sometimes, despite our best efforts, we fall prey to circumstances which hinder our performance and threaten our progress. Illness, injury, and mental health issues can plague us. EKU has many resources that you can call upon to assist you; Student Health Services is one of them.

Staffed by physicians, nurse practitioners, RNs, and CMAs, SHS sees students for problems such as sore throats, ear aches, cough and cold symptoms, headaches, stomach upsets, urinary tract infections, gynecologic problems, rashes, etc. SHS evaluates and treats injuries, opens and drains abscesses, diagnoses and treats sexually transmitted infections, and performs a number of simple lab tests.

➲Visiting Student Health Services (SHS)

Student Health Services is located on the first floor of the Rowlett Building; its front entrance faces the intersection of Kit Carson and Park Drives. The phone number is 859-622-1761. All visits to the SHS are confidential; protected health information is not shared with anyone without your consent.

Fees for Services

All services provided at SHS, with the exception of immunizations and TB skin test, are free to all enrolled students.
All tests obtained at an outside facility or sent to Quest Diagnostics will incur a charge, which must be paid for by the student.

Recommended Vaccinations for College Students

- Meningitis (especially for freshmen living in residence halls)
- Hepatitis B *
- Flu (yearly)
- MMR—Measles, Mumps, and Rubella *
- Pertussis (whooping cough) *

*Available at the Student Health Center at a cost. (The flu shot can be obtained at the local health department.)

➲ATTENTION:

For life-threatening emergencies, injuries, or illnesses, please dial 911.

■ STUDENT WELLNESS RESOURCE CENTER

The Student Wellness Resource Center enhances the health of EKU students through health promotion, educational programs, services, and resources including those below.

HEAT

The Health Education Action Team (HEAT) Peer Education program is geared toward empowering students with knowledge and facts concerning health issues. HEAT Peer Educators coordinate campus health awareness events and provide health education programming upon request to residence halls, student organizations, and college classes.

"The greatest of follies is to sacrifice health for any other kind of happiness."

Arthur Schopenhauer
German philosopher

Free Health Screenings

- Diabetes management information
- Dermascan skin testing
- Blood pressure and cholesterol screenings
- Alcohol screening
- Body mass index testing
- HIV testing

Wellness Coaching

Coaches work with students one-on-one to help with nutrition and meal planning, smoking cessation, exercise/fitness planning, stress management, and general wellness.

Cooper Clayton Smoking Cessation Program

This program is available to all EKU students; cost reimbursement is available.

WELL 4 U @ EKU

Throughout each semester, you will have the opportunity to participate in a variety of fun health- and wellness-promoting activities. Participate in these activities and earn WellPoints that are used to earn prizes at the end of each semester!

Student Health 101 Newsletter

This monthly newsletter is distributed via EKU Students Today. The newsletter covers health and wellness topics including alcohol and other drugs, stress, family and mental health issues, sexual responsibility, body image, fitness, nutrition, study habits, and more.

For links to these great wellness resources, visit: http://www.campusrec.eku.edu/wellness

Be Safe at EKU

➲Make a few good and trusted friends, and stay close and connected; watch out for each other.

College campuses are full of potential for fun, new experiences, but it is important that you make smart decisions to stay safe. No matter how secure a place appears, your personal safety is in your hands. Avoid behaviors that place your immediate safety at risk, such as driving after drinking alcohol or after taking drugs, riding in a car driven by someone who has been drinking, or walking alone in an isolated, poorly lit area. Now that you're likely living in a housing community where your actions have a direct impact on others, it is also important to be aware of fire safety precautions. The following section outlines precautions you can take to keep yourself and others safe.

For more information on services the Police Department offers, visit http://www.police.eku.edu

■ FIRE AND LIFE SAFETY

The Environmental Health & Safety (EH&S) Department is a part of the Division of Public Safety. The department is responsible for overseeing the environmental, health, and fire and life safety needs of the University and its extended campuses. Fire and life safety is an important aspect of your well-being. The following is a list of basic steps you can take to help protect yourself:

- Know at least two ways out of every structure.

- When the fire alarm sounds, get out and stay out until the all-clear is given. A building occupant is required by law to evacuate the building when a fire alarm sounds.
- Never use an elevator during a fire or fire alarm. Only use stairs.
- Check closed doors for heat before you open them. If you are escaping through a closed door, use the back of your hand to feel the top of the door, the door knob, and the crack between the door and door frame before you open it. Never use the palm of your hand or fingers to test for heat—burning those areas could impair your ability to escape a fire (i.e., ladders and crawling). Crawl low under any smoke to your exit—heavy smoke and poisonous gases collect first along the ceiling.
- You should only consider using a fire extinguisher if you have been trained to use one and only if you feel confident that you can use one safely.

Other information to help keep you safe while on campus:

- Do not overload electrical circuits by piggy-backing surge protectors.
- Do not plug high voltage use equipment, such as space heaters or hair dryers, into anything other than directly into the wall outlet (no extension cords or surge protectors). Space heaters are not permitted in residence halls.
- Open flames are prohibited under most circumstances.

POLICE DEPARTMENT

University Police provide 24-hour patrol of the EKU campus buildings, parking lots, residence hall exteriors, and campus grounds. Patrol is conducted by motor vehicle, bicycle, and on foot. The department does not provide patrol services to the regional campuses but may provide other services to include investigations and crime prevention programs. Eastern Kentucky University has sworn police officers who have full law enforcement authority on all University property and concurrent jurisdiction on all roads and streets adjacent to the campus. They also have the authority to investigate crimes committed on University property anywhere in the state.

➲Don't Be a Victim of a Theft of Opportunity

- Do not leave your valuables unattended for any period of time.
- Always lock your office or residence hall room when it is unoccupied.
- Remove all valuables from your vehicle and ensure that it is secured when parked.
- If you notice any suspicious activity in or around University facilities, contact the EKU Police Department immediately at 622-1111.

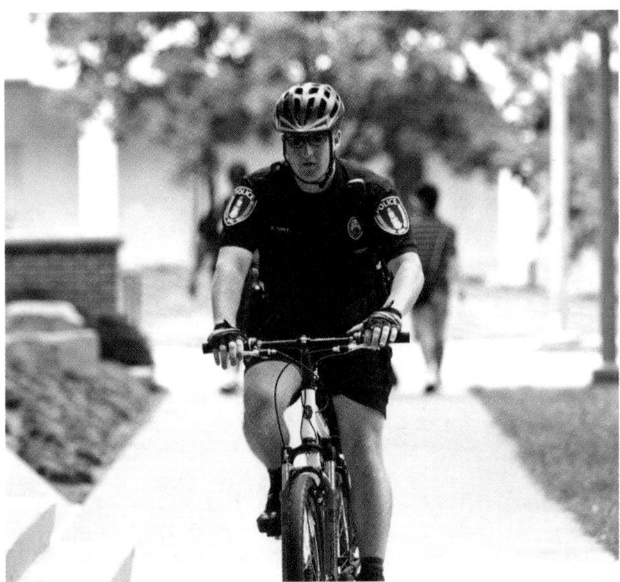

The EKU Police Department provides the following crime prevention services designed to make the campus safer:

Escort Service: The department operates a campus shuttle van service during evening hours. Students, faculty, and staff are encouraged to use this convenient service. The shuttle can be accessed by using telephones located in several parking facilities and areas around campus or by calling 859-622-1111.

Emergency Telephones and Call Boxes: The University provides emergency telephones and blue-light call boxes at strategic locations on campus so persons can immediately and easily report crimes and other problems.

Alarm Systems: The department provides alarm systems and alarm system monitoring for alarms for fires, elevator safety, and area intrusion security.

"You know, all that really matters is that the people you love are happy and healthy. Everything else is just sprinkles on the sundae."

Paul Walker

American film actor

Rape Aggression Defense (RAD) Classes: The Police Department offers Rape Aggression Defense classes for female students, faculty, and staff. The course is twelve hours long and is taught over multiple days. Announcements for upcoming classes are posted on EKU Today and EKU Students Today.

PREVENTING VIOLENCE ON CAMPUS

When we think about violence, it seems like something that is happening around us, something that we can't control. We are horrified when something happens, and we have a feeling of helplessness.

- Every two minutes a woman in the U.S. is raped.
- One in nine women in Kentucky is sexually assaulted during her lifetime.
- Women or men of any race, age, class, religion, or sexuality can be victims of sexual assault.
- Rapists can be acquaintances, friends, family, intimate partners, or strangers.

You may be wondering, "How can I stop violence from happening?" An awareness of the various types of violence is the first step in being prepared to help prevent it.

Types of Violence

Stalking: A pattern of repeated, unwanted attention, harassment, or contact that would cause a reasonable person to feel fear. Stalking includes unwanted phone calls, letters, emails, or text messages; following or spying; leaving unwanted gifts; or spreading rumors about the victim on the internet, in a public place, or by word of mouth.

Domestic violence: A pattern of abusive behavior in a relationship that is used to gain or maintain power and control over an intimate partner. Domestic violence can be physical, sexual, emotional, economic, or psychological actions or threats of actions.

Dating violence: Violence committed by a person who is or has been in a romantic or intimate relationship with the victim but is not married to or living with them. Dating violence includes the same behaviors as domestic violence.

Sexual Assault: Any type of sexual contact or behavior that occurs without the explicit consent of the recipient of the unwanted sexual activity.

Bystander Intervention

The basic idea of bystander intervention is that you become a part of the solution. This is not about making decisions for people or getting into a fight. It could be as simple as telling a friend that you don't like the way he or she is acting, checking in with a person you are concerned about, or interrupting a situation. Asking "Where's the bathroom?" could provide an opportunity for someone who is feeling cornered to slip away. At times it could mean calling the police.

The action steps for bystander intervention are to:

1. Notice the event
2. Identify event as intervention appropriate
3. Take responsibility
4. Decide how to help
5. Choose to act

The point is, if you see or know of a violent or abusive situation, do something—because it could change the course of someone's life forever. If someone you know tells you they were sexually assaulted, it is important to believe him or her.

If an assault has been reported on campus, EKU Public Safety recommends taking the following precautions:

- Immediately report suspicious persons loitering around University facilities.
- If you become the victim of a crime, do not try to physically detain or apprehend the criminal. Report the incident immediately to the EKU Police Department at 911 or (859) 622-1111.
- On or off campus, walk/jog/bike in groups of three or more in well-lit and well-traveled areas. After dark on campus, call the campus shuttle or the campus police for a walking escort.

- Scan the area before you exit or approach your vehicle/building and while you proceed between sites.
- Have your key ready in hand to quickly access the door of your building.
- If strangers approach, maintain a distance and be observant. If they are in a vehicle, get the license plate number, if possible.
- Lock doors and windows of your room/building. Do not prop open doors or let strangers in.

Green Dot @ EKU

If you've been the victim of violence, Green Dot @ EKU is here to help. Green Dot @ EKU can provide you with information, referrals, and support on campus. Services are available to any University community member—student, faculty, or staff—who has experienced sexual assault, relationship violence, stalking, or harassment on or off campus.

Services of Green Dot @ EKU

- Bystander intervention training
- Peer educator training
- Coordination of campus crisis services
- Advocacy
- Information and referral
- Workshops on healthy relationships
- Opportunities for community service and activism

➲ **Green Dot @ EKU is located in Keith 129.**
Call 859-622-9999 or email GreenDot@eku.edu for additional information.

If you are sexually assaulted:

- Get to a safe place
- Call 911
- Go to the Baptist Health Emergency Room (Pattie A. Clay Hospital)
- Call the Bluegrass Rape Crisis Center at 1-800-656-4673
- Call Green Dot at 622-9999

If you need medical attention:

- Don't change clothes (if you must change clothes, bag and bring the clothes you were wearing at the time of the assault)
- Don't shower or douche
- Don't brush your teeth or hair
- Don't eat or drink
- Don't smoke

Chapter Summary

College is a time of transition, and oftentimes, your health and wellness will be compromised as you make adjustments. Although it may seem easier to take short cuts when it comes to your overall well-being, failure to take adequate care of yourself will ultimately lead to more problems than benefits. In this chapter you learned about the six dimensions of wellness: physical, intellectual, social, emotional, spiritual, and environmental wellness. All these dimensions are interconnected with each one affecting the others, and you learned about some of the specific aspects to each of the dimensions. Some of the areas discussed more in depth were nutrition, physical activity, and sleep; stress, anxiety, depression, and counseling; alcohol, low- and high-risk drinking, and other drugs; and sexuality, contraception, and STIs. Then you looked at protecting your overall wellness by learning about staying safe on campus. All along the way you found links and directions for accessing resources online and on campus concerning all aspects of your wellness.

There is much more to learn about this broad topic, but now you have begun to learn the basics. Using the tips mentioned in this chapter will help you learn how to prioritize your life and make responsible decisions as you begin your college career. Sometimes, though, you may need help from others. There are numerous resources and services available for you at EKU to help you manage your well-being and protect yourself. Take advantage of the valuable resources in this text, online, and around you on campus as you begin to discover more about your own personal wellness while here at EKU.

"Get action. Seize the moment. Man was never intended to become an oyster."

Theodore Roosevelt
American President

KEY TERMS

Anxiety: A state of unease, apprehension, or worry often triggered by uncertainty or fear about future events

Binge drinking: Consumption of five or more alchoholic drinks in a single sitting with the primary intention of becoming intoxicated

Blood Alcohol Content (BAC) or Level (BAL): The ratio of alcohol to blood in your body. This is normally reported as a percentage

Depression: A mental state of prolonged depressed symptoms, such as sadness and despondency, loss of motivation, disturbed sleep, etc.

Lifestyle: The habits, attitudes, morals, values, and actions which constitute the way a person lives

Mental health: Refers to a state of well-being in which one can cope with everyday stressors, have a good command of one's own strengths and abilities, maintain active and fulfilling social connections, and be productive in everyday tasks

Sleep deprivation: The lack of restorative sleep over a period of time causing physical or psychiatric symptoms and affecting routine performance of tasks

Stress: Pressure or tension experienced in life which can be positive or negative

Wellness: A dynamic and multidimensional characteristic that describes one's quality of life and that is closely associated with one's lifestyle

NOTES

"Health nuts are going to feel stupid someday, lying in hospitals dying of nothing."

Redd Foxx

American comedian and actor

CAMPUS RESOURCES

Alphabet Lounge
Miller Hall, basement

Campus Recreation and Intramurals
http://www.campusrec.eku.edu
Fitness & Wellness Center, room 105, 859-622-6751

Community Service Office
http://www.communityservice.eku.edu
Powell Student Center, room 128, 859-622-3855

Education Pays Center
http://www.soto.eku.edu/epc
Weaver Building, room 202, 859-622-6684

EKU Counseling Center
http://www.counseling.eku.edu/services
Whitlock Building, room 571, 859-622-1303

EKU Psychology Clinic
http://www.psychology.eku.edu/psychology-clinic
Cammack Building, room 5, 859-622-2356

Environmental Health and Safety
http://www.ehs.eku.edu

Green Dot @ EKU
Keith Hall, room 129, 859-622-9999

Meditation Chapel
http://www.studentaffairs.eku.edu/chapel
Powell Student Center Plaza, 859-622-1723

Registered Student Organizations
http://www.studentlife.eku.edu/rso
Powell Student Center, room 128, 859-622-3855

Religious Life
http://www.firstyear.eku.edu/familyresources

Student Assistance and Intervention Team (SAIT)
http://www.sait.eku.edu

Student Health Center
http://www.healthservices.eku.edu
Rowlette Building, room 103, 859-622-1761

REFERENCES

Abouserie, R. (1994). Sources and levels of stress in relation to locus of control and self-esteem in university students. *Educational Psychology, 14* (3), 323–330.

American Academy of Sleep Medicine. (2007, February 15). New study in the Journal of Clinical Sleep Medicine finds that sleep disturbances affect classroom performance. *AASM News Archive*. Retrieved December 1, 2010 from http://www.aasmnet.org/Articles.aspx?id=282

American College Health Association. (2002). *Healthy campus 2010: Making it happen*. Baltimore, MD: American College Health Association.

American Institute of Stress (AIS). (n.d.). *Effects of stress*. American Institute of Stress. Retrieved March 18, 2011, from http://www.stress.org/topic-effects.htm

American Sexual Health Association (ASHA). (n.d.). *Male and female condoms*. Retrieved March 18, 2011, from ASHA website: http://www.ashastd.org/pdfs/Male_and_Female_Condoms.pdf

Banks, S., & Dinges, D.F. (2007, August 15). Behavioral and physiological consequences of sleep restriction. *Journal Clinical Sleep Medicine, 3*(5), 519–528.

Blanco, C., Okuda, M., Wright, C., Hasin, D.S., Grant, B.F., Liu, S.M., & Olfson, M. (2008, December). Mental health of college students and their non-college-attending peers: Results from the National epidemiologic study on alcohol and related conditions. *Archives of General Psychology, 65*(12), 1429–1437.

BrainyQuote. (n.d.). *BrainyQuote.com*. Retrieved June 9, 2011, from http://www.brainyquote.com/

Brougham, R. R., Zail, C. M., Mendoza, C. M., & Miller, J. R. (2009, June). Stress, sex differences, and coping strategies among college students. *Current Psychology, 28*(2), 85–97.

Budney, A.J., Moore, B.A., Vandrey, R.G., & Hughes, J.R. (2003, August). The time course and significance of cannabis withdrawal. *Journal of Abnormal Psychology, 112*(3), 393–402.

Centers for Disease Control and Prevention (CDC), Division of STD Prevention (DSTDP). (2010, November). *Sexually transmitted disease surveillance, 2009*. Atlanta, GA: U.S. Department of Health and Human Services. Retrieved March 18, 2011, from CDC website: http://www.cdc.gov/std/stats09/default.htm

Centers for Disease Control and Prevention (CDC), National Center for Chronic Disease Prevention and Health Promotion (NCCDPHP). (1999, November). *Surgeon General's report on physical activity and health*. Atlanta, GA: U.S. Department of Health and Human Services. Retrieved March 18, 2011, from http://www.cdc.gov/nccdphp/sgr/index.htm

EKU Substance Abuse Committee. (2010). *2010 CORE alcohol and drug survey*. Richmond, KY: Eastern Kentucky University.

Furr., S.R., Westefeld, J.S., McConnell, G.N., & Jenkins, J.M. (2001). Suicide and depression among college students: A decade later. *Professional Psychology: Research and Practice, 32*(1), 97–100.

Greenberg, J.S., Bruess, C.E., & Conklin, S.C. (2011). *Exploring the dimensions of human sexuality* (4th ed.). Sudbury, MA: Jones and Bartlett Publishers.

Hingson, R.W., Heeren, T., Winter, M., & Wechsler, H. (2005). Magnitude of alcohol-related mortality and morbidity among U.S. college students 18–24. *Annual Review of Public Health*, 26(1), 259–279.

Hingson, R.W., Heeren T., Zakocs, R.C., Kopstein, A., & Wechsler, H. (2002). Magnitude of alcohol-related mortality and morbidity among U.S. college students ages 18–24. *Journal of Studies on Alcohol, 63* (2), 136–144.

Holmes, T.H., & Rahe, R.H. (1967). The Social Readjustment Rating Scale. *J Psychosom Res, 11*(2), 213–218.

Hughes, A., Sathe, N., & Spagnola, K. (2009). State estimates of substance use from the 2006–2007 National Surveys on Drug Use and Health (Office of Applied Studies, Substance Abuse and Mental Health Services Administration, NSDUH Series H-35, HHS Publication No. SMA 09-4362). Rockville, MD: Substance Abuse and Mental Health Services Administration. Retrieved March 18, 2011, from U.S. Department of Health and Human Services, Substance Abuse and Mental Health Services, Office of Applied Studies website: http://www.oas.samhsa.gov/2k7state/2k7state.pdf

Kempner, M., & Rodriguez, M. (2005). *Talk about sex*. New York, NY: Sexuality Information and Education Council of the United States (SIECUS). Retrieved March 18, 2011, from SIECUS website: http://www.siecus.org/_data/global/images/TalkAboutSex.pdf

Mayo Clinic staff. (2010, July 23). *Stress management: Identify your sources of stress*. Mayo Clinic. Retrieved March 18, 2011, from Mayo Foundation for Medical Education and Research (MFMER), Mayo Clinic website: http://www.mayoclinic.com/health/stress-management/SR00031

National Institute on Alcohol Abuse and Alcoholism (NIAA). (2010, April). *Rethinking your drinking: Alcohol and your health* (NIH Publication No. 10-3770). Bethesda, MD: National Institute on Alcohol Abuse and Alcoholism.

National Institute on Drug Abuse (NIDA). (2010, Sept.). *Marijuana abuse* (NIH Publication Number 10-3859). Bethesda, MD: National Institute on Drug Abuse.

"Health is not valued till sickness comes."

Thomas Fuller

English historian

National Sleep Foundation (NSF). (2009). Myths—and facts—about sleep. Retrieved December 1, 2010 from National Sleep Foundation website: www.sleepfoundation.org/article/how-sleep-works/myths-and-facts-about-sleep

Nihira, M.A. (2010, March 24). Birth control and Depo-Provera. In *WebMD*. Retrieved March 18, 2011, from http://www.webmd.com/sex/birth-control/birth-control-depo-provera

Office of Student Life Studies. (2000, November). Noncognitive factors that influence student learning. *A Quarterly Summary of Challenges to Student Learning*, *4*(1), 1–4. Cape Girardeau, MO: Southeast Missouri State University. Retrieved March 18, 2011, from http://www5.semo.edu/stulifestudies/nov00.pdf

Paykel, E.S., & Cooper, Z. (1992). Life events and social stress. In E.S. Paykel (Ed.), *Handbook of affective disorders* (2nd ed.). New York, NY: Guilford Press.

Pollack, W. S. (2004). Parent-child connections: The essential component for positive youth development and mental health, safe communities, and academic achievement. *New Directions for Youth Development*, 2004 (103), 17–30.

Pollack, W. S. (2006). The "war" for boys: Hearing "real boys'" voices, healing their pain. *Professional Psychology: Research and Practice*, *37*(2), 190–195.

Pollack, W. S. (2010). Gender issues: Modern models of young male resilient mental health. In J. E. Grant & M. N. Potenza (Eds.), *Young Adult Mental Health* (pp. 96–109). New York, NY: Oxford University Press.

Public Employees Benefit Board. (2009, May 29). [Photograph of fruit]. In *Oregon.gov*. Retrieved January 6, 2011, from http://www.oregon.gov/DAS/PEBB/news/Wellness/Cancer.shtml

Sax, L.J., Lindholm, J. A., Astin, A.W., Korn, W.S., & Mahoney, K.M. (2002). *The American freshman: National norms for Fall 2002*. Los Angeles, CA: Higher Education Research Institute, UCLA.

Schlaug, G., Aslop, D., Gaab, N., & Stickgold, R. (2005, June 29). Study shows how sleep improves memory. In *ScienceDaily*. Retrieved December 1, 2010 from http://www.sciencedaily.com/releases/2005/06/050629070337.htm

Substance Abuse and Mental Health Services Administration (SAMHSA), Office of Applied Studies. (2010, September). *Results from the 2009 national survey on drug use and health: Volume I, summary of national findings* (NSDUH Series H-38A, HHS Publication No. SMA 10-4586 Findings). Rockville, MD: Substance Abuse and Mental Health Services Administration. Retrieved March 18, 2011, from U.S. Department of Health and Human Services, Substance Abuse and Mental Health Services, Office of Applied Studies website: http://www.oas.samhsa.gov/NSDUH/2k9NSDUH/2k9ResultsP.pdf

U.S. Department of Health and Human Services (USHHS), Office of Disease Prevention and Health Promotion (ODPHP). (2008). *2008 physical activity guidelines for Americans*. Retrieved March 18, 2011, from HHS, ODPHP, Physical Guidelines for Americans website: http://www.health.gov/PAGuidelines/guidelines/default.aspx#toc

U.S. Department of Health and Human Services (USHHS), Office of Public Health and Science (OPHS). (2009, July 24). Common sexually transmitted diseases (STDs). In *4Parents.gov.* Retrieved January 18, 2011, from http://www.4parents.gov/sexrisky/stds/common_std/common_std.html

NOTES

"…I am constantly thinking about my own health and making sure that I'm eating right and getting exercise and watching the aches and pains. I want to be this really fly 80–90 year old."

Michelle Obama

First Lady of the United States

EKU Resource Guide

Appendix

Appendix

EKU RESOURCE GUIDE

EKU Phone Numbers

Academic Advising	2-2276	Lost and Found	2-3855
Academic Affairs	2-3884	Meditation Center	2-1723
Admissions	2-2106/1556*	Multicultural Student Affairs	2-4373
Alumni Relations	2-1263	NOVA (Student Support Services)	2-1047
Athletic Tickets	2-2122	Panhellenic Council	2-2050
Bookstore	2-2696*	Parking and Transportation	2-7275
Campus Recreation/Intramurals	2-1244	Police (EKU)	2-2821
Career Services	2-1568/1567*	President's Office	2-2101
Computer Help Desk	2-3000	Public Relations & Marketing	2-2301
Developmental Education	2-1892	Records Office	2-5078/2410*
Dining Services	2-2179	Registrar	2-2320
Disabilities Services	2-2933	Registration Center	2-2320
Diversity Office	2-6587	Residence Life Council	2-1724
Eastern Progress (Student Newspaper)	2-1881	Residence Halls	2-1515
Employment (Student), On-Campus	2-1760	Scholarship Office	2-8032
Employment (Student), Off-Campus	2-1568	Sororities	2-2050
Enrollment Management	2-3047	Sports Information	2-1253
Financial Aid	2-2361	Student Accounting Services	2-1232/1236*
First Year Courses	2-7322	Student Affairs	2-2642
First Year Programs	2-1682	Student Life	2-3855
Fraternities	2-2050	Student Government	2-1724
Graduate Programs	2-1742/1745*	Student Health Services	2-1761*
Health Services	2-1761	Student Organizations	2-3855
Housing	2-1515	Student Senate	2-1724
ID Cards (ColonelOne Cards)	2-2179	Testing	2-1281
Information, General	2-1000	Traffic Violations	2-2821/6279*
Inter-Fraternity Council	2-2050	Transcripts	2-2384
International Education	2-1478	University Programs	2-2222
Library	2-1790/6594*	Veteran's Affairs	2-2345
		*Indicates TTY Services	

➲ Dial 859-622 followed by the 4 digit extension when calling from an off-campus number.
Visit http://www.eku.edu/contact-us/offices-department-listing for the complete EKU Phone Book.

NOTES

Where to Find It…

A few important places that you might need to visit while at EKU.

ALUMNI COLISEUM
Athletic Ticket Office

CASE ANNEX
Honors Program

COMBS BUILDING
Eastern Progress (Student Newspaper)

MATTOX BUILDING
Parking and Transportation
Parking and Traffic Violations
Police
Vehicle Registration

POWELL STUDENT CENTER
ColonelOne Card Office
Dining Services
Food Court
Fresh Food Company
General Information
Greek Life
Lost and Found
OWLS Nest
Residence Life Council
Student Government Association
Student Life
Student Senate
Technology Commons

WHITLOCK BUILDING
Academic Advising
Academic Testing
Admissions
Billings and Collections
Center for Career & Co-op
Counseling Center
Disabilities Services
Enrollment Management
Financial Aid and Scholarship Offices
First Year Programs
Graduate Programs Office
Housing and Residence Life
International Education
Registrar and Transcripts
Student Affairs
Student Employment
Student Outreach and Transition Office
Study Abroad

➲Can't find what you're looking for?
Visit http://www.eku.edu/siteindex

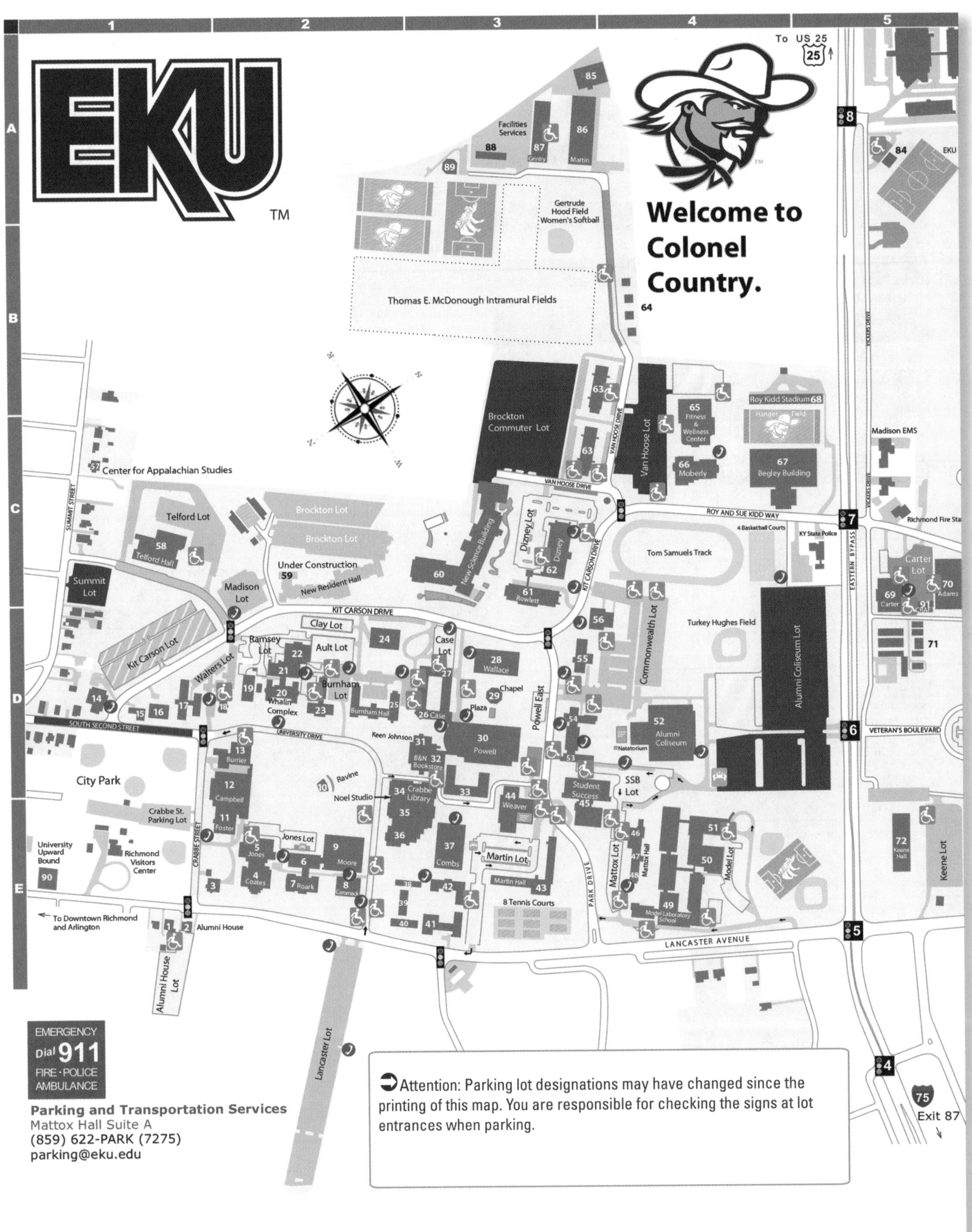

Parking and Transportation Services
Mattox Hall Suite A
(859) 622-PARK (7275)
parking@eku.edu

Attention: Parking lot designations may have changed since the printing of this map. You are responsible for checking the signs at lot entrances when parking.

6
7
8
Pattie A. Clay Hospital
Women's Soccer Field
McKinney Training Complex
Handicap Building Key
Sample:
Keith Building S- PAD, E, C, R
N- North, S- South, E- East, W- West
PAD Power Assist Door
E Elevator
R Accessible Restrooms
Telescope Deck
81
83
Cross Country Woodchip Trail
Ashland Lot
82
80
Bizzack Skills Training Complex
75 Springs One Room Schoolhouse
Stratton Lot
79
76 Perkins
Hummel Planetarium
77
Business & Technology Center
73
KIT CARSON DRIVE
Stratton
78
Perkins Lot
74 Center for the Arts
Center for the Arts Parking
Leach Driving Range
HALL DRIVE
Information / Emergency Call Box
Handicapped Parking
Commuter and Employee Carpool Parking
Map Legend
Commuter Student Parking
Resident Student Parking
Brockton Student Parking
Employee Parking
General Parking
Visitor Parking - Permit Required
Dual Lot Parking (Resident/Employee)
Dual Lot Parking (Commuter/Employee)
Buildings in Alphabetical Order
70. Adams Building/Tennis Center - C5 N- R
52. Alumni Coliseum - D4 W- PAD, E, R
2. Alumni House - E1
82. Ashland, Inc. Building - C6 S- R
22. Ault Building (Whalen Complex)- D2 E- E
14. Baptist Student Center - D1
32. Barnes & Noble Bookstore - D3 W- PAD
39. Beckham Hall - E2
67. Begley Building - C4 N- PAD, R
80. Bizzack Skills Training Complex - C7, C8
88. Black Building - A3
3. Blanton House - E1
63. Brockton Family Housing - B3, C3
25. Burnham Hall - D2
13. Burrier Building - D2 N- PAD, E
73. Business & Technology Center - D6 E- PAD, E, R
8. Cammack Building - E2 E- PAD, E, R
12. Campbell Building - D2 N- PAD, E, R
69. Carter Building - C5 W- R
26. Case Annex - D3 S- E, R
27. Case Hall - D3 S- E, R
16. Catholic Newman Center - D1
57. Center for Appalachian Studies - C1
74. Center for the Arts - D6 E- PAD, E, R
29. Chapel of Meditation - D3
24. Clay Hall - D2 W- PAD, E
4. Coates Building - E2 S- PAD, E, R
37. Combs Classroom Building - E3 N- PAD, E, R
41. Combs Hall - E3 E- PAD, R
56. Commonwealth Hall - D3 N- PAD
34. Crabbe Library - D2, D3 E2, E3 W- PAD, E, R
91. CRAFT Research - D5 W- R
62. Dizney Building - C3 S- PAD, E, R
51. Donovan Annex - E4 E- PAD
49. Donovan Building/Model Laboratory School - E4 W- PAD, R
54. Dupree Hall - D3 N- PAD, E, R
65. Fitness & Wellness Center - C4 N- PAD, E, R
20. Fitzpatrick Building (Whalen Complex) - D2
11. Foster Music Building - E2 N- E, R
79. Funderburk Building - D7
85. Gabbard Building - A3 E- PAD, R
87. Gentry Building - A3
21. Gibson Building(Whalen Complex) - D2
71. Greenhouses - D5
77. Hummel Planetarium - D7 E- PAD, E
5. Jones Building - E2 N- PAD, E, R
50. Kearns Gymnasium - E4
31. Keen Johnson Building - D3 W- PAD, E, R
72. Keene Hall - E5 E- E
42. Keith Building - E3 S- PAD, E, R
35. Little Building - E2, E3 N- PAD, E
86. Martin Building - A3
43. Martin Hall - E3 E- PAD
46. Mattox Hall - E4 N-PAD, R
40. McCreary Hall - E2
33. McGregor Hall - D3
83. McKinney Training Complex - B6
6. Memorial Science Building - E2 W- E, R
15. Methodist Student Center - D1
38. Miller Hall - E2
1. Million House - E1
66. Moberly Building - C4 W- PAD, E, R
49. Model Laboratory School/Donovan Building - E4 W- PAD, R
9. Moore Building - E2 S- PAD, E, R
59. New Resident Hall (Under Construction) - C2
60. New Science Building - C3 W- PAD, E, R
55. Palmer Hall - D3 N- PAD, E, R
47. Parking Office - E4 N- PAD, R
76. Perkins Building - D6 S- PAD, E, R
48. Police Department - E4 N- PAD, R
30. Powell Building - D3 E- PAD, E, R
89. Presnell Building - A3
19. Ramsey Building - D2
7. Roark Building - E2 W- R
61. Rowlett Building - C3 E- PAD, E, R
68. Roy Kidd Stadium - B4, B5, C4, C5 N- PAD, R
75. Springs One Room Schoolhouse - C6
78. Stratton Building - D7 W- PAD, E, R
45. Student Success Building - D3, E3 N- PAD, E, R
23. Sullivan Hall - D2
81. Telescope Deck - B8
58. Telford Hall - C1 W- R
53. Todd Hall - D3 N- PAD, E, R
18. Turley House - D2
36. University Building - E2 N- PAD, E, R
90. Upward Bound - E1
64. Van Hoose Drive Houses - B4
10. Van Peursem Pavilion - D2
28. Wallace Building - D3 W- PAD, E, R
17. Walters Hall - D1 S- PAD, E, R
44. Weaver Building - E3
20,21,32. Whalen Complex - D2 N- E, R
84.Women's Soccer Field - A5

NOTES

Index

A

B

C

D

E

F

G

H

I

J

K

L

M

N

O

S

T

U

V

W

Y

Z